14 Days

AMAVAND
3,934

TAR LA

ND
3,934

KHOSRAVAN

BESARD   JAPAN

SORKHDEH

KILAN

MOGHANAK

ARD

SAID ABAD

SARBANDAN

SARKHAR

MT. SHAPLAGHI

TO FIRUZKUH

52°15   52°30'E

35°45'N

52°15'E.   52°30'E.   THIELE

REVEILLE *for a* PERSIAN VILLAGE

by Najmeh Najafi with Helen Hinckley

As a child, Najmeh Najafi determined that her life was to be spent helping the villagers of her native Persia to a better existence within the pattern of their ancient culture. It was this determination which sent her to America to study. And it was this determination which took her home again to Persia fired with plans to realize a dream.

Advice and offers of help were not lacking. But what Najmeh had to do required her own particular way, a way rooted in the conviction that progress must be based on the familiar, the important, the loved. And so she came eventually to the village of Sarbandan, in the hills several hours from Teheran, where modern ideas from the West had not penetrated, where people lived as their fathers and grandfathers had lived before them. Armed with love, intelligence, determination and very little money, she set up clinics, put into effect a sanitation program, gathered the girls into classes for study, coaxed the fathers into giving land for a school, re-educated the women in

(*continued on back flap*)

ALSO BY NAJMEH NAJAFI AND HELEN HINCKLEY *Persia Is My Heart*

Najmeh Najafi with Helen Hinckley

REVEILLE FOR A PERSIAN VILLAGE

DECORATIONS BY MASSUD

HARPER & BROTHERS, PUBLISHERS NEW YORK

For men and women
engaged in compassionate service
everywhere in the world

Contents

Reveille for a Persian Village

One ⚙ HOME TO PERSIA

Far beneath our plane, the greenness of Lebanon merged into the sandy sweeps of Iraq. The man beside me closed his magazine and leaned forward to look out past me. After a moment he settled back again, apparently determined to find something more interesting inside the plane than out. I had known when he boarded the plane that he was American—an American from the West. If I had not guessed this, his first words would have told me.

"Beautiful country, Lebanon. Nice town, Beirut." I knew he thought that I was Lebanese.

"Yes."

"Good. You speak English. Very good. A man gets lonely ripping through the sky by himself." I looked out of the window but I knew that he was studying the tawny patches of freckles on the backs of his hands, wondering how to push our conversation further.

I did not want to talk. Ever since the plane had lifted at Beirut, my heart had been turbulent.

He disregarded my withdrawal. "Planning on quite a trip, young lady?"

"I'm going home. To Teheran."

"That so? Been away long?"

"Four years."

I

He whistled. "Four years? Well, that's quite a spell. England?"

"England, yes, and Europe; but specially America."

"Ever get down to New Mexico?"

"No, I never did. Arizona, but not New Mexico."

"Quite a place, New Mexico. Quite a place." Silence; then, his good nature taking the rudeness out of his words, "Looks like if you'd wanted to stay in America some young fellow would have been glad to marry you and make you a citizen."

"Iran's my country."

"Must have something real special to come back to." I knew he meant some special man. Although I meant something entirely different I said, "Yes. Yes, I have."

"H'm, a four years' journey!"

And I thought, I wonder what he would say if I told him that I have really been on this same journey for twenty years; ever since my nurse, Zahra, took me into a hungry village and I knew deep inside myself that someday, sometime, I must do something for my country. This feeling had come again and again to me, as I grew up in Teheran, as I visited the villages, as I decided to study in America, and as I attended classes there, gaining the skills I would need to work with my people.

It was the eve of Mohammad's birthday, the seventeenth of the month of Rabi'ul Awwal of the Hegira Lunar Calendar. Mohammad's birthday is to Moslems something like Thanksgiving is to Americans. "The earth is the Lord's, and the fulness thereof." Everything which man has, has been given him by God. It is the custom in my country to take meat to the poor people on this special day so that all may share in gratitude to God.

Early Zahra spoke of taking a barbecued lamb to the people in a near-by village. At once I began to beg to go with her. "It is good," Mother decided. "Najmeh should know that life in the villages is not like life in our home in Teheran."

I jumped around with delight and insisted on helping with the preparation of the lamb. This our cook, an impatient, parchment-dry old man, would not hear of. Nevertheless I stayed close to the kitchen, being careful to keep out of his reach. The whole lamb is purchased dressed and ready for cooking. It is placed in a great earthenware vessel over a charcoal fire. With it are water, tomato, onion, herbs. All day long it cooks, sending out delicious fragrance.

Late afternoon we went in the family car to this village, maybe ten, maybe twelve miles from Teheran. I had seen nothing in Teheran to prepare me for this village. I had been with Zahra to her home so that I knew that families could live in one room, that the window openings could be closed in winter with rags and paper, that the floor could be made of hard-baked earth. Still, even this part of Teheran was luxurious compared with the barrenness of the village.

First I saw trees, poplars I think, leafless because it was late autumn. Then I saw the homes, dome-shaped huts of sun-dried clay, unbelievably small and standing close together in a naked dirt field. At the center was the home of the kadkhoda. The kadkhoda, as headman of the village, had three rooms: one for receiving visitors, one for the sleeping, cooking, eating and living of his large family, and one for the animals: an ox, a donkey, a cow and a goat. There was not a hut in the village, not even the kadkhoda's, with a door or a window. Strips of woven rug hung before the single open doorways.

The driver helped us out of the car and I hung to Zahra's skirt, unable to understand the strangeness, the ugliness. Our driver distributed the meat. I peeked inside the houses. There was absolutely no furniture. These people slept on the floor, ate on the floor, lived on the floor. In some homes there were samovars and in one or two a bright piece of carpet. I heard Zahra and our man-servant mumbling about how things used to be better; how the samovars and carpets of the villagers had gone for taxes to build roads they would never ride on.

But the people who crowded around us were beautiful, especially the children and young men and women. There were shining, shining hair, white teeth, deep soft eyes. Too little food had made the fine bones of their faces and hands visible. I let go of Zahra's skirt and escaped her reaching hand. I wanted to touch these people. Deeply and unexplainably I felt that they belonged to me. I was happy, but the happiness was a sorrow.

When the lamb was gone I got reluctantly back into the car. Zahra settled down, tucked the robe around me and sighed, "Thank God that there is no one hungry in Persia tonight."

Why was anybody hungry, ever, I wondered. During the fasting month of Ramazan, of course, but why any other time? Hunger hurt—hunger was evil. Abruptly my eyes filled with tears. If every person is a child of God why should some live in an ugly village and some in beautiful Teheran? Later, when I asked my mother and my older sisters this question, their answer was: "That is the way things are, Najmeh-jun."

And then one day I found an old woman who lived in a hut very much like those in the villages, but right in Teheran, only a few blocks from my home. At that time I had a regular source of income. The older members of my family would often ask me to dance or sing for company. In repayment they'd give me a penny. With the coin damp and hot in my hand, I'd slip away to the home of this old woman. "Tell me a story," I'd beg, and I'd put the money in her palm. Wonderful were the stories she told me—stories of golden days when there were no hungry in Persia, when anyone could go directly to the king and tell him his troubles and be heard. These stories I neither believed nor disbelieved, but they comforted me.

Once when I was traveling with my sister, Fakhri, and her husband and son, Ali, a flash flood forced us to stay with some poor villagers in a one-roomed hut. We shared our lunch with them and they gave us tea and shelter. Fakhri sat up all night by the fire. In the morning her eyes were red and her face was sagging from weariness. "How could you, Najmeh? How could you lie down with those children? On that floor! They might have had lice!"

I was very rested and happy. "We are all people. All alike," I told her.

Fakhri's voice snapped. "You are without a mind!"
But I was not.

Sitting in the Teheran-bound plane, my head back, my eyes
closed, my loosely folded hands in my lap, it seemed to me that
all my life I had been coming unexpectedly upon pieces of a great
jigsaw puzzle, which, when they fell into proper place, would
make a picture of what God expected of me.

There were that first sight of village poverty, the stories of the
dim-sighted old woman, the night spent in the tight mud house
while outside the storm raged around us. There were other ex-
periences, too. Whenever I had an opportunity to go into a village
with some gift, I went. Each seventeenth of the month of Rabi'ul
Awwal, I took our family gift, sometimes accompanied by Zahra,
and later by our manservant and my nephew, Ali.

One New Year's time—in Persia the New Year is on the first
day of spring—my friends planned a skiing expedition to the
mountains of Azarbaijan, Iran's northernmost province. We went
by rail to Zenjan, from there by horse to the tiny snow-bound village where we were to stay.

We had brought a mutton as a gift to the people and we gave
it to the kadkhoda, the chief official of the village, to distribute to
the needy. He protested, as he accepted the gift, that no one in the
village was in need. While the others skied I talked with this
very intelligent man and his wife. They served me a glass of tea
and as I put my spoon into the sugar bowl I discovered that it was
filled with paper with a thin layer of sugar on top. They were
so proud they could not have me know that this was their whole
supply; they could not let me scrape a spoonful from the bottom of
the bowl.

I soon discovered that everyone in the village was in need and
that dividing the mutton would be a difficult task.

"Is the soil poor here? The water scarce?" I asked.

"The soil is rich and the water plentiful."

The wife, in a full-skirted dress of dark blue cotton, bent over the samovar scarcely listening to our conversation, but she said, "It is the long cold months."

"Yes," the kadkhoda agreed, "so many idle months!"

I sipped my tea, holding the glass in my two cupped hands. Now the deep feelings which had always pushed in on me seemed to take form around the nucleus of the wife's words: "It is the long cold months." If there could be some way of using these months profitably, the village people could end their suffering themselves. Zahra and I had taken a gift of food, food enough for one night, and Zahra had thanked God. How much better would be a gift of a way to earn food.

Later, when I had finished school, I opened a modiste shop in Teheran. In the front room sat the most wealthy women of Teheran, going through the fashion books lately come from Paris or from America. In the back room, the workroom, sat the girls I had recruited from the humble quarters of the city. These girls, sweet and beautiful every one, taught me something of importance: Give a Persian woman an opportunity to learn, a chance to trade her labor for the money which she and her family so desperately need, and no better needlewoman can be found. And this faith in the ability of my sisters was another piece in the puzzle. In my shop I could employ only a few, less than twenty, and many asked for an opportunity. I grew impatient helping by spoonfuls when a power shovel was necessary.

And then, abruptly, I decided to go to America. The picture of my life as it should be was taking shape but I did not know how to take the first step. To learn I must leave Teheran.

I went to America knowing no English, with no well-laid plan for study, yet my college experience there was rich and meaningful to me. For a time I was a borrowed daughter in the Jones family. Often I talked to Mrs. Jones of the puzzle that life was slowly completing for me, and my purpose became articulate in the book *Persia Is My Heart*. Many readers wrote to us. These friends entertained me as I crossed the country on my way home to Iran. They made it possible for me to meet people engaged in the work of the Ford Foundation, the Near East Foundation, UNICEF

and the American Point Four. They even gave me valuable intro-
ductions to people in my own country who might help me live
my dream.

My seatmate leaned forward to watch the desert slide away
under us. When he settled back he fixed me with his keen, red-
veined blue eyes. "Meet any likely men in America?"

"Too many," I said, and laughed.

"Teheran'll look different to you. Like it's been hit in the head.
Home town always does when you first get back."

Again I smiled, but didn't answer. I wondered if he were right.
I had been wondering this ever since I had sailed from America.

"I'd like to put up a bet that there'll be times you'll wish you'd
stayed where you were well off."

I thought of the number of foreign students, not Iranian alone,
who were quite frank about their desire to change their student
visas for permanent status in America. And I thought of the
afternoon I left Pasadena. Eight of the people I loved most in the
world were at the station to put me on the shuttle bus that would
carry me to the train in East Los Angeles. I was gay as I could be,
and the minutes which I wanted to hold on to forever, but para-
doxically wished would speed by, passed like hours. At last the bus
came in. I kissed each in turn, wondering in spite of myself which
of these eight I would never see again. I got on the bus, still smiling, though the tears in the eyes of these eight had shaken me.
Just as the bus started I heard my Pasadena "Mommie" cry aloud.
Her husband put his arm around her shoulder. "There, there,
Babe," he said, and my control broke. I put my head on my arm
on the seat in front of me and cried all the way across California
and half across Nevada.

No, leaving had not been easy, and now as I thought of it I
felt the tears gathering in my throat. "Perhaps you're right," I
told my seatmate. Then we chatted until the twin rivers, the Tigris
and Euphrates, came into view and the brilliant domes, the heart-
tearing minarets, the palms of Baghdad lay beneath us.

"Well, here's where I leave you," he told me. "If you ever

come back to God's country look me up."

"If you're in Teheran, look me up," I told him.

After we left the plane we shook hands; then he turned and walked away. He was a stranger, but unaccountably, as I watched him shoulder through the crowd, I felt that all America had slipped away, and for a time I was desolate.

After fifteen minutes in Baghdad the plane took off for Teheran. Over Kermanshah. Now we were in Persia. Over Hamadan, where the great physician Sina is buried and the bluest pots in the world are created by loving artisans. Over Ghom (Qum), famous for its salt, its perfumed soap, its school for mullahs. Oh, my mind was whirling and filled with revolving fragments of sensation and memory. While I felt the taste of the slightly salt melons in my mouth, I smelled the delightful little soaps and heard the strident voices of all the mullahs in my life. Now just a few heartbeats to Teheran.

As I left the plane, in spite of myself I looked about for someone to greet me. I had not told anyone just when I was coming. I knew my sisters would have planned a big homecoming celebration, that there would have been a noisy crowd at the airport to greet me. I did not want to return home in this way, so my family thought me still in Beirut. A strange disquiet had made me want to know just why I was returning to Iran. Had I missed my family? Had I hungered after the familiar beauties of Teheran? Did I really love the poor of Persia and hope to serve them?

Standing by the dull brick wall of the airport I looked around for a taxi and selected one driven by a weathered old man. "Go slowly, slowly," I told him. "I am searching for my home."

The way from the airport to the city, which when I had left four years before had been wasteland, was now built up entirely. On one side a motion-picture studio hid behind high walls. On the other, beautiful new homes of European style stood in cultivated gardens. These things did not hold my eyes. I wondered vaguely what other changes had touched my country in my absence, but I was looking for old things, familiar things. I directed the driver to take the street on which stood my mother's house. She would not be there. While I had been in America my brother Mohsen's wife had died and my mother was taking charge of his family. But I needed to see my home. We found the street, but the house was not there. Everywhere there was change. I moved in a troubled dream in which one walks and things are familiar but disturbingly different.

We drove back to the bazaars. I left the taxi and walked through the covered corridors. How dear were the raised voices of the bargainers. Purposely I brushed my shoulder against others. I had not remembered how dingy the bricks, how broken the tile, how thin and pitiful the beggars, how many the flies. But I loved the antiquity of the ancient bricks and tile. I loved the beggars with a feeling mixed of affection and compassion. I loved the—no, I did not love the flies. Too long I had been in America!

When it was almost evening I called another taxi and gave the ancient driver the address of my sister, Fakhri, who lives in the Shemiran area in a modern apartment. Now impatience to see my beautiful sister, who had always loved me next to her own son, Ali, seized me. How slowly the taxi moved—how long it was before the driver let me off at her door.

"Najmeh," my sister screamed when she came running to meet me. She held me close and cried against my cheek; then she held me at arm's length. "What have they done to you in America? Najmeh, what has happened to your shining eyes? To your beautiful hair?" Again she cradled me in her arms. "Little sister, little sister," she crooned.

Soon my brother Mohsen and my mother came. Mohsen's face was shining with welcome but he stood back while my mother took me in her arms and cried as if her heart were broken entirely. "Najmeh-jun. Baby!" she whispered. And I was crying, too.

"I came back," I said foolishly.

"Yes, yes, yes," she whispered, still crying and stroking my hair.

Finally we sat together on Fakhri's mile-long modern sofa, our hands entwined. "Najmeh, what have they done to you?"

"I have grown older," I said gently, "just as you have, Mother."

"See what your going away did to our mother," Mohsen said, and I could see. Her hair had been white when I left but now it had lost the wonderful color of living silver. Her face was still round and soft but no longer smooth.

"I am home," I said. I knew what Mohsen meant but I could not say, "I will never leave you again." I knew my life might be a series of goings away and returnings.

"What has happened—"

"Perhaps I am tired," I said. I thought, No one asks me what I have put in my head and heart during my four years in America. They want me just as I was.

At this moment Ali, my handsome tall nephew, always my playmate, came through the door. Without saying a word he turned on his heel and started away.

"Najmeh is home," his mother said unnecessarily.

"That this should have to happen to me," he groaned. "Well, how long are you going to be using my room?"

"You clown!" his mother chided. But we needed to laugh. We were all soggy with tears.

Even after Fakhri asked that dinner be served, my mother and I sat with our hands locked together. And many times she said, almost childishly, "I thought I would never live to see this day."

The next day the other members of the family came early bringing fruits and flowers. In the afternoon friends came. Carefully gloved and hatted and wearing the latest Paris styles, they sat stiffly in Fakhri's living room and tried not to show disappointment at the simplicity of my dress. Having just returned from America, having there been the guest of people of prominence, I, too, should have been dressed in stylish elegance.

"Did you see Hollywood?"

"Yes, I saw. There is very little to see. It is another American city."

"But didn't you see the stars?"

"Not a single movie star," I told them.

And they were disappointed.

"What are they wearing in America?"

"Seldom did I see ladies as elegantly dressed as you," I told them, and they were pleased with the compliment but disappointed in America. American motion pictures, which are very popular in Teheran, give a picture of American life very different from reality, but why should I tell them this?

No member of my family, not one of my friends, asked about the courses I had taken, the schools I had attended.

"Isn't she simple!" they exclaimed to Fakhri when I was not in the room.

"Well, she is still tired," Fakhri told them. "She has been traveling for a long time."

The next day was the same, and the next and the next. It was all very pleasant, but I was restless. I was a visitor. I had not really come home.

After three days I said impatiently to Fakhri: "I could sit here for a month accepting gifts, hearing and saying nice things. Then I could rent a car and return all these calls. Fakhri, I can't do it!"

She sat down beside me on the long white sofa. "Najmeh, have you forgotten? This is the way we live!"

"But I must work!" I began to tell her haltingly of the work I had always wanted to do for my people.

She silenced me with a finger on my lips. "Najmeh, you are just one woman. One not very strong, small woman."

"Even a tiny candle sends its light a long way when the night is very dark," I said.

"I will invite Dr. Birjandi to dinner," Fakhri promised. "Please don't do anything until you talk with him and a few other people who know about these things."

Dr. Birjandi, whom our family had known for some time, was the one man I could count on to understand that I must begin to help my people. He is a government official in charge of the Development Bongha in Iran.

He accepted the invitation. His wife, an excellent psychiatrist, was in America so he came alone. The two of us, seated side by side, had the evening to ourselves. We sat alone on the island of our mutual interests, washed by a sea of conversation and laughter from the rest of the guests.

Dr. Birjandi is a cultured, widely educated man who is oh, so human. He asked of my years in America and I saw interest glimmer in the eyes behind the bone-rimmed spectacles. I told him of the Los Angeles Trade College, where the factory machinery of nearly every trade hums, and young people, without cost to themselves, learn to print, to bake, to sew, to build machines, to make cabinets —to do endless practical things. "If I could just rub a magic lamp I know what command I would give when the genie appeared," I told him. "Genie, set this whole school down in my country!"

Dr. Birjandi smiled. "With you first comes the donkey leading the man! When all of these young men and women finished where would they be employed? First we must expand our industry."

I shrugged my shoulders helplessly. Even Dr. Birjandi seemed afflicted with Fakhri's feeling that one person could do nothing. But I told him how the puzzle of my life had ended in a pure picture. I knew what I wanted to do.

For more than two hours we talked. He told me about the Development Bonghas and what they were trying to do in the rural areas. He told me about the work of American Point Four, of the Ford Foundation, of the Near East Foundation.

"I not only want to work with my people. I know how I want to begin. I have—"

He stopped me with a quieting hand on my arm. "I know you want to help our people, Najmeh. I know that. But you have too much heart. You will have to educate it to be strong, not soft. I have had to do this. Often you will want to see the incident instead of the outcome. If you fail in this work it will be because you love—too much."

His words made me uneasy. I had felt that I was prepared to live my dream. Now I knew the most difficult battle was still before me.

"You will have to educate your heart to be strong, not soft."

Two ❧ ZEMESTAN

How wide, how white is the desert under the merciless October sun. Soon the rains of Zemestan (winter) will come and coax life from this dead land. Now the soft, loose dirt of the footpath drags at the feet and the sameness of the dun-white landscape drags at the heart. The village of Ghaleh Nou was left behind me. I looked back over my shoulder but its mud huts had sunk into the eternal flow of sand. I was trudging in what I hoped was the direction of the village of Hajiabad; but I was beginning to fear that I had taken the wrong footpath. In the summer, when the trees in the desert oases are green, the poplar spires catch the eye and break the unending monotony of sky and sand. But in October . . .

Perhaps if I had been lighthearted I would not now have felt so uneasy; but the past weeks had been the most miserable of my life.

Before I left America I had talked with representatives of the Ford Foundation and the Near East Foundation. The Ford Foundation had spoken hopefully of assistance in the project I wished to initiate on my return. I had told them that before I launched my project I would like to try myself. Perhaps in the four years I had been away I had lost touch with my people. In the years I had been away these Foundations had made advances of which I knew nothing. Perhaps I should work with an already established agency, I thought, while I adapted myself to the life of my people.

13

The past weeks had been filled with a series of unproductive interviews. I was ready to give myself, and there seemed to be no place to begin the giving. The people I needed to see seemed to be shut away from me; many of those with whom I talked had no power to make decisions.

But now I was living, my food and bed furnished by the Near East Foundation, at the nearly completed girls' school across from the village of Ghaleh Nou; and sponsored by the Foundation, I was beginning a study of the place of women in the primitive villages.

I lifted my eyes from the path before me and saw a shepherd following a few bedraggled sheep. The sheep raised a cloud of dust. The sun was reflected from each grain of dust and the sheep seemed to move in a cloud of fire.

"Whoo-oooh!" I called, and beckoned to the shepherd with a wide gesture of my arm. He came toward me, looking curiously at the European knapsack I carried on my back. He offered me a drink of water from his jug. Even though he herded sheep far away from the cities he had heard of strange things happening in his country.

"Are you of Point Four?" he asked. "Are you of the Bongha?"

"I am a teacher," I told him, "and I wish to reach Hajiabad."

He raised a thin arm to point the way to me. "Then you are not a Communist?"

"I am not a Communist," I told him.

"May God speed you then to Hajiabad."

When I neared the village I saw at once that unlike the villages near Teheran, there was a mud wall surrounding it. I stopped near the first hut. "Whoo," I called. "Anybody home?" A score of dogs rushed toward me, barking. I drew back away from the wall and the dogs jumped against the wall and made a frightening chorus. A woman came to the doorway of the dome-shaped hut.

"Jump over the wall," she called to me. The dogs, hearing her voice, stopped barking. "Jump over the wall," she invited again.

"If you will call in your dogs," I shouted back. I am not afraid of small dogs but any one of these could have matched a hundred pounds of weight against my eighty or ninety.

She called the dogs and they went bounding to her and at a firm word groveled into the house. I climbed the wall and went toward her.

"Did the Bongha send you here?" she asked as I came near enough to talk without shouting. "We don't have any girls here to go to your school to learn."

"I did not come to take girls away to the school. I came to teach."

"Well, there are no girls here," she insisted. But she consented to take me to the kadkhoda.

"I am not forcing anything," I told him and the woman. "I am a teacher. I love to teach. I am not charging for the instruction."

The kadkhoda beckoned to his wife, who had sat down in a distant corner, her face nearly covered with her chador. He ordered her to prepare lunch for us, then he turned his attention to me.

"Our girls do not need the school," he said.

"You are the headman here," I told him. "You know best."

Soon the wife brought a simple lunch. The dishes were not clean and there was dirt in the water she had used for making tea. I was grateful for my immunization. I said nothing. Iranians love company; they love hospitality too, and the climate grew warmer as we ate together.

"We do not care to read and write," the woman told me.

"Do you like to sew?"

"We like to sew."

"And would you like to learn to weave on a loom?"

Now the wife came into our circle and sat down, relaxing her hold on her chador. "I would like that," she said. There was eagerness on her thin dark face. "That is what we like."

So we chatted a long time and I made a proposal. Any woman or girl who would come to me to learn reading and writing would also be taught handicrafts and sewing.

That was the end of the interview for that day. The next time I came, thirty-five girls and women waited for me. Thirty-five from a village that "had no girls"! At first two gleems (tribal rugs) for us to sit upon were brought into the yard of the kadkhoda. Later

the villagers gypsum-plastered a room. To this room I came once
a week. Even after the weather grew cold the only heat we had
in the hut was the heat from our own bodies; but we were warmed
by a feeling of love. I brought my lunch and shared it with the
class. We talked together, and our hearts were open. They told
me about their most intimate relationships, about their income,
about many things which gave me an opportunity to study their
standard of living, their ideas of sanitation. Especially I discovered
how dear to them were their customs, their superstitions, their religion. It was while sitting in this makeshift classroom, glasses of
tea between our hands, that I learned that for these people *progress must be based on the familiar, the important, the loved.*

After I had walked back and forth from Ghaleh Nou to this
village many times, the villagers provided me with a horse and a
little groom. Ali was about nine or ten, simple, naïve, and oh so lov-
able. As I rode I often had him mount the horse behind me and
I taught him how to count, how to read the first literacy book.
Sometimes we sang the songs I had learned when I was a child.
When I went to Teheran I brought back for him a new hat with
ear muffs and a pair of warm fur gloves. "Sometime," he told
me, "I am going to be very, very rich. Then I will buy a horse for
you and one for me."

"If I ever become very rich, Ali, I'll buy you a horse," I
promised.

Soon my hours, my days, my weeks fell into a pattern. After I
had begun my classes at Hajiabad I made the same beginning in
the villages of Upper Gheshlagh and Lower Gheshlagh and Ghaleh
Nou. Early mornings I was busy at the girls' school. Midmorning
I began my four- or five-mile walk to one of the villages. In the
village I drank a glass of tea and ate the lunch I carried with me.
I conducted the classes until late afternoon, then I walked back
to Ghaleh Nou. Thursday afternoon I did not teach in a village
but walked seventeen or eighteen miles to the bus line or caught
a ride on a supply truck in order to spend Friday in Teheran with
my family and my friends.

How healthy I was at that time. My face was a shining brown from the long hours under the sun, and my body, hardened by the constant exercise, was slimmer than it had ever been.

But when the rains of Zemestan set in, these long walks were hard for me. Now I trudged through soft, deep mud as I went from Ghaleh Nou to each of the villages to teach crafts and literacy and sanitation, trying to reach not only the minds but the hearts of the people. Sometimes the work was rewarding, sometimes it was discouraging. Always I was very tired. A friend in Pasadena offered to send me a bicycle. A bicycle in all that mud! Later he offered to send me money for a horse or a donkey; but these animals would need food and shelter. Besides, and this was the point, the fact that I went among the people walking gave them confidence in me, let them know that my work with them was not a selfish thing.

Even a jeep to take me from one village to another would not have given me rest, really. I was tired from thinking of the enormous problems my country faces in rural development. One pair of hands can do so little, I often thought. And then it seemed that Fakhri might have been right about the helplessness of one woman—one small woman—trying to carry a candle in a dark world.

One day I returned to Teheran for a few days' rest and I stayed, as usual, at the home of Fakhri. "You are tired, Najmeh. You are killing yourself." She took my hands and held them between hers.

"There is so much to be done, Fakhri."

"What can one person do, then, Najmeh?"

"Fakhri, the Near East Foundation is doing a great thing. They are teaching many to teach. Perhaps I should not be working in the villages. Perhaps I should be preparing others to do this work."

She leaned over and kissed me. "Najmeh-jun, you weren't made for public life. You were meant for marriage, for home, for a husband's delight."

A pain which I thought I had put away from me forever engulfed me. "I have turned my face away from that kind of love, Fakhri. For me, it is finished."

"When did this happen?"

"In—America."

From that time Fakhri did not try to dissuade me from my work.

I slept in the school dormitory with twenty-two girls. Sometimes at night I heard someone crying, "Carry me back to my mother." These girls, many of whom had never been outside a great city, who had never spent one night away from the crowded room where all of their family slept in closeness and security, were homesick in this distant village living among strangers. When I would hear this crying I would creep like a conspirator to the girl's bed. Perhaps I would lie down by her and put my arm around her. "Now Mooshi (little mouse)," I would whisper, "you are not going to cry. At home your family prays for you. They are so proud. Perhaps you are going to school for your whole family—the only one with this opportunity. When you finish and become a teacher they will say, 'See, this is my child! How wise she is, how intelligent!' And then you will have money in your pocket and you can buy food for your family, new shoes for your little brothers." Or perhaps I would tell a funny story and leave the girl chuckling as I crept back to bed; chuckling and feeling that she was not as far from home as she had thought.

Many of the girls told me, "We do not like you to go to Teheran." And when I asked why, they'd answer, "There are no bedtime stories when you are gone."

But there were those in authority in the school who did not sympathize with the bedtime stories, the midnight visits. "These girls must learn discipline," I was told. "They are women. Your softness spoils our work!"

There was Dr. Birjandi's word again. "Soft."

I agreed. What else could I do? But even as I nodded my head, I knew that no girl who cried in the night should remain uncomforted.

We had one girl in the school, more intelligent than most, who was always sad. At last she confided in me. "Lady Najafi"—in our language we have no Mrs. and Miss, only *Lady*—"I cannot live if I do not see my baby!"

"Your baby?"

Then she told me the story. She had married very young a boy who was no more mature than she. One day they had had a great, childish quarrel and she took the examinations for entrance to the school. She passed the examinations so she packed her things and came to Ghaleh Nou. Now, of course, the quarrel was long over and she cried, "This place is a prison to me! I hate it."

"But you have begun the study here. It is a great opportunity."

"Lady Najafi, it is killing me. I must see my baby." Then she told me that her child was in the home of her husband's parents just two villages away.

"Can they not come on Friday?" Some Fridays were visiting days at the school, and friends and relatives walked many miles through the deep sand to visit these girls.

"My brother-in-law will bring the baby to see me, but he cannot come on Friday."

Each week the principal of the school, Mrs. Zhianbod, and I took the girls to a neighboring village for a bath, since the bath at the school was not completed. We went by station wagon. Since the bath was small she took eleven girls and waited while they bathed. The girls under my direction washed clothing, then boarded the second station wagon and went into the bath when the first group came out. "We can arrange for you to see your brother-in-law and the child on the day we go to the bath," I told her, and she danced around and sang as she did her share of the work.

But this promise, too, was a mistake, I was told. She was denied this privilege, and after I had left the school I heard that she too had left. I do not know whether or not she stayed long enough to graduate, but I do know that she is not now engaged in teaching or village work.

Life in the school was not all dull. Sometimes we had a party and the girls entered into the gaiety with complete abandon. I introduced the American game of bobbing for apples in buckets of water and the girls screamed with excitement. Sometimes the games were planned with a point in mind. Two relay teams lined up. Each girl in turn took a plate, saucer, cup, knife, fork and spoon that were stacked together and placed them in the correct order for place setting, then they stacked them up again and ran back and touched the next waiting team member. This I learned about the girls: They were more eager to get through than they were to do things right. But perhaps this is true of girls everywhere.

Perhaps the most fun the girls had was over the beautiful seven-basic-foods charts which were placed in the dining room. The girls loved these posters with their bright pictures, but they couldn't help but notice the difference between the food shown on the charts and the food that was available in Ghaleh Nou. "When do we eat all this food?" the girls would giggle. One of them kissed the cheek of a red apple in the picture and said, "I don't taste a thing!" Another who had come from Teheran and had seen many American movies said, "If we eat these things we look like Ava Gardner!"

I laughed, but I was sad. I knew then that although the study of nutrition was most important—many of the girls had come to the school undernourished—the instruction would have to be fitted to the food that was available, not to American dream food.

I loved all of the girls at the school, but one was especially close and dear to me. Moneer.

One day I was sitting in the dining room making some notes on a report which I hoped to write for the Ford Foundation, when suddenly the kerosene heater exploded with a deafening roar. The windows on the one side of the room were shattered and soot descended like a pall over me. For a moment I was too stunned to realize that my skirt was burning, that the room was filling with smoke. I screamed. It was Moneer who came running and opened the door so that I could flee from the flames. With her naked hands she beat out the flame from my skirt. I would have done this thing for her, had she been in the room. This we both knew.

The education of Moneer became my greatest interest. At every point I gave her additional instruction. I hope that someday she may go to America and continue her education.

Through the months of Mehr, Aban and Azar (October, November and December) I worked in the villages, organizing the classes; then these schools were turned over to the Bongha (the Near East Foundation) and a tall, capable young woman whose name was Mahin took my place. I was not satisfied with my work in these villages of the Varamin area. To me the people were like the taste of water—no salt, no sweet, no anger, no joy. In these villages there seemed to be little warmth, little movement, and not even the faces of the children were mirrors of inside happiness. I found myself praying, "God, never let me be empty. Let me sorrow if I must, but never let me be without emotion."

I do not know why this is true of these desert people. It is not true of the mountain people of Iran.

When I was no longer working in the villages I had more time to work at the school. I acted as interpreter for the American teacher, planned the menus and the preparation of the food, and helped to organize the girls to do the daily work in the buildings and the compound. In addition I conducted a study of my own. I made notes on the things that were good in the program, classwork, and management of the school; the things which I felt did not fit the needs of my people. When the time came that I could organize my own school I would remember these things.

Organizing such a school became my dearest dream. Moneer I would take with me. Oh, I had many plans. I had even talked with Her Royal Highness, Princess Ashraf, about it.

Princess Ashraf is the twin sister of the Shah. She is small, perhaps as small as I, but in some way she is regal. In repose her face is veiled, but when she lifts her eyes there is a current of energy which charges those who meet those eyes. People say she has the eyes of her father, Riza Shah, who brought the ways of the West to Iran.

When I had an audience with her she was not alone. With her were twelve men of importance—the Minister of Finance, the

Minister of Education, others. She listened to me briefly, then she made suggestions. I might research some charities in which she was interested, I might—

I did not know that I should not speak so I opened my mouth. "Princess Ashraf," I said, "of these things I know very little. Of my own plans I know a great deal. I want to remain just Najmeh." And so we talked of the school and she turned the ideas over to her ministers for their consideration.

I told her I realized that if I were ever really to do good for my country I must train others to harrow where I had plowed, to harvest where I had planted.

After the conference I was not satisfied, but I was hopeful. The Near East Foundation was doing excellent work; but I felt that any educational program must preserve the highest Iranian culture as well as raise the standards of living, sanitation, child care, nutrition and literacy. Many of the Americans could not see this point. How could they? You must be born in any culture, you yourself must have your roots firmly planted in it, in order truly to appreciate it. It is no wonder that people who come from a very different country with a totally different culture should put the gaining of progress in tangible things first on their programs.

At Ghaleh Nou I was restless, and I knew by my own restlessness that I was not using my time and strength in the best way. Always when I am doing what is best, I know it. Deep inside me someplace I can feel the difference.

Zemestan had passed; now it was Farvardin, April, and I knew that I must begin my own work. Not the organizing of the school, of course, because that would take financial resources that were not possible to me, but preliminary work in some village.

When I left the school Moneer came to me at night and begged to come with me. "No," I told her, "you must graduate from this school." Perhaps I made a mistake. Still she coaxed. But when I asked if I might take her with me and be responsible for her completion of the year's study the director was adamant in her refusal. "Not with Najafi!" she said, and I understood why I had been restless at Ghaleh Nou.

When I returned to Teheran, bringing my knapsack, my sleeping bag, my few articles of clothing with me, Fakhri looked at me with questioning eyes, but she said nothing.

"I am going to find a virgin village," I told her. "Here I am going to try the methods that I deeply feel will work."

"Are you going alone?" she asked.

"The Ford Foundation will give me some assistance. But yes, I am going alone."

Three ⚘ FARVARDIN

In the month of Farvardin in the little Iranian village of Sarbandan, the air against the cheek is like the first bite into a new apple, the mountain flowers carpet the slowly greening earth, and the yellow leaf buds climb to the very end of the soft purple apricot willows. Sarbandan is high, so spring is late in finding it. But the sky, tucked in behind the mountain's snowy crown, is as blue and quiet as a summer pool.

I clambered out of the ancient automobile which had brought me fifty-six miles from Teheran, north along the old Mazandaran road. Leaning against the car I looked over the roof tops of the village to the apricot and cherry orchards fanning up over the foothills; my eyes followed the clear stream of mountain water, which we Persians call the jube, as it flowed through the center of the village. Along this stream I could see people going and coming. My people.

My heart shook me for a moment. Perhaps, I thought, perhaps this is the place!

Very near was a teahouse. Before it was a small, partially enclosed court where tea was served outdoors. I went in, kneeling to wash my hands and face in the icy water of the jube which ran through it.

When I looked up a boy of about seventeen or eighteen stood

watching me. "May I serve you, my lady?" he asked in the quiet voice that villagers always use with strangers.

I smiled but his face did not reply. "I would like to speak to the owner of this place."

His eyes studied the long black coat I wore, the quiet kerchief that covered my hair. "I will bring my brother," he said, and hurried away on silent feet.

In a moment the owner stood before me; a man past middle age, dressed in a brown suit and linen that was clean but no longer white. On his head was a chapeau, a sort of hat which gentlemen in the villages wear.

"I would like a tea," I told him. "Bring one for yourself, too, so that we may talk together." As we drank our tea he told me that he was called Mash'hadi Mokhtar (his name signified that he had taken a pilgrimage to Mash-had) and that he was the owner of the place. I looked about me. In addition to the outdoor pavilion where we stood, there was an enclosed coffee shop in one end of which was a meat market. Around the walls of the coffee shop ran a sort of bench of sun-dried brick, dirt and stone. A strip of carpet and a samovar were marks of affluence.

"It is a fine place," I told him.

"Oh, yes, I am very rich." For the first time the curtained look left the brown eyes under the magnificent eyebrows. He smiled broadly, and under the magnificent mustache the gold in his teeth gleamed. I could *see* that he was very rich.

"Mashdi Mokhtar, you own a very fine teahouse. But who owns the village?"

"Many own land here."

"No landlords?"

"Some landlords. A few big ones. I am one of these."

"You are a man of importance," I told him.

The man had taken my sincere words for dangerous flattery. Again his eyes were veiled. "Another tea, my lady?"

"Another tea. A tea for each of us, please."

Again he came with the tea. I curtained my eyes, too, and we were strangers.

"Well, Mashdi Mokhtar, what about the population of Sarbandan?"

"Almost two thousand—in the summer."

"And in the winter?"

"When there is no work there is no food," he told me with dignity.

"How much snow do you have?"

Mash'hadi Mokhtar pointed to a little tree. "This very tree you see before you has been covered," he said, "when we have two and a half meters of snow." He gestured toward the dark interior of the coffee shop. "See. We still have korsee. We have it eight months of the year." In the gloom of the coffee shop I saw the stool that Iranian villagers place over a small fire, usually of dung but sometimes of charcoal. Over it was spread an ancient blanket. In the cold weather people sleep on the floor with their feet toward the korsee. Now, in the coffee shop, three old men sat with their feet warming. I could hear only the murmur of their voices but I knew that they were talking about philosophy, or crops, or telling the tall tales that Persians love to tell.

"But you are growing tired, my lady. Let me get a rug for you."

"No, thank you, Mashdi Mokhtar, I won't bother you."

"It is no bother at all," he told me as he unrolled a rug for me to sit upon.

"How do people live through such a long cold winter?"

"They do not stay in this place."

"They go to Mazandaran, perhaps?"

"If they did not go, cold and hunger would kill them," he said defensively. "They work in the rice fields of Mazandaran. Only women and children and old men are left here."

We talked for a time and I asked if the people had a bath. "Bath? How could we have? Our forefathers made one about a hundred years ago but it is ruined now. Its pool is so unclean that no one has the desire to go into it." Then he looked at me with a flash of anger. "My lady, why do you ask these questions of me? Why?"

At this moment I loved Mash'hadi Mokhtar. I loved him because I saw the fear leap in his eyes and I understood this fear. My people are proud and they have much to be proud of. How can they be happy when so many people want to change them?

"Because I think I might want to make my home here, Mashdi Mokhtar," I said very quietly. "I think perhaps Sarbandan is the place for me."

He left me and returned with his chopogh, a sort of long pipe. He drew on it two or three times, then, wiping the mouthpiece first with his fingers then against his cheek, he handed it to me. I drew two or three small suffocating breaths and returned it to him.

"Do you have a school, Mashdi Mokhtar?"

He smiled. Again the gold in his teeth glittered. "Indeed we do. Four years ago we built the school. We turned it over to the Ministry of Education. We have grades one, two, three and four. Next year, perhaps, we will have five and six. If not next year, at least some year."

"And is there a school for the girls?"

"What are you talking about, my lady? A school for girls!"

I changed the subject. "Tell me, does Sarbandan have a clinic?"

"Clinic? What is this clinic?"

"A place for the care of the sick."

"How could we have such a place when there is no doctor?" Again there was anger in his voice.

"I am hungry, Mashdi Mokhtar. What can we eat?"

"Abgousht," he told me, and went to get me a serving of the always delicious Iranian broth.

Sarbandan is the place for me, I thought, while Mash'hadi Mokhtar prepared my lunch in a dark corner of the teahouse. All the time that I had been working in the villages of the Varamin area I had been deciding on exactly the sort of village in which I wanted to live and work. In the mountain villages where the growing season is short and the winters are long, hunger sits at every korsee. Perhaps, I thought, the women in a village like this could be trained to make things in the home—modern things that might sell in world trade, ancient things which could be objects of beauty—the winter, like the summer, could be a period of productivity; and I thought of the wife of the kadkhoda in the Azarbaijan village who had first said to me, "It is the long cold months." There are many such villages in my country, but while my work was beginning I wanted to be near Teheran so that a village clinic would be close to the hospital facilities of a great city; I needed to be on a main road so that transportation would be possible and I hoped that there would be other villages near by. This, because there was a very quiet deep dream in my heart. I could see my work extending into other villages; I could see myself walking from village to village to start schools or clinics; I could even see all of the villages joining together in a great co-operative fair or harvest market. Oh, I had had wonderful dreams when I lay between sleeping and waking. Sarbandan seemed to meet all these needs.

I was glad, too, that Sarbandan was owned by many small landholders and by several landlords, because I thought that co-operation would be more easily achieved.

Since there was no school for girls, I could organize the very special kind I had dreamed of. This school was to be the foundation of my whole plan. In it I would teach literacy, of course, sanitation, nutrition, child care. But I would also train girls to work with their hands; to emancipate themselves from poverty through their own skill. In it, too, I would train the brightest village girls to carry on my work.

Above all I wanted a village in which other organizations had not begun work. The Ford Foundation, the Near East Foundation, the United States Government's Point Four—all had done many good things, but I wanted my work to be different. I wanted to work "heart by heart," not in the mechanized way that I had found organizations must move. Besides, I did not want to make a little America in the mountains of Persia. I wanted my people to stay as they were, keeping the feeling of security that goes with doing things in the sweet, almost sacred, accustomed way. I wanted to see if a better way of life could be built on a foundation of native customs and mores. For my people I wanted happiness rather than that colder goal that is sometimes called *progress*.

When Mash'hadi Mokhtar returned with the abgousht we sat on the rug and ate in silence. I felt satisfied with Sarbandan, and already in my mind I could see the white walls of a school and clinic rising beside the jube.

Finishing my abgousht I asked, "Do you have a village council?"

"Yes, we have. But the members seldom see each other. When they meet there is nothing but quarreling at the teahouse."

"Tell me, why do the old men quarrel?"

"My lady, in Sarbandan the people are divided into two factions. We even have two kadkhodas."

"Two kadkhodas?" A kadkhoda is a responsible man selected by the large landholders to keep order in the village. After he has been selected he is given a piece of paper by the government empowering him to assist the state mounted police. Technically he is nothing, being responsible neither to the government nor to the people, but practically he is everything. "Two kadkhodas? That is incredible!"

He spread his clean, thin hands, palms up. "But we have. You see, we are of two tribes. And our landholders . . ."

The walls of the clinic and school which I had just built in my mind crumbled away. Two factions. Two tribes. Co-operation,

which is always hard to achieve with people as individualistic as
my people, might be impossible. I would have to spend time and
energy avoiding petty jealousies, ironing out petty disputes. I could
not afford to waste myself that way. I was defeated before I began.

"Come," he said, standing. "Allow me to show you the village,
my lady."

Half reluctantly I followed him along the banks of the jube.
Women were washing clothes along both sides. The crying of a
lamb drew my eyes upstream. Two men were killing the little crea-
ture and its blood was flowing into the water. Between the lamb
and the women bent over their washing, a half-grown girl dipped
a jug into the stream and lifted it dripping to her shoulder.

Sarbandan needs me, I thought. I looked at the faces of the
women and children. Their skin was transparent, their cheeks
like spring petals. Again my heart shook me.

"I think I have found my village," I told my sister Fakhri when
I returned to Teheran that night. And then I described Sarbandan.

She looked thoughtful. "Najmeh, dear," she said, her beautiful
face serious, "you are very crazy."

Four days after my visit to Sarbandan I got up early and took
my knapsack and lunch with me. I went to Fouzieh Square and
waited until I found a charcoal truck that was going north on
the old Mazandaran road. The driver was not unwilling to have a
passenger so I climbed up in the cab beside him.

The Mazandaran road at that time was rough beyond imagination. Wheels had worn deep ruts. Every now and then some road
worker with a shovel was moving the dirt from the side of the road
back into the ruts in that halfhearted manner that one always has
when a job is so great that it will never be finished. But I could
look away from the looping road, away from the dusty-bearded,
charcoal-blackened driver, to the green freshness of the mountain.
Everywhere there were wild flowers, lupine and columbine and
larkspur. Sometimes we passed a flock of sheep, body-deep in the

fresh mountain salad. Sometimes we passed villages surrounded with early-blossoming orchards.

After four hours of travel—a passenger car could make the trip in two, and now that the road has been improved and covered with smooth asphalt as far as Abe-ali, even less—I got stiffly down at Sarbandan. In the four days since I had been there the orchards had changed. The cherry trees were now frosted with opening blossoms and the leaf buds on the apricots had changed from yellow to green.

When I went into the teahouse of Mash'hadi Mokhtar the boy who had first spoken to me on my other visit came quietly toward me.

"Where is my friend Mashdi Mokhtar? I wish to see him."

The boy's face was impassive but his eyes were friendly. I thought, Mash'hadi Mokhtar has spoken of me to the others. "Today he is not here. Another day perhaps."

My body ached from the springless ride in the charcoal truck. "Some other day will not do. Is there a center in the village of Sarbandan?"

"Yes," he said, and going out to the road beside me, he pointed the way.

For a time I stood alone in the center of the village. There were three or four little shops—a shoe-repair place, a barbershop, a house that stocked a few grocery staples—beside the life-giving jube. Some women and children looked at me curiously and hurried away. Finally some old men appeared, urging each other forward, and asked me what I wanted of them. Evidently Mash'hadi Mokhtar's brother had sent them to me.

There is nothing to be gained by moving too slowly, I thought, so I said boldly, "I have come to start a girls' school in Sarbandan. That is, if you wish me to."

"Are you Point Four?"

"No."

The men talked together, then the same spokesman came forward again.

"Are you from the Ministry of Education?"

"Nobody sent me here. I came myself. I will live in Sarbandan and teach the school—if you wish me to."

The spokesman withdrew again and there was muttering among the old men.

"If you have a village council you could discuss a school in your council meeting, then tell me what you decide." This way they will either unite in favor of a school or against it, I thought. In any case they will unite.

The old man came forward again. "We do not see any harm in your proposal," he said. Then a sharp light flickered in his eyes and his voice changed. "Since you are going to live in Sarbandan you will need to find rooms," he suggested, and I thought that his eyes turned toward my purse.

"Surely for a school rooms will be given me for my use."

They looked at each other. They had no intention of giving.

"Oh well," I said. "This is not of importance. Show me some rooms."

So, trailed by the old men, I walked through the village. From the outside many of the houses looked livable, from the inside they seemed impossible. Finally I said, "Perhaps I will build me a new place. Or I may repair an old house in return for a year's use."

They nodded wisely and walked back to the road with me. Here I drank a tea and waited until the charcoal truck came back from the pits.

My bones ached when they thought about another journey to Sarbandan by charcoal truck, but I had promised the old men I would be back in a week to select the room which everybody wanted to rent to me, and no one wanted to give for the school. When my friends began to plan an out-of-town picnic I suggested, "Why not some place along the old Mazandaran road? There are wild flowers, sometimes almost waist high, now. I passed that way just the other day." (I did not say "by charcoal truck.") "Everywhere along the 'road of a thousand curves' the mountain slopes and the valleys are incredibly green."

So the next Thursday we took the Mazandaran road; two carloads of us. Everybody was gay, laughing. We had enormous lunch baskets. We were like picnicking young people any place in the world. Only I was dressed in the black silk duster, the long black gloves, the head scarf of the traveler.

When we reached the village of Abe-ali I suggested that the others wait for me while I went on up to Sarbandan to complete a business arrangement.

"We'll all go to Sarbandan," somebody shouted, and laughing they piled back into the cars.

"No, really," I said. "That would spoil everything."

I did not want the village people to think of me as belonging to the city. I must come from nowhere into the village. Almost as if God sent me. That way I would seem to belong to them, and that was necessary.

So my friend Forough Farschi drove me to Sarbandan. His sister, Dr. Faraj Farschi, is one of the finest obstetricians and gynecologists in all Iran. As we rode we talked about my plans for the village of Sarbandan. He, like the villagers, asked, "Are you working with Point Four? With the Ford Foundation? With the Near East Foundation?"

There came a quiet quiver at the ends of his lips. "What are you going to use for money?"

"I am working with heart, not money. I am giving energy and thought and love."

"Love and thought don't buy vaccine, nor build schools, nor equip clinics," he told me.

"I know that." The Ford Foundation had granted me a small scholarship, fortunately with independence of action, which would keep me alive while I worked. I had some money in the Persia Is My Heart Corporation from the sale of my first book, but that must be kept for building, not used for operations. "I think the necessary money will come," I told him quietly. "God gives. He has never disappointed me."

In Sarbandan the villagers were waiting for me. They took me directly to the home of the chief of the council. "We will not be more than an hour," I told Forough; then, turning to the old men, I said, "Let me talk with the householders who showed me rooms last week."

In an incredibly short time the owners of the houses were gathered, each explaining loudly the advantages of his own property. Above the clatter of voices I could not make myself heard. It was as if these people were having a tug of war and I was being torn apart between them. Forough took my arm. "Najmeh, let us go. There are other villages, hundreds around this highway, where people can co-operate."

The voices which at first had sounded like those of traders at the bazaar now became angry. Words of praise about their rooms gave way to quarreling, personal recriminations. But I knew why, and I was not angry. I knew that my presence in a home, my pitifully small rent, would mean the difference between food and hunger for an entire family. These men would be ashamed to face their wives and children if they did not at least put up a good battle.

I shook my head at my friend, and for the villagers I put on a sorrowful face. "I have come for peace," I said. Then when they did not hear I turned to him. "I am not giving up at the first difficulty. This quarreling shows more than anything else that the people need me. They can't understand any better. They can't appreciate what they haven't known."

So we waited until the men had quarreled themselves out. Then I talked with them, one by one, telling them that the good I would bring to Sarbandan would not rest only under the roof that covered me, but would spread like morning mist to everyone. Finally I rented a house, and contracted to have it gypsum-plastered during the next week. When I asked them to shake hands, kiss and be happy, they did so, some still muttering under their black mustaches.

Forough and I ate cheese, bread and meat in the kadkhoda's house. When we left to rejoin the picnickers we had been five hours in Sarbandan, not one, and though I had finally smoothed out a part of the trouble and rented a house, I was as limp as wet cotton.

"Najmeh," Forough said, "this will be too much for you. You will see. Why should you fight with these people when others would reach out toward your hand?"

I would not let myself think of fighting with these people. People were not my enemies. My enemies were ignorance, greed, superstition, fear. Mostly fear.

"Someday these people will love and trust me. You will see."

Four ⟐ ORDIBEHESHT

In the language of my country the month of May has a beautiful name: Ordibehesht—heavenly month. The Moslems imagine heaven to be a beautiful green garden, fresh and fragrant with flowers and grasses, the air cool and sweet from the spray of fountains. In heaven there is a beautiful pool, called Kowsar. Near this pool the pure in heart, the innocent, may live forever.

The afternoon that I rode into Sarbandan beside the driver of a rented car, all my possessions packed carefully in the back, I was glad that I was beginning my new life in Ordibehesht. Sarbandan, which moves slowly toward summer because it is so high on the great body of the mountains, was so sweetly green. The blossoms, standing with light feet on the branches of the cherry trees, with their soft whiteness made the green seem even newer and cleaner. There was, of course, no Kowsar here, but Sarbandan looked like Behesht to me.

"This is the place," I told the driver. And a mighty leaping of my heart in my forehead and throat told me truly that this must be the place.

In the heaven of the Moslem imagination, beautiful nymphs are always ready to serve. In Sarbandan nobody came to help the driver take my things from the car. Even a group of little children who were playing in the dirt near the kadkhoda's house, just

36

upstream from mine, looked shyly from the corners of their eyes and went on with their play. When the driver had finished unloading my things I put his pay in his hand and he drove away. I stood in the center of the one room that was my home and looked at my things piled around me.

The people of Sarbandan and other northern villages build their houses of dirt, straw and water. The mud is placed little by little so that each day the new mud will be placed upon mud which has dried enough to support the additional weight. The walls are built very thick. Probably two feet or three. All around the room alcoves, sometimes a foot deep, sometimes nearer two, are hollowed out. The effect is of a room surrounded by shallow closets. The thickness of the wall between these alcoves helps to strengthen the building. My room, including the alcoves, was rather small and of a dull white color. The walls were so new with the fresh gypsum plaster that I had to look up to the ceiling made of woven willows, once green and pliable, but now dry and nearly rotten with age, which supported the mud roof, to realize that my home was more than eighty years old.

I knew that I should get settled. The two kerosene burners which I had imported from Germany I would place in one alcove. This would be my kitchen. Above the burners a few shelves would take care of my utensils and my food supplies. I would shelve another alcove for my books because I wanted them to be ready to my hand. My very few simple garments would hang in another niche. I had brought many yards of a blue cotton material with a small red design—the villagers love red—to curtain the alcoves. A braided mat of wheat straw, dyed red with color from the jackets of nuts, would cover the floor of hard earth.

There were many things I could do to begin to make this room into a home, but suddenly I felt very small, very alone, almost frightened. I had been very bold about saying that a little candle may shed a large light when the night is very dark. I knew that in Sarbandan there was much darkness. But now I wondered if I were a lighted candle at all.

I turned my back on the tasks I might have done and walked up toward the mountains, keeping my eyes on the higher reaches.

As a student in an American college I had sung: "Lift thine eyes, oh lift thine eyes to the mountains; whence cometh, whence cometh, whence cometh help." Then with all the voices weaving their melodies in my brain: "Thy help cometh . . . Thy help cometh . . . Thy help cometh from the Lord, the Maker of heaven and earth."

This is a Christian song, and I am a Moslem, but I knew in a manner that is deeper than knowledge that my help would come from "God, the Maker of heaven and earth."

Always after that, when I seemed much too small for great tasks, I took that walk again. Many times I took that walk.

After many minutes I turned my eyes from the mountain back toward the village. I could see my own little home, looking very much like the others, drab and without character. Soberly dressed men, women wrapped in their chadors, children, streamed out of the mosque. This was the fifteenth day of Ramazan and the afternoon service was just over.

Ramazan, for all Moslems, is a month of fasting, a month for drawing near to God. It was in this month that most of the Koran was revealed to Mohammad; it was during this month that he himself went without food in order to share with the humble the pangs of hunger and to purify himself to listen to the voice of Allah.

I sat down near the mountain path, my legs folded under me, and thought of all the Ramazans of my own life.

Even before I was old enough to keep the fast my nurse, Zahra, had awakened me at two in the morning to hear the beautiful male voices singing a prayer from the roof tops. Sometimes I had sneaked down to the kitchen to be under the feet of Osta, our cook, or my mother as they prepared breakfast to be served two hours before sunrise. In my mother's home eggs and tea, sugar, rice and fruit were served. In the homes of the poor there is often only rice and tea.

After this meal, during the hour before sunrise, our family prayed together as do all other Moslem families that are living in the faith. It is no accident that family ties are so tight in my country. It is in hours like these that the cords are wrought—sweet, quiet hours. And at sunrise, again there is singing from the roof tops.

All day we fasted and once we went together to the mosque, where the mullah, sitting upon a menbar draped in rich green material and lifted three steps from the floor where all we others sat, taught us with prayers and exhortations and sometimes with simple, straightforward good advice.

At about four we came out of the mosque. My nose always took me again to the kitchen where Osta was preparing the meal to be served after dark. As the sun set there was again a family prayer. Each of us put his finger in salt, then in his mouth. We each drank half a glass of warm water and then ate a light supper of tea, cheese, bread or rice with perhaps dates or other dried fruits. Restraining oneself gives a strong character. He who can control his appetites can control his thoughts and thus his destiny.

I could remember all the details of every Ramazan; how I had missed the spiritual surge it gives even an exhausted spirit the years that I was studying in America. I thought of the fashionable women in Teheran and the other large cities who keep the fast not for spiritual reasons but to reduce their weight so that they will look glamorous in the latest French fashions.

Now as I watched the people of Sarbandan being swallowed by their small mud houses I wondered about them and their worship. Did these village men know the prayers to sing from the roof tops? Did the women know how to perform their ablutions before offering up a prayer?

My work in the village was to be influenced by the answers to these questions for I intended to build all my work on the secure foundation of religious faith.

After a time I walked slowly back to my little home. When I entered a sheep was already there. He was looking with some curiosity at my folding cot. Very soon I must wind my shuttle with string and knot a mesh curtain for my open doorway, my two narrow, unglassed windows.

"How do you do?" I said to the sheep. "It is not yet dark or I would offer you a tea."

At dusk I waited for the singing of prayers in rich, warm men's voices; but there was no such singing. I opened my folding bed and lay alone in the darkness. Soon I saw the flicker of lanterns as the women, wrapped in their chadors, went toward the mosque or to the home of a neighbor. I had not prepared an evening meal for myself and I was hungry. I wanted to be hungry. I wanted to begin my great experiment with extreme humility.

There was no call for prayer during the night, but I heard the soft thud of bare feet as someone passed my door.

As soon as it was light I got up, dressed, carried water from the jube to cleanse myself, then went toward the latrine, downstream from my house. It was on my property but I could see no other near my neighbors' dwellings. I went in. In daylight it was more disgusting than it had been in the darkness. There was no roof, just three and a half shoulder-high crumbling walls. In the center was a large opening over a filthy pit up from which the great flies buzzed with the drone of a hundred small engines. No wonder, as I had observed, the people preferred to use the gardens and the orchards!

I went quietly to the teahouse of Mash'hadi Mokhtar. Again Mash'hadi was not there, but his young brother greeted me with a smile that was small on his lips but very shining in his eyes.

"Malek," I asked, "where can I find a mason? I have walls to be mended."

"That is easy, my lady. I will send one to you."

I went to my home and began putting my things in order in the alcoves. Very soon a mason stood before me.

"Can you build walls?" I asked him.

"This is the month of Ramazan. We do now only that which is needful," he told me with reproach.

"This is needful," I told him with emphasis. Then I took him to the crumbling latrine. "We will build it as far as possible from the jube. We will build a floor and a roof and in the floor will be only a small opening to the pit below."

"This is Ramazan," he repeated.

I clenched my hands in my skirt. "This is Ramazan," I agreed.

I knew that I would have no new latrine today nor tomorrow; but I would have it in due time. I reminded myself that many, many times I would have to hurry slowly.

Alone I went back to my house. First I brought my D.D.T. spray to the latrine and stopped the buzzing of the flies and the crawling of other little creatures along the walls. Next I brought an aftabeh of water strong with antiseptic and D.D.T. and a broom and cleansed the inside; finally I brought from my stores a curtain to hang before the opening, half a wall wide. The little children from the next door, three of them surprisingly blond under the dirt, had gathered to watch me work. "You may use my rest room," I told them. This was a joke because the pit was so wide that none of them had legs long enough to reach from side to side. They scattered off to use the garden space behind my house, instead.

Nearly all day I worked on the rest room, then in a basin of water from the jube I cleansed myself for prayer. Shortly after dusk I set out the things for supper: tea, rice, cheese and sugar. In the villages a cone of sugar, harder than the cubes in the American market, and perhaps eighteen inches high and nine inches in diameter at the base, is considered the most desirable possession in the world. I had one of these cones and I was busy breaking some of it into smaller pieces with a tiny hatchet made for that purpose when I heard the shuffle of bare feet just outside my home. Three women, wrapped in their chadors, each carrying a lantern, were coming to call on me.

They stood shyly outside the doorway until I said, "Won't you come in and have a tea with me?" Glancing covertly about them, they came in and stood awkwardly just inside my house. "I am breaking sugar," I told them, not because they could not see me do it but because I must say something and I could not speak the questions that were in my head. *Who are you? What names do you have? Are your children healthy? Why do you not keep them clean? How much money do you have for food in a year? Why does no one in this neighborhood ever use a rest room?*

I thought of some of the Near East Foundation social workers asking people who were almost starving for a handful of rice if they were serving their families the seven basic foods every day.

So I might have asked, *What do you know about nutrition?* I could ask none of these questions. Some would never be answered. Some would be answered later—much later.

I said, "I am breaking sugar."

"May I help?" the youngest of the three, a woman of about thirty, asked.

"I would be so grateful. Now I can prepare the tea." I turned the cone over to her. In villages sugar is such a luxury that for a special guest the glass is filled half with sugar, half with strong tea.

I lighted my samovar and we all sat upon the mat.

With little urging, after the tea was served, the three began to talk. The youngest woman's name was Masoomeh, and she was the sister of the kadkhoda who lived upstream from me. (The other kadkhoda lived in the mountains and came down to the village center only occasionally.) Masoomeh was beautiful, with a smooth oval face, light in color, framed by the folds of her chador. Her lips were thin but with a softness of expression. It was not until she opened her mouth that I discovered that she had only two teeth, and these were long and pitted.

It is the diet, I told myself, but I kept my eyes away from those tragic teeth. The young girls have beautiful teeth, straight and white and shining, but with each baby the mother's teeth go. No ordinary person in the village ever has a tooth filled. Men like Mash'hadi Mokhtar have gold in their teeth to prove their wealth rather than to preserve their teeth. The village barber is also the dentist. When a tooth aches he yanks it out without benefit of even a pill to deaden the pain. But then he is used to suffering. He also lets blood from those who have fever, or applies the hungry leeches to the veins of the sick. Cleanliness of the mouth is unknown. No one in the village has ever seen or heard of a toothbrush.

The other younger woman was called Banu (Lady). She was the wife of the kadkhoda. Very soon I heard a story about her. In the old marriage customs of Persia a man must make a large wedding gift to the parents of the girl whom he is to marry. This gift may be money or something else of value. In order to buy Banu the kadkhoda—then not the kadkhoda, of course—had given all his farm land. The girl's father turned the land to her as a dowry. So now the kadkhoda was working land that belonged to his wife. Banu put on an air of superiority with the others. Was she not the only woman landholder in the village? But I sensed insecurity deep in her nature.

The older woman was the mother of my landlord, Madar-i-Kadkhoda, and this was the only name I ever heard her called. Much of the conversation that evening was about Madar-i-Kadkhoda. She was the midwife of the village, the source of all the old racial knowledge. She knew how to read the moon so that the planting of the beans or the potatoes could be done at the most propitious time, the hen could be set upon the eggs, the farm animals could be bred. She knew where the wild weeds grew that were good for food and where to find those that were good for medicine. She knew how to use every part of the body of a sheep, drying some for meat in the spring and fall, freezing it in the winter, cooking it and covering it with tallow in stone jars. She could squeeze the juice from the tiny white mulberry and boil it until its pectin made sweet, flavorful jelly to be eaten with bread as a special delight. She knew how to bring the baby, and if it presented an arm or a leg how to coax it to return that limb to the womb by touching it with ice or snow. She was the village matchmaker, carrying word of marriageable girls to the parents of marriageable boys and knowing words of praise for both. And once the match was made she knew exactly the amount of rice and oil that would be needed for the wedding feast.

I looked at Madar-i-Kadkhoda in the flickering light from the kerosene lanterns. From what she said she must have been almost eighty, but she looked strong and muscular, more like sixty. She could be a powerful ally to me, or my worst enemy. In her was the wisdom of the village, a wisdom deep as the race, as old as the generations. It was not until they rose to go and I watched her walk flatfooted across the mat that I noticed her aged toe bones, saw that her feet were set down wide apart as are the feet of the aged in every country.

This was my first contact with the women of Sarbandan, and it was with the women and children that I intended to work.

The next day they came again. This time Masoomeh had a baby folded in her chador slung on her back. Over her head was a shawl, tied under the chin. I studied the village dress with quick glances, since I didn't wish to stare and always before the women had been completely covered with their chadors. She wore trousers, as nearly all village women do, to her ankles; they were skimpy, but not tight. Her skirt of bright printed cotton stuff was exceedingly short and very full, exactly like the brief skirt of a ballet dancer. Over this, not tucked in, but hanging to the hips, she wore a shirtlike blouse. I praised the village dress and the two younger women smiled with satisfaction.

That evening, after prayer time, I served tea to a roomful of chattering women.

On the twenty-sixth of Ramazan my mother came to Sarbandan. The end of the month of fasting is the time in my country for visiting people you love. With her came my nephew Ali. All day Mother and I cooked. With butter, flour, sugar and zafaran spice we made halva, a kind of sweet that Persians like better than any other, for the twenty-seventh of Ramazan marks the closing of the fast and in the mosque it is a time for feasting. The halva we baked in a long covered baker of clay in a charcoal fire out of doors behind my house. We would bake again on the twenty-seventh, for I planned to take enough halva to the mosque for everybody.

At sunset Ali climbed to the roof of my house. With one of the most beautiful voices in all of Persia he began to sing the song that my heart had hungered for:

Praise be to God, Lord of the worlds,
The compassionate, the merciful,
King on the day of reckoning.
Thee only do we worship and to Thee we cry for help.
Guide Thou us on the straight path,
The path of those to whom Thou hast been gracious;
With whom Thou art not angry, and who go not astray.

At that moment the deep meaning of the words, the man-voice of Ali singing for all the young men in Islam, the simplicity of the way of life that I had adopted, my mother with her hair whiter than silver and the serene face of an angel, all combined to produce in me the strangest of emotions. The tears flooded my eyes, tears of happiness and sadness. All this that was so deeply ours we must not lose for a sewerage system, for electric lights to replace our kerosene lanterns, not even for food for the always-hungry body of man.

I could not share this complex emotion with my mother sitting beside me. I kissed her on both cheeks and made a foolish joke about my swaying willow roof, which was unprepared for the weight of my heavy nephew.

At eftar, sunset, Mother and I and Ali took the great copper trays to the mosque. On them we had placed small plates of halva, and fruit, and slices of cucumbers which Mother had brought from Teheran, available there because they had been trucked in from the warm southern countries.

Ali took his tray to the men's side of the mosque; Mother and I took ours to the side where the women and children were waiting.

This was the first time I had been in the mosque at Sarbandan and now I saw it by the light of hundreds of lanterns. It was a very large room with a red brick floor and a flat ceiling supported by wooden pillars which had once been covered with stone and brickwork. Now some of the bricks had crumbled and the wood was visible. We knelt upon straw mats on the floor, the men on one side of a tattered curtain, the women and children on the other.

The walls were broken by five doorways and by niches in which the lanterns, giving off their orange-red glow, were placed. The mullah, the chattering women had told me as we drank tea together, came only two months out of the year from Ghom, from a sort of seminary or training school for mullahs. He was young, fresh-faced, devout and sensible. I wished that he might be with us through the year.

Many times I have knelt in a mosque at the closing of the month of Ramazan; but never in a simple mosque like this. Yet the flickering light and shadow that cross the faces of those who kneel is as beautiful to me as the light from a thousand electric bulbs in the ornate chandeliers of the mosque in Teheran where I had most often prayed. We are kneeling in long lines, our faces toward Mecca. From the pulpit come the words of the young mullah, but it is not his voice alone, but his voice amplified by the concentration of a multitude of hearts. Tonight he talks simply but solemnly. He speaks often of God and each time he mentions the Name we put our faces to the floor with a great sound. The sound is a muttered response from the many throats but it sounds to the ear like a jube of music. Tonight, kneeling on the mat beside my mother, I am not "my lady." I am truly a human soul to whom God will show His everlasting love and mercy, but who never, worlds without ends, will be more important to Him than the soul of any other who has learned to reach upward.

"God is great," the mullah reads.

"God is great," we repeat, and again we put our foreheads to the red brick earth, the earth from which the body of man is made.

And now it is time for each to make quietly his own prayer— a prayer which he has saved in his heart for this very auspicious time. Do you want land of your own? A son? A husband? A wife? A new chador? A plow? Relief from pain? Now is the time to ask it, because the body is cleansed by the fast and the spirit is very close to the spirit of God. I had not saved my prayer for this occasion. I had been asking it in my heart for a long time. "God, give me wisdom, and strength, and maybe enough money to carry out my work. But above all give me understanding."

After the service I stood in the doorway with a reed basket filled with halva which I offered to the women as they left. It was rich and delicious, and in the lantern light the oil which had come to the surface glistened like dew. The gaily dressed young girls giggled as they reached into the basket. The women searched my face. I heard one of them say as she turned away from me, "She is young, but she is a good Moslem."

I now belonged to Sarbandan.

The next day Ali and my mother returned to Teheran and I began to study my village. I walked through it, sometimes stopping beside the jube to visit with the women who were washing their clothes or their dishes, sometimes stopping at a doorway to speak to a woman making food for her family or caring for her children. The dirt was depressing. It seemed that the women were always washing and never clean. But the little children were never washing and so were always dirty.

One week passed, and every evening I gave tea to the women who called at my home. It was not my plan to open a school and then urge them to come to it and learn. Rather I planned to grow slowly into their lives so that they would come to me and ask for the school.

After a week I visited the school for the boys. The schoolroom of which Mash'hadi Mokhtar had been so proud was a mud-brick room little larger than my home. The walls were not plastered and were moldy with the dampness that works its way out of the mud. The only light in the room came from the always-open doorway and the two unglassed narrow windows. Here about forty little boys bent over their studies.

I made a rapid calculation—forty boys from a population of sixteen hundred. There must be many many boys not in school.

The young teacher welcomed me warmly. I could see that he was proud of his school. He came from another area and did not have the education to teach where the position was really desirable. But he was trying, and he invited me in. When my eyes became accustomed to the half-darkness I looked closely at the little scholars, reciting two grades at a time to the young teacher. I noticed on the heads of most of the boys the white blisters and patches of baldness that are evidence of the dread scald-headedness of the Middle East.

I went from the school to the bathhouse. Outside, the sun was bright and warm. Inside the long corridor which led to the bath, it was so dark that even after ten minutes I had to light a lantern to see my way, and the air was cold and damp and unhealthy. As I rounded the corner the stench from the putrid water struck me like a wall. I went forward, holding my lantern, and came upon the pool itself. Mash'hadi Mokhtar had told me about this pool, but, since only the day before I had heard a wedding party going toward the bath with singing and with the dong, dong, de-dong of the donbak, I thought that he had exaggerated.

Slowly I turned away and walked back down the passageway. Once again I felt helplessness take me by the throat.

That night as I lay on my camp bed, lifted above the little creatures that in spite of D.D.T. often scurried over my floor, I wondered where I should begin. Is it education that is the foundation for progress in every nation? But of what value is education without sanitation? Is it sanitation? But why keep the poor alive if later they must starve? So, perhaps, I should start as I had at first dreamed, with teaching the women to make salable articles with their hands.

I got out of bed and went to my doorway, looking up toward the mountains dark as a pasteboard cutout against the deep blue of the star-pierced night sky. "God," I said, and I heard my own voice speaking, "open my mind to the truth, my eyes to the path that I must follow."

Five ❀ KHORDAD

Now is the month of Khordad—June. No longer is Sarbandan veiled in pink and white. Petals fall like summer showers, and hidden in the greenness of the tree the tiny fruit waits for the season of its maturing.

And when the trees no longer are in blossom, the young girls by two or threes, their print dresses new bright flowers on the green hillside, search for the tiny edible spring greens, delicate in texture and flavor. Their chadors tied about their waists make bags at their sides. Their eyes and their hands are quick, their speech as fluid as the sparkling jube, their laughter high-pitched, happy summer music.

During the month of Ordibehesht the frost has reluctantly left the earth and now the men are turning the waiting soil. Sometimes, using the plow of their fathers, the men work by twos, one pulling the plow, one following it. Sometimes a plowman urges a cow, harnessed to the plow, to forget her calf and move forward. Birds follow the turning of the soil. It is as if each man has a plume of feathers trailing him across the brown field.

Beside the houses, the old women sit in the sun, deftly cutting potatoes, readying them to be put inside the open furrow. Younger women, sometimes with babies slung in their folded chadors, disregard the crying of their infants and bend over the waiting soil and with the hands of faith and hope gently pat in the beans and the potatoes.

Here is the life of the village. A life centered around the growing of food, planting a bulwark against famine.

I wondered why the yards of the houses were left dry and hard; why no one planted a dooryard garden. I, at least, would plant spinach, onions, leeks, parsley; but first I must have someone to help me.

When I had been packing my things to come to Sarbandan, Fakhri and my older sister, Fatemeh, had stayed close, making many suggestions and worrying about the simplicity in which I planned to live.

"Take a servant with you, at least," Fatemeh had urged. "Why not Asghar?"

Asghar was a smiling young man with solid round cheeks like rosy apples, with wide questioning brown eyes and with a body built for labor. His mother had been brought to Teheran as a servant from a province where Fatemeh's husband, Sang, was governor. She was an excellent servant and her two sons and one daughter were trained for service in Fatemeh's home.

I appreciated Fatemeh's offer but I scoffed at my needing a servant in Sarbandan. Now I saw that Asghar could save me a great deal of energy which I could use for something besides gardening, scrubbing and cleaning.

Down to the teahouse I went with a letter to Fatemeh. Mash'hadi Mokhtar could give it to any traveler going down the road to Teheran and eventually it would reach my sister. The letter had good fortune. In less than a week Asghar arrived by charcoal truck.

Willingly he turned the soil, and protesting against woman's work planted in my yard a half-dozen packets of seeds and six fruit trees. Already there was in the yard one great cherry tree, fifty or sixty years old, bending under the weight of the growing fruit. Another year I would plant flowers and shrubs, but this first garden must be only useful.

While Asghar worked outside I sat inside making my plans. I

knew that I had much to learn and that I would have to learn as I worked, but I was determined to start out in an orderly way. Although I did not know well the strange sea I had embarked on, nevertheless I needed to chart my course and decide upon my destination. Carefully I drew a map of the village. On it I placed every home. Starting from the west and moving toward the east, street by street, alley by alley, house by house, I would visit every home. Sometime, and that very soon, I would know the names of everyone in the village. I would know which families were rich, which ones were poor, which ones owned land, which were tenant farmers, actually almost serfs left over from an outmoded feudal system. Each night after a day of visits I could check off the houses I had visited on the master map and add to my case-history files information about each family. It would have been easier, I know, to start in haphazard fashion, visiting those who lived near me, but that way I would have immediately aroused the feeling that some were favored, others were not. Now if people asked me why I had not visited their home I could explain that I wasn't yet on their street, that when the turn came I would be there.

The map looked beautiful on paper, the plan that I would follow seemed businesslike and perfect. I had forgotten how strong ignorance, suspicion, fear could be. Or perhaps I thought that because I was a Moslem and loved the people suspicion would not wall me out.

The first day I dressed carefully for my visits. I did not wear the dress of the women of Sarbandan; that would have been effrontery. The dress belonged to them and I was a stranger. I put on a full long skirt of bright print, a long-sleeved, high-necked blouse that matched it. Over my hair I put a kerchief.

You do not knock on the door in Sarbandan. There are no doors. "Yoo-hooh. Anybody in?" I called at the first house.

"Who is there?" came the question in an almost sullen voice.

"I am Lady Najafi," I answered. "I am a teacher."

"I am Eshrat. Come in, my lady," the voice answered.

I went in, my eyes growing accustomed to the darkness. The walls, the floor were of dried earth. The woman who peered at me through slitted, suspicious eyes was feeding a young child from a bowl about which the flies buzzed in a humming spiral.

Sanitation, I thought. *God, put words in my mouth.*

She brushed at the flies with a careless hand. "Flies," she said. "Always flies in the summertime."

"Yes," I said, thoughtfully. "But there is a way to kill the flies." I thought of the latrines of Sarbandan, too few, too seldom used; of human excrement being used to fertilize the fields, of animal filth in every dooryard. "There is a spray," I told her. "Material called D.D.T. I have used it at my home and it is very good."

Her eyes passed from my kerchief to my simple sandals and came to rest on her own rough bare feet. "If I had what you have I'd kill flies, too," she said with growing sullenness.

"You may use my spray," I offered.

"I'll keep my flies."

I might have walked out of that hut defeated but I resolved to find a path to the woman's mind, a way to reach her that would conquer for the time at least her fear of the new.

I tried a careful approach through our religion. I reminded her that Moslems never eat anything unclean. Mohammad taught that unclean things are not good for the body. The law is in the Koran. I showed her the tiny copy of the Koran that I wear on my breast suspended from a chain around my neck.

She sat cuddling the child against her, her eyes watchful but less suspicious. Then I explained how food on which the fly has lighted is no longer clean and fit to be eaten. Reaching out a quick hand I seized a fly and imprisoned it between my thumb and middle finger. I showed her the nature of the fly's legs, and described his flight from his breeding place in a pile of manure, from filth heap to filth heap, to the food of her baby.

"If you know so much about the Koran answer me this," she said, and almost sneeringly propounded a theological question for which I had no answer.

"Do you know rugmaking?" I asked her. She smiled, thinking that I was avoiding an answer by changing the subject. "No, I don't. That is the wisdom of the tribe people, I believe."

"Do you know how to cut potatoes for planting?"

"Of course."

"There is some wisdom for the mullah and some wisdom for me," I said. "I know about the uncleanliness of the fly. You must ask the mullah about—"

Finally when I left the woman had consented to borrow my spray. In my plan for the day I had allowed fifteen minutes for each call. With my first woman I had spent an entire morning. I went back to my home, got out my map of the village and checked the house. On my case history I wrote, "Suspicious, somewhat crafty. She is a complex character. She both loves and hates, both hungers for knowledge and fears it."

I did not know how many times I was going to write those words after a name.

It was midafternoon when I stopped at the home of Fatemeh. There was no answer to my call, no sign of life when I peered inside the house. Somewhere I could hear the mewing of a sick child. I went around to the back. A slender young woman, dressed in a bright cotton print, holding a whimpering child in her arms, was bent over a black kettle hanging above an open fire.

"Salaam," I said quietly. She didn't turn, just kept on stirring. "May I help you?"

She turned her face toward me. There was a look of complete despair in her red-rimmed eyes and I could trace the tracks of tears down her smoke-grayed face. I took the child from her arms and looked down into his yellowing face. He was six months old perhaps, but unbelievably thin and dry-skinned.

"He isn't going to die. Six I have had that died, but Ali will live!" There was hysteria in her voice. "I won't let him die!"

"What are you making?" I watched her rough hand, white-knuckled around the shapeless iron spoon.

Her glance at me said, "Why, you stupid woman! How is it that you don't know?" Her lips said defiantly, "Medicine."

"And what is this medicine?"

"The blood of a living raven boiled with crushed beetles." Her eyes, wide with fear, came to my face for a minute. "It is a good medicine?"

"No, no, no!" I wanted to cry out. "It is not a good medicine!" Instead I said as calmly as I could, "It is a strange medicine for one so small. So helpless."

I did not know how to answer her. All I knew was that I must save this little one from that horrible brew. I moved to overturn the kettle, but I stopped myself. What right had I to do this? The baby's father had probably spent hours in snaring a living raven so that the blood could drip from it while it still lived.

I reached for the child and the mother put him in my arms. Think of something, think of something, I told myself as I hushed him against my breast. But I could not think; I was feeling too much. There were tears on my cheeks, a dread fear of death clutching at all my muscles, making them like useless rope. This might be my baby, I thought, as I felt the heavy beating of his heart against me. He is my baby.

Abruptly his body tensed in my arms. He coughed, grew rigid, coughed again. With the cough there was a high-pitched gasp of strangulation.

The mother seized the child from me and covered his little purple face with kisses. "He isn't going to die," she cried again. "Not this one."

She turned her desperate eyes to me again but I could not help her. I shared her panic.

I thought then of Dr. Birjandi's words. "You are too soft. You must educate your heart." And I knew in this first crisis that I had failed. I had been merely a woman, any woman. "God," I prayed, "lead me. Guide me. Direct me."

Abruptly into my mind came a memory that I did not know was stored there. In the tiny village of Japon, about five or six kilometers from Sarbandan, the government had opened a small, well-stocked clinic. I did not know who was in charge there. I didn't even know that I knew there was a clinic, but I trusted this moment of inspiration. "Come," I said. "You hold the baby and I will go rent a donkey. We will take him to a doctor."

With decision, strength returned to my body. Half running, I hurried to the teahouse of Mash'hadi Mokhtar, my bureau of information. He told me where a donkey could be had for a small rental; even sent his brother to procure it for me. Almost at once the mother with the baby in her arms was mounted on the donkey and I was walking beside her.

The June sun was hot on my face but I was not tired. The distance seemed long because of my concern for the baby, the mother's continuous whimpering, and the fearful spasms of coughing that shook the emaciated body of the baby.

After more than an hour of walking we reached Japon. My inspiration had been right. We found the clinic in part of a small gypsum-plastered house. The old man who was in charge, by courtesy called a doctor, had been apprenticed to a physician in his earlier days and then had begun practice on his own. When the clinic had been opened he had been given a short course in common ailments, taught to give hypodermic shots and to do certain mechanical things like reducing fractures. That he was a doctor was an assurance of competency to the mother. She put the child willingly into his arms.

I described the cough. Croup, he said, with a respiratory infection. He studied the yellow face, the yellow eyeballs of the child. "Give plenty of boiled water and as much milk as he will take," he said. The mother put her hands on her shrunken breasts, a mute gesture that said the milk had left her breasts and she could not feed the child.

The doctor put a package of dried milk into my hands. "You'll know what to do with this," he said. Then he gave the mother a small bottle of medicine. "When the child coughs give him a dose of this every few minutes until he vomits," he said.

"Vomits?" she questioned.

"Yes, that will clear his throat for breathing." I stole a glance at the medicine. It was ipecac.

"What is the charge, Doctor?" I asked.

He shrugged.

"I wish to pay for the examination, the shot, the milk, the medicine."

The doctor's eyes didn't meet mine. "Miss Najafi, when I saw you coming, walking beside that donkey, I was shamed. You may count on me to help you all I can. No charge."

We slowly returned to the village. Now the mother was singing a soft little song to the baby, who still mewed now and then.

When we got back to her house she put the baby in my arms while she poured the magic medicine compounded of the blood of a living raven into her yard, where it left a dark damp stain. She had other medicine, and she was content.

I had not noticed the long walk to Japon or the long walk back; but when I reached my home my legs were like floss. They trembled and would not hold me. I was very, very tired.

The next morning I took, as was my habit, a walk toward the top of the mountain. Just a little way up, where I could be away from the sound and movement of the village, I could stand in the stillness and drink strength from the clean blue sky and the hills. When I returned my home was full of women with children in their arms. "You helped Fatemeh's child," they told me. "My child, too, needs help."

So now God had answered my question. I had asked Him where I should begin. Was it to be with education, with industry, with sanitation? Now I knew. Unprepared as I was in the field of medicine I must begin with a clinic.

I thought of my friend Forough's words, "Love and thought don't buy vaccine, nor build schools, nor equip clinics." And I wondered where I should turn.

I could not turn to the Ford Foundation. With them I had already discussed my problem and had received enough for me to live while I worked in the village. Neither could I call the Near East Foundation, because, though our real aims were very similar, our methods of accomplishing those aims were often very different. When I had left the Foundation to begin my own work, a superior in the organization had said to me, "Don't start your work too near any of our villages. You'll ruin what we are trying to do."

I thought of the Imperial Organization of Social Services and decided to turn to them for help. But now the mothers waited impatiently for me to do the magic thing for their babies. I explained that later I could do these things; that now I did not have the medicine but that I would get it. Then I talked to them of boiling the water, of giving clean milk, of keeping the children bathed and clean, of the importance of good nutrition.

As soon as I could find a ride into Teheran I went.

In a country where misappropriation of funds is not an unusual thing, the Imperial Organization of Social Services stands above criticism. The Shah is the honorary head of the organization but his sister, Princess Ashraf Pahlavi, is the honorary director. She attends the board meetings; she has her finger on the pulse of the needy in the nation. The director is Dr. Ashtiani and his assistant is Dr. Kasemi. These people were to be the godmother and godfathers of Sarbandan. They listened to my problem and approved the formation of a clinic in Sarbandan.

A visitor would have smiled if he hadn't become apprehensive at my lack of knowledge. I learned to give shots: vitamin, antibiotic, penicillin. I got a large medical book with symptoms plainly described. I took the first-aid materials and the simple medicines that were given me. And scared to death, I opened the clinic.

I had been in my little home less than two months and now it was no longer mine. While I was gone on my visits, getting acquainted with the people of my village, the sick gathered in my one room. When I returned I had to step over them to reach my medical book, my aspirin tablets, my first-aid supplies that were neatly shelved in one of the alcoves.

"I am not a doctor," I told all of the patients. "I can give only first aid." But they were happy with first aid, especially if a shot was included. They had such faith in a shot that if a needle happened to hit a nerve and the shot was painful, they grew well overnight.

And yet running the clinic must not take all my time. I had not come to Sarbandan to run a clinic.

One Friday morning a group of my friends drove into Sarbandan. The summer is cool in Sarbandan; it is a pleasant place to escape the heat of the city. Among these friends was a doctor, Dr. Zolnasr. I had left a roomful of patients to go out to greet my friends. What more natural than that I should invite him in to look at them.

"Najmeh, these folks needs more than aspirin tablets," he told me. "Look." He called me over to look into one child's eye. "Glaucoma. It happens to be in the first stages so I can show you how to treat it here." His face was grave as he went from patient to patient. Finally he sat down on the mat with a pad of paper on his knee and listed the drugs I should request from the Imperial Organization of Social Services. I took the list and looked it over hopelessly. "But I am not a doctor."

I had said this so much the repetition tired me.

"Of course you aren't." He was serious for a moment, then his face brightened. "Look. I have been taking Friday from my own work. I will come here each Friday and see the sickest of the patients while you care for the others."

And so the clinic was closed except on Fridays, though I never turned away someone who needed my help. Friday morning Asghar would go down to the old bathhouse, take the megaphone from its nail, and go through the village calling, "Clinic is open today. Clinic! Doctor will be here today. Doctor!" And suddenly, out of the little huts all over the village would come a thin, broken stream of the sick.

I watched the doctor work and made myself an unusual reference book. With his help I wrote down the symptoms of each disease that might be found in Sarbandan. By the symptoms I put the instructions that I could follow in giving temporary aid; the instructions the patient could follow at home to speed his recovery. This special notebook was of more value to me than the big book with its long involved names and its treatment which called for materials which I did not have.

Later, other doctor friends agreed to give a Friday to the clinic and they took turns so that no one doctor had to come too often. "Najmeh," one of them told me, "I never thought I'd live to see the day when I would examine a hundred patients!"

"Why do you do it now?" I asked him.

"Because you don't stop so I can't," he grinned.

With the clinic running smoothly I decided it was time to build a classroom for the women. Perhaps, I thought, I can build such a room onto this little house. The money which I would pay for a year's rent to the kadkhoda would hire the contractor and pay for the material. When I suggested to the kadkhoda that I would build this room onto his house instead of paying him the rent for a year he objected noisily. I spoke to him of the increased value of this house when it would have an additional large room with glass windows and a heavy wooden door. He argued, he explained, he argued some more. *He* would build the room to my specifications; and I would pay the rent as usual.

I drew the plans, a large room with big windows to give plenty of light. The windows would be of glass and there would be real doors. The kadkhoda was not at all frightened by the details of my plan. His mother, his wife, his sister came with him one morning ready for work. I was assigned to carry the water; they would make the bricks of mud and water and straw and place them. Everybody worked. Asghar, cleaning my house and doing the cooking, grinned cheerfully every time he saw me pass with my full jar.

But one morning, when the walls were about waist high, the whole building collapsed and the kadkhoda and his assistants withdrew from the building industry. With the help of Mash'hadi Mokhtar I found brickmakers and masons and set them to work on my plans. This time I didn't carry water. I went on with my visits to the people of the village, with my work in the clinic.

I had learned by one more experience that one person cannot do any important work alone. It is better to know where to turn for help than to be self-sufficient.

Six ⚜ **TIR**

Khordad ripens into Tir (July), and in the orchards of Sarbandan thousands of fresh-faced little suns look up through the greenness of the apricot trees' foliage at their life-giving father, riding free and high through the quiet, bright blue of the Persian sky. The cherry trees, the tips of their lower branches almost sweeping the earth, are weighted with clusters of enormous black jewels.

Little Rabbit, the blond, two-year-old son of my neighbor, the kadkhoda, stands with his feet wide apart, his round little stomach protruding from the ragged short shirt which is his only apparel, his hands locked behind his back, and with his teeth and lips picks off the fruit from a low-hanging limb of my ancient cherry tree. In Iran, as in other Eastern countries, one may eat as much as he wants of another's fruit or vegetables or melons, or grain. It is only when such produce is taken out of the field that a wrong has been done. A hundred cherries in a stomach is all right; one in the pocket and the owner of the pocket is a thief.

I smile as I watch Little Rabbit, so dear, so dirty. I think: His method of harvesting is much more sanitary than picking the fruit with the hands.

As I call at the homes in the village I often find them empty. The cherries must be picked for the truckers to take to the city. The crop has been contracted even before the trees were in bloom. The apricots must be picked, sorted and cut for drying. Every farmer dries his own crop on his own roof top. The women are never too busy to chat, but I know that they should be, so I speak cheerily when I see them at work with their knives and go on.

Now the growers of cherries will be able to pay the landlord part of what they borrowed during the lean months of the winter so that soon they can borrow again, keeping themselves forever in debt, and thus under the control of those who have money to lend.

It was evening, and I was picking a bowlful of my cherries for my supper when a strange cavalcade stopped in front of my house. I put down the bowl and went to the front of my yard. The middle-aged man, gray with worry and fatigue, spoke:

"Are you Lady Najafi?"

"Yes, I am."

The man signaled to four boys who were carrying a small rug on which a girl of about fourteen was lying.

"We have brought you Batool," he said. "I am Batool's father and these are her brothers."

I waited for more explanation, but there was none. "What has happened to Batool?"

"She was working in the orchards. Some snake bit her."

"Would you like to show me the place, Batool-jun?" I asked,

but the girl only moved restlessly on the ragged bit of rug. Since the father and the boys made no move to help her, I knelt by the rug. One foot was swollen. I turned back the bottom of her trousers. The foot was black, the leg was black, too, halfway to the knee.

"When did this happen?" I asked sharply.

The father made a deprecatory flourish with his hands. "We did not know that it was serious," he said.

"I am not a doctor. I cannot help her."

"But, Lady!" It was the youngest of the brothers who had spoken.

"I cannot help her but I will find one who can," I promised.

Quickly I sent Asghar to rent a donkey for me. We made Batool, now feverish and moaning, as comfortable as we could and started for Japon, where a car might be available, six of us walking beside the donkey. The father and the boys were silent. Now and then I tried to reassure the girl, but mostly I was silent, too.

In Japon we found a jeep which could be procured to take Batool to Teheran. Her father would go with her and I assured him that any patient I sent with a note to one of the doctors who was my friend would be given every attention and at once. I wrote the note and pinned it to Batool's blouse. She moved her head backward and forward restlessly as if she were no longer conscious of what went on around her.

The jeep was drawn up to the door of the clinic and we lifted Batool from the rug where she had been resting while I arranged for the car and wrote the note. But now she began to scream and fight. "I will not ride in a car. If I ride in a car I will die. I will not sit in a car."

Finally I overpowered her, not with force but with a sedative by hypodermic needle. In a few minutes she was calm and we put her carefully in the car.

"Come with us, my lady," the father begged. But I had work to do in Sarbandan and besides I knew that in the busy hospitals of Teheran a woman with no special knowledge would be only in the way.

It was almost winter when the father, the four brothers and Batool came to see me again. Batool was still riding on a donkey.

To save her life the doctors had amputated her leg to the knee joint, leaving the joint so that sometime an artificial limb could take the place of the one she had lost through delay in treatment. I put down *One artificial limb* on the list of things that I must somehow acquire—a list that I carried in my mind.

Four days after Batool had first been brought to me, as I went on my usual visits, thinking that even here, high in the mountains, the day was warm, one of the kadkhoda's sons came running to overtake me. "My lady," he cried, "there are many in the clinic. Come. Hurry."

I wondered if I had visitors from Teheran so I turned and followed him. There were many in my little room, but my visitors were village mothers with whimpering and crying children.

"This is not the day for the clinic," I said, but seeing the panic in the women's eyes and the sick, listless appearance of the children, I knelt on the mat beside one of the sick babies.

"It is the summer sickness," said Zivar, one of the more intelligent young mothers. "It comes every year with the ripening of the fruit."

I did not need to look in my homemade medical book to know that she was right. Diarrhea. Child after child with the green, stringy, profuse bowel movements. Since village mothers do not diaper a baby many times in one day, as American mothers do, the stench in the little room became sickening and we moved the clinic outside under the tree.

For one panicky moment I wished desperately that this was Friday. Then I conquered myself. These mothers were looking to me for help, and if I had none to give, then next door was Madar-i-Kadkhoda with her store of marvelous and dangerous medicines.

"This is not too bad," I said cheerfully. "But we must all work together."

"Children die of it," Zivar said, in that peculiarly dead tone of voice that only the hopeless use.

"No one needs to die," I told them. Then I talked to them again about sanitation. I knew that there was not much use in asking them to boil all of the water they used. To them boiled water and water fresh from the jube *looked* alike so it must be alike. I explained how a little rice was to be boiled in much water and this rice water was to be given not only to the sick but to the well to ward off the sickness. The milky appearance of the rice water was distinctive. This difference they could believe because they could see it. I sent them home with instructions to wash their hands carefully before preparing or serving food and I called after them as they left, "Remember, a little rice in a great deal of water!"

As soon as I had sent them to their homes I gave Asghar money and sent him to find a ride to Teheran. If he could get into Teheran that evening he could come back on a charcoal truck the next morning. He negotiated the trip successfully and in the morning he was back with perchlorine.

Now with Asghar carrying the perchlorine and I a spoon, we went from house to house measuring the purifying factor into each family's water jug. Ordinarily this great jug is filled at sunrise and its contents last through the day.

"You are not going to put that foul-smelling medicine into my water!" several of the women told me fiercely. I did not fight with them. I did not even argue. I simply said, "Then don't bring your children to the clinic. I won't see them." I did not have time to explain. I had an epidemic to waylay if I did not already have one to battle. When I walked out of the house with Asghar carrying the perchlorine usually the mother came running after me. "I'm sorry, my lady. I'm sorry. Come give medicine to my water jug!"

I knew that many people had come to the clinic. Sometimes by six in the morning there would be a line in my back yard waiting for the clinic to open. But I did not know until now that the confidence of the women in the clinic had actually begun to surpass their fear of the unknown.

But chlorinating the water in the jugs would not be enough. Too many people used water directly from the stream. Most any time you could see some child stretched out by the stream, face down, drinking directly from it.

In the afternoon I walked up and down the stream talking with the women. "You must carry the water away from the stream to wash your clothes, your dishes," I told them.

"But both the water and the sand are here," they would argue. I looked at the white sand which the village women use as an abrasive in both clothes and dishwashing. It looked clean but I had seen half-naked children sitting on this very sand instead of seeking a latrine.

"We must keep the water in the jube as clean as possible," I told them. "Besides, this sand is not good for washing. It is unclean. There is something much better than sand."

In Sarbandan there was no soap. How could there be? Thrifty farm women throughout the world pull the fat from the entrails of butchered animals and reduce it to oil for soap-making. But in villages like Sarbandan every bit of such fat is used for food. I had already discovered for myself the value of wood ashes for cleaning. With the help of my friends in Teheran I would substitute clean cans of ashes for the polluted sand along the bank of the stream. I longed to go to Teheran and get this project under way, but I was afraid to leave the village before the summer sickness had subsided.

Two days after the outbreak of the sickness a young couple from a village downstream from Sarbandan came to my home, the girl carrying in her arms a year-old child. The little one's curls were tight against the sweet baby-roundness of her head, but my eyes went first to the tear-stained faces of the young father and mother. The girl was perhaps fifteen or sixteen, and the boy perhaps seventeen.

"My lady, they say you can cure our baby," the father said as he put the baby in my arms. I knew the minute that I touched her that she was dead. I put my fingers on her wasted wrists, my ear against her chest, a mirror before her open mouth.

"I cannot help your baby." I made my voice gentle because these words never can be. "She is dead."

"Give her a shot," they begged. "Please, please, give her a shot."

"I would give her many shots if shots could help her," I said still more gently. And then I tried to say the useless, comfortless things that can be realized only a long time after an abrupt bereavement. "God gives all. He may take what He chooses. But death is not forever. It is a journey, and you yourself may sometime overtake this little traveler." Then I looked at the carefully made curls and I knew that this little one would be lonely starting on such a journey without her mother. It was the first time since I had come to the village that I had met with the finality of death. Now I prayed again, the same prayer, "God, put words in my mouth!"

But this day He did not put words in my mouth. Abruptly I knew that words could not touch these sorrowing parents. I asked Asghar to heat water for me and bring me one of my own new towels. I bathed the child, as the Moslems must do before burial, and wrapped her in sweet clean muslin. As I worked I talked quietly, using the figures of speech that all Persians love and understand. Before they left I had Asghar serve them lunch.

When I finally put the child back in their arms they were comforted. I knew that many times the girl mother, preparing food, would save a choice thing and say to herself, "I will put this by for the baby," and the thought would be followed closely with the intolerable realization of loss. Or perhaps in the nights to come, half aroused by some small sound out of the silence, they both would listen for the breathing of their baby and then the realization would seep through them that she was dead and again they would cry in each other's arms.

And I thought as I saw these children going from my door, carrying the empty vessel which for a year had held all their hopes, that this world will be different only when everyone feels in his heart that no death anywhere in the world is a statistic.

Downstream from Sarbandan. The baby had died from drinking the water our village had helped to pollute. I resolved again that unnecessary pollution of the stream must stop. And it was this afternoon, shaken by the death of the child, that I walked toward the mountain and came upon Eshrat washing the wrappings of her sick child in the stream. She had had the child in the clinic. She had heard me tell the women to carry their washing away from the stream. She turned to me the same sullen face that she had shown me when I talked with her about the filth carried by flies; then she picked up her washed and unwashed clothes and flounced toward her house. I knew that I would be unwelcome there but I followed her in.

I wanted to strike out at her. I wanted to call her stupid—stupid and cruel. But I knew that to show anger builds a wall between the speaker and the one who hears. I sank down upon the dirt floor of her house and tried to talk calmly to her. I told her of the germs (unclean little animals too small to see) that lived in the excrement from her sick child. I tried to make her understand that all of these germs were now set free in the stream and would be carried as far as the jube ran. They would be in the water of a hundred water jugs and mothers who loved their children just as she loved hers would give their little ones this water to drink.

Grudgingly she listened to my story and accepted the logic of what I said, but she could not be defeated easily. "You talked with me about the fly before. My lady, if you had told me about these unclean things I would have carried my washing away from the jube." Her words were civil enough but her tone of voice and manner were insolent and clearly said, "How can you possibly blame me for something that is entirely your fault?"

I took a deep breath. One cannot be taught the whole world's knowledge in one day. This lesson she would have to learn. "Do you have bread in your house?"

"I do."

"Please bring me a piece."

She brought me a piece of black bread.

"Where did you get this bread?"

"I made it."

"On what fire did you bake it?"

"My husband brings wood from the mountain when he has time."

"Did he bring this wood today?"

"He brought it last autumn before he went to the rice fields of Mazandaran."

"And the flour?"

"It is grown from my father's wheat."

"When did you plant this wheat? When was it harvested? Did you wait for the right phase of the moon for the planting and harvesting? Did you wait for the sun and rain to give it growth? Did you wait for the wind to blow the wheat from the chaff?"

"Why do you ask so many questions? Questions, questions, questions!"

"This piece of bread, simple as it is, was not made in a day. Many months ago this bread had its beginning in wood from the mountains, in a wheat seed put under the ground at the proper time. There was a time for everything. And that is the way it is with education. I cannot teach you all that I know in one hour. I myself cannot learn all I need to know in less than one lifetime."

I returned the slice of bread to her. My hands were clean and a slice of black bread is of importance in Sarbandan.

When the doctor came to the clinic on Friday I told him about my week. "We are fortunate in places like this not to have typhoid," he said.

"What can we do?"

"Well," he considered, "you did the right thing. Perchlorine is the safest purifier." Then abruptly he said, "If we could just pipe this water from the springs to the village and have the jugs filled from a faucet. If we could safely dispose of our waste in septic tanks."

I smiled and he looked at me curiously. I knew that at this time even if there were water pipes and a faucet in each part of the village there would be many who would hurry out before sunrise and dip the water for their jugs from the jube. They liked the old ways best. "Well?" he asked.

"It is nothing," I said. "Only my new latrine is now finished and people still prefer the fields."

"I know. Education is more important than money."

As we took care of the day's patients we talked from time to time about preventive medicine. I decided to ask the Imperial Organization of Social Services for material for vaccination and immunization. The organization approved the request at once and our immunization program was begun.

Now when Asghar took the ancient megaphone from the nail in the bathhouse he called, "Friday. Doctor here today. Bring all of your children. Shots today. Shots today."

I had some fears for the project but the people were already converted to hypodermic shots. The superstitious ones were willing to think that the strange treatment was some sort of charm against evil; the intelligent ones appreciated the real purpose.

Every Friday the children lined up in the yard, each holding a number. Five hundred people were vaccinated for smallpox; thirty-eight small children for whooping cough and diphtheria. This was just a small start in the necessary immunization program, but the work was well begun.

Now I no longer had to fight for the clinic nor persuade people to see the doctor. Rather I had a great deal of trouble keeping the people from misusing the privileges. The clean white room with its red mat and blue curtains was a cheerful place to chat with one's neighbors. Even sitting under a tree waiting for a turn to go inside was preferable to staying at home. It began to seem like a social club, too full of the well to take care of the sick.

I talked with Mash'hadi Mokhtar and others about this problem and we decided to charge a small fee for each visit. For a long time we argued about this charge. The fee must be large enough so that people would not come to the clinic who did not really need its services; but small enough so that even the poor would have the proud feeling of paying their own way. Those who were entirely without funds would not be turned away. The door would never be closed to anyone.

We decided on five rials (six to eight cents) for each patient treated. Since the doctors were donating their services at this time and the drugs were furnished by the Imperial Organization of Social Services and the Public Health Co-operative Organization the small fee we collected could be used for emergency services. More and more frequently people were coming a long way from other villages for treatment in the clinic. For these people I wanted to prepare food at noon: shirbrendy (milk and rice), ash (a sort of soup), tork chin (rice and yogurt), or abgousht. The fees which did not need to be used for these lunches could be saved toward the building of a real clinic.

"When does the village council meet, Mashdi Mokhtar?" I asked one afternoon as I sat in his teahouse with a glass of tea.

"Thursday."

"I would like to meet with them."

He raised his magnificent eyebrows. "You, my lady?"

"I wish to ask them to build a clinic."

"We have a clinic."

I thought of the one room rented from the kadkhoda which I had outfitted for a clinic. The classroom beside it was going up ever so slowly because this was the time for the harvesting of the fruit, the cutting of the first crop of hay. I thought of the everlasting arguments of the old men when I had rented this room. "The year for which I have rented my home will be over, Mashdi Mokhtar," I told him, "before we have another building to take its place."

He nodded gravely. "The council meets on Thursday."

"What Thursday, Mashdi Mokhtar?"

"Any Thursday."

"Where?"

"At some home."

"But what home?"

Mash'hadi Mokhtar's shoulders went up in their expressive gesture. "Any home. Perhaps the home of the kadkhoda. Perhaps this teahouse. Someplace."

"When you see the council members will you suggest that they meet this Thursday at this teahouse?"

"Yes, my lady."

But though Thursday came the members of the council did not

come to the teahouse. Mash'hadi Mokhtar and I sat alone.

"Who belongs to this council, Mashdi Mokhtar?"

He raised his shoulders and his gold teeth glittered under his carefully groomed mustache. He was friendly, but obviously I had asked an impossible question.

"Perhaps I can find out from the kadkhoda."

Reluctantly he capitulated. "I will give you the registration," he promised. "But there is no use in a meeting of the council. There is nothing but quarreling and angry voices for many hours in the teahouse."

So he gave me the registration. Several, I found, were unavailable for the meeting. Some were busy with harvest; some were out of town; some were dead. Those that I could find I invited to my home the next Thursday evening for tea. On Wednesday I sent Asghar to their homes to remind them that the next day was Thursday.

Thursday thirteen men came. Some were members of the council, others were just curious. First we must decide who really belonged. There was loud and bitter wrangling. Even my tea, sugar, cakes, and most pleasant persuasive way did not prevent this.

I have spoken of the village council. Perhaps I should say more about what it is and how it works in Iran.

Every man in Iran, no matter how humble, knows a great deal about politics. In the teahouses of the villages old and young men who can neither read nor write discuss politics intelligently—not local politics, but national and international problems. An average American college student knows much less of history, international incidents and international policies than these so-called illiterate men.

This is because politics touches them on every side. Their economic life, their rice and milk and bread depend upon the relation of their state to its ruling powers, the relation of these powers to other great powers. Always these people have watched Russia, England and, since World War II, the United States with a mixture of interest and suspicion. If one man in the village can read, that is enough to keep the entire village informed. Where some other people discuss personalities or the relative value of the Edsel and the Chrysler, our people discuss political blocs, secret pacts, hidden intentions.

But until the time of the council all that these men could do was talk.

The council was meant to give the people practice in democratic procedures as well as assist in rural development. Ordinarily its membership included representatives of the landlord or landlords; of the villagers, free landholders or tenant farmers; and of the government. The council is supposed to study the needs of the village and make application for consideration of these needs to the proper governmental authorities. In other words, it has absolutely no legislative or executive power. It can only advise and request. I determined that our council would not be impotent.

When the wrangling had subsided I talked with the men about their opportunities, their responsibilities. I wanted them to feel pride in their position, to feel status, so that these feelings could blossom into a willingness to do more than talk.

In this way the first evening was spent.

At the next meeting I told them at once about the need for a larger, better-equipped clinic. I told them of the number of patients we had treated, of the vaccinations and immunizations, of the arrangements I had made to have the dangerously ill treated in Teheran hospitals, of my concern over the scald-headed boys at the school.

They nodded their heads and agreed with each statement. When I was through they simply said, "But we have no money." I remembered that when I first came to Sarbandan and asked for a gift of a room for a school there wasn't one available at all; when I said that I wanted to rent one, there were many at my disposal. But now I was resolved that this village council would have to begin to solve its own problems.

"Surely you have *some* money," I told them.

Then began such wrangling and quarreling as I had never heard in my life. Each faction said that if the other faction had not been so stupid, so stubborn, so impossibly ignorant there would be much money now. I got little out of the argument since I knew nothing about the occasion they were referring to. Sometime soon I would ask Mash'hadi Mokhtar. He always knew all. After I had sat quietly for an interminable time, I got up and walked out and began counting the voiceless stars. When they finally realized that I was gone they fell silent and I returned.

"This project will take little money," I promised. "I will apply to the Ministry of Health for assistance in the building, but first we must have the ground. We must have land upon which to build— much land. Not rented land but land that will belong to the clinic."

Now there was deep silence in the room. The men thoughtfully drew the smoke through the long looped tubes of their ghalians, their eyes upon the carafes of water which sat on the floor mat under the bowls of burning tobacco.

Even the promise of government help did not open their purses.

Ever since I had begun my visits in the village I had heard a rumor about Mash'hadi Mokhtar. The story differed in minor ways from telling to telling, but always the essentials were the same. His father had died, willing a piece of ground to the village for a site for a school. According to the story, Mash'hadi Mokhtar was trying to keep this information hidden while he continued to farm this piece of land with the rest of his fields.

Sarbandan lies above the old Mazandaran road. Below the road were the wheat and hay fields—the wheat and hay fields of Mash'-hadi Mokhtar. It was on this side of the road that I hoped to build the clinic so that other villagers traveling the road would say to themselves, "This beautiful and good thing we must have in our village."

Mash'hadi Mokhtar had told me a great deal about Sarbandan but he had never told me about his father's will. I studied him, his eyes half closed under the eaves of his brows; his mouth so tightly drawn that his gold teeth did not glitter in the flickering light of the kerosene lantern. I wondered how to approach him. I knew that under that chapeau of his there was a great war being fought. Mash'hadi Mokhtar, the rich man of property, was battling with Mash'hadi Mokhtar, the great philanthropist. I knew that anything I might say could throw the victory to the former, so for a time I was silent.

Finally I spoke. "Mashdi Mokhtar, ever since I came to Sarbandan you have helped me in all things. Now help me in this. Who owns the wheat fields that are below the Mazandaran road?"

The eyes of the other council members turned toward him, and he must have read knowledge there. "That land belonged to my father, Lady Najafi," he admitted, not looking at me.

"It did!" I cried with incredulous joy. "That is wonderful because now it belongs to you, I suppose, and of all men you are the most willing to improve this village."

For a second or two he dropped the veil of inscrutability over his eyes and I could not read his thoughts. Then his smile flashed and he reached up a deft hand to twist the end of his mighty mustache. "I would gladly give this land but it is not mine to give. My father made a will—"

I almost sighed with relief, but he was not through talking. "The land was given for a *school*. It must be kept for that purpose." Again the voices of the councilmen rose like waves and battered against him. "A clinic is as important as a school." . . . "Your father did not know the value of a clinic when he lived." . . . "We already have a school, now we need a clinic.". . .

Finally I hushed them. "Mashdi Mokhtar," I said, "do not let these gentlemen decide for you. You are a great man, a good man, who loves Sarbandan." He was a "careful" man who would love to keep this land for himself, too. This I knew. "What do you read in your own heart and mind?"

The room was so quiet that the gurgling of the water in the carafes of the ghalians could be heard.

"I will give the land for the clinic," he said, and then added grandly, "and a field for something else besides."

Abruptly I saw in my mind the white-walled clinic, and round it lay an experimental garden of vegetables, berries, flower-bordered.

"Mashdi Mokhtar, tonight you have done a great thing!" I said, and suddenly in the room there was a new rush of voices. Each of the councilmen was promising to do what he could in labor or in money. The meeting ended with kissing and well-wishing, less formal and more warm than usual. "You have all promised great things," I told them. "Great things."

And so the foundation stone for the clinic was laid July 24, 1955. It was four months from the time that I had stopped in the tea-house of Mash'hadi Mokhtar that afternoon in Farvardin. So soon can the people of the villages learn to co-operate to gain things of value.

Seven MORDAD

Mordad, August, is a month of two phases. The first weeks are a time of waiting. The fruit has gone from the orchards; and the leaves of the cherry and apricot are turning yellow and brown and falling from the listless branches. Although the potato vine is beginning to lose its greenness it is not yet time to bring the potatoes from the earth. Some of the "good" is still in the vine and the harvester must wait until it descends into the tuber. The wheat is yellow but not yet golden, and the hay is not yet tall enough for the sickle. Sarbandan seems to hold its breath as it rests under the bright summer sunlight or the soft grayness of a summer shower.

Now is the time, I think, for completing the schoolroom, but village workmen cannot be hurried. All day they can talk, talk, talk about the work before them; but only the promise that I will go into Teheran and bring back the wooden door and glass windows puts them to work at all.

In Teheran the heat is unbearable after the mountain coolness of Sarbandan. Only in the shaded courts that surround the ancient buildings and under the many-domed pavilion of the bazaars is it at all pleasant. And I am not in either of these places. I am hunting for used doors and windows from the commercial wrecking establishments, and standing around in Fouzieh Square trying to

76

contract for their delivery by charcoal truck. The trucks that pass Sarbandan to the charcoal pits always go up empty to return loaded with charcoal. These, of course, are the cheapest means of transportation for heavy items being taken to Sarbandan.

While I am in Teheran I ask my friends to save their empty cans, and to ask their friends to do the same. I want a can to hold ashes in every home in the village to use for cleansing and whitening the clothes and for purifying the dishes.

After two days I return to Sarbandan. I am surprised at the lift in my heart as I turn the final bend in the road and see the village, my village, all green and brown and gray and golden in the early-morning sunlight.

I had scarcely changed into my village clothing when I heard a man's voice calling, "Anybody home?" I recognized the smiling young man who filled my doorway, not by name of course, as one of the construction engineers whom I had met at a convention of the specialists of the Damavand Development Bongha.

"I am Abolhassan Mozaffari, do you remember me?"

I said that I did.

"We, my parents and I, have come to Sarbandan to spend a day away from the heat of Teheran and to visit my mother's aged aunt and uncle. We wondered if you would like to pay a call with us."

My hands itched to measure the doors and windows and draw up the plans and specifications for making the frames, but I quickly agreed. My work in Sarbandan had been with the poor. I wondered about the relatives of this young engineer.

"For many years my uncle had his own apothecary shop in Teheran. He built a summer home here to escape the heat of the city. Later, when he retired, they came to this little house to make their home. Perhaps you have seen his shop in the village."

"Yes," I said, remembering the genial old man and his shop where herbs and other traditional medicines could be purchased.

We walked together toward the teahouse, where he introduced me to his father and mother. "Two Mr. Mozaffaris might be confusing," he said. "My friends call me Shapoor."

Seated in the neat little home of Shapoor's great-aunt we drank tea from fragile glasses in filigree silver holders. Her husband would soon be home, she said. When the eighty-five-year-old man came to his door he called in a lively, robust voice, "Madam, your servant is here." And she, blushing like a young girl, patted her kerchief and blouse and hurried to meet him. I looked at the young engineer—Shapoor—and found his eyes on me. We smiled together.

Perhaps, someday, I thought as I returned to my work, Sarbandan might attract many city people like this charming old couple. High in the mountains, it has the perfect summer climate. Maybe, after several improvements were made in the village, we could—My mind was so busy with this new project for Sarbandan that I was astonished to look up and find a crowd of interested observers and would-be technicians watching as I measured, wrote down numbers, and measured again.

When I handed my specifications to the carpenters they smiled knowingly and assured me that they could do very well with the frames—without my figures. They insisted that their eyes "told them" and that measuring by meters was absurd. Three times they built those frames and took them to pieces. The fourth time they were measured and put together according to my specifications. Even though my patience was as ragged as an old garment I let them take their time and build and rebuild. Only in this way would they learn that accuracy is essential. Had they used my specifications from the first they would have always thought, and told each other, too, that their way was best had they just been given an opportunity to prove it.

During this waiting period, too, was an excellent time to begin the treatment of the scald-headed children, some of whom I had noticed the first day that I visited the boys' school. I had requested treatment for these children from the Imperial Organization of Social Services and they had granted my request. The only requirements were that I should have the children in Teheran at six any Monday morning, and that we should do everything we could do to prevent reinfection after the condition had been cured.

Scald head is a fungus disease in which the hair roots are affected. In the old days the only way of curing it was to pull out
one hair at a time from the affected area, scrub the head with
natural agents and finish with a coat of pitch. The treatment was
painstaking and painful, and was successful some of the time.
Today the sick hairs are removed by radiotherapy which burns the
roots and kills the fungus. Such a change!

Getting the boys to Teheran was my problem. The first step was
to visit the home of each child and talk with the mother. I had
to convince her first that there would be no expense connected
with the treatment, second that the condition was curable, third
that I could not take care of it in our own little clinic, and fourth
that her child would be returned safely to her arms.

Village people love their children with a sort of fierce pos-
sessiveness that at times seems to be almost angry and belligerent.
Perhaps this is because they have no other interests. They do not
have to divide the love they are giving Hamid with their affection
for a new car, an automatic refrigerator, a back-yard barbecue.

Getting the boys to the clinic at six would mean taking them to
Teheran the night before, feeding them supper and breakfast. This
just didn't seem possible. We—the kadkhoda, who had offered
his help in the project, and I—decided to leave in the early morning
hours. For transportation I borrowed a sort of station wagon which
was meant to hold eight but which for our trip would have to hold
twenty-four children, the kadkhoda and me.

At two-thirty Monday morning I went from door to door. "Come
now. It is time to rise. It is time to get ready to go to Teheran to
the clinic. Come, Abbas. Come, Mahmood. Come, Abdolah."

The parents wakened from their sleep grumbled sleepily that
they had changed their minds. The little boys set up a wailing, half
from drowsiness, half from fear.

"Come, Abbas. Come, Mahmood. Come, Abdolah."

Finally the shivering boys trickled out of their houses, holding
tightly to the hands of their mothers. Overhead the sky was deep

navy blue filled with more stars than are ever seen in the city skies. As we waited for the car I noticed that each boy had a pair of shoes. If there were shoes in the family they had been loaned to him for this occasion. If not, he had borrowed from his cousin or his aunt. Few had small shoes intended for small boys. Some were very big men's shoes suitable to be worn in the army. Some were high-heeled women's shoes. But a trip to Teheran demanded this dignity.

As we waited for the bus, the boys wiped their eyes on their mothers' skirts, gave their shoes to their mothers' keeping, and began to frolic around, tagging each other, racing breathlessly, shouting, kicking up the soft dry earth.

The kadkhoda cut two switches from a near-by tree and handed one to me. I laughed inside of me to see him twitching that switch as if he were herding ducks or chickens.

At last the conveyance came in sight and immediately the fun was forgotten. Again the boys howled and clung to their mothers. The mothers wept and clung to their boys. The driver impatiently waited for the load.

Finally all of the boys were packed in. "Don't forget to put on your shoes. Don't forget your shoes!" the mothers called.

Barely had we gone around a dozen curves when most of the boys, who had never been in any sort of vehicle before, began to grow dizzy with the unaccustomed motion. They were hungry, too, excited and more than a little afraid of the unknown. At first we tried to get the most disturbed boys to the outside near the windows but the effort was useless. Each boy was returning his supper rice. The smell in that bus! It was fortunate that the fresh air swept through.

Near Teheran, goaded by one or two of the older boys, each child tried to put on and tie his shoes. In the crowded bus that was quite a problem. As soon as we reached town and unloaded the boys they saw that there was asphalt. "Why, shoes are unnecessary!" they cried, and taking them off they tucked them under their arms. The kadkhoda, armed with his switch, shepherded them to a washroom.

Six o'clock and we were at the clinic. Now we waited only until seven for the treatment to begin.

First each child's head needed to be shaved. I had not known this or the shaving could have been accomplished at the village barber's. I explained why it was necessary and since the cost of shaving was not part of the clinic treatment I paid for this service.

Next each boy was placed under the powerful X ray. Obediently they turned their heads first for a time one way, then for a time in another. Only the smallest boys wiggled and received unintentional burns on their faces.

It was evening before the boys were again packed into the tiny bus. I had bought lunch for them, and for supper each was chewing on a magnificent bun. They would all have to return in a month for a checkup, but most of them were cured completely by the one treatment. Cured if we could prevent reinfection.

As we chugged home, the bus laboring on the steeper grades, my thoughts were divided between methods for preventing reinfection and dreams of the time when a mobile unit, carrying its own power, could make scald-headedness a thing of history in the Iranian villages.

"Come, Abbas. Come, Mahmood. Come, Abdolah. Waken now. We are in Sarbandan. We are home."

The bus drew to a stop before my house and there was a greeting committee of every father, every mother, many brothers and sisters. The sleepy travelers were hauled out of the bus, checked for the all-important shoes and hurried away to their homes. I truly believe that some of these mothers did not expect to see their sons again! "He who was lost has returned again home."

In each cottage the lantern burned late. For this young man who had seen more of the world than his mother ever would see there were tea and sugar, and perhaps a sweet cookie. With interest and wonder the bar of soap, a disinfectant soap, that had come home with each boy was passed around, smelled, and admired. The shaved head was to be washed daily with this soap. I must see that it was used for this purpose and not kept for a memento of a wonderful adventure.

The homemakers of Sarbandan are good housekeepers—in their fashion. They are very neat. First thing in the morning the bedding used at night is picked up and packed away. The samovar is polished every day and kept marvelously shining. Yet there are many things about housekeeping that these women do not know.

In the village, people sleep with their heads on sort of a pillow. It is really a bag of wool and doesn't have a removable pillow case. The bags grow dirtier and dirtier. I spent the week visiting the homes of Monday's patients making certain that all of these pillows were washed and dried in the sun. I had dreaded this work, because when a villager gets used to his dirt he never sees it or smells it. However, to the mothers of these boys, the cure of the scald-headedness was a miracle. No more itching, no more burning, no more falling out of whole patches of hair. Since the treatment can't be given to anyone under seven, the big point in life to look forward to for many little children is the day when they can have the treatment. It is wonderful to be seven!

"Thank you, my lady. This was magic," the mothers told me. "Only cleanliness can maintain the magic," I told them, and almost without exception the people co-operated.

Now the waiting phase of the month of Mordad is over. The village draws a quivering sigh and wakens for the harvest. The potatoes, the beans, the wheat, the hay, all are ready. And besides the harvesting and the laying away of food there is something of even greater importance to be done. The last of Mordad (August) and the first of Shahrivar (September) are the time for marrying.

And because in the Moslem marriage customs the bathhouse is most important, it is the time for a new project for me. The old, broken, dirty bathhouse must be cleaned.

All summer I had carried the thought of that filthy bathhouse in my mind. I had chafed against waiting for a trip to Teheran before I myself bathed, but the job had seemed just too big, too impossible. Now it must be done.

At a meeting of the council we organized the work on the bath. One council member was to see that the water was drained from the pool, another that the emptied pool was thoroughly scrubbed and disinfected, another that the long corridors were scrubbed and mended with new mud. Really, dividing this way, the work was not too great. My part was to put perchlorine in the water to keep it safe.

After all our work the bathhouse was still dark, still dank, but it was clean and sanitary. There was no way to arrange in this old bath for a little water to go and new water to come. Each time it was cleaned it would be the same job of total change.

The bathhouse was ready for the marriages.

In Sarbandan, as in other Persian villages, marriage is the climax of one's life—the only really wonderful thing that ever happens. Toward the money gift to the mother of the bride for each son, or the dowry for each daughter, fathers and mothers plan, save and borrow. Mostly borrow. And the young bridegroom is responsible for the payment of this debt. For seven years after a young man marries, his life will belong to the moneylender. But who would want a poor wedding?

Still, in the cities, those who live the traditional life expect a young girl to marry an older man, a man who has money, public office or social position. In the villages young girls marry young boys. These are the happiest marriages I have ever seen.

The people in the villages believe in long engagements; sometimes four months, sometimes four years. This engagement period is not for becoming better acquainted as in America, but for preparing for the wedding. During this time the intended bridegroom must buy everything, even clothing for his betrothed bride. On each special day, such as New Year's or the birthday of Mohammad, he must send gifts.

In the cities there are many who hold to the ancient traditions and depend upon matchmakers to bring a boy and girl together. In the village there is always a matchmaker. In Sarbandan, Madar-i-Kadkhoda has been busy acting as go-between or agent for the two families. But here there is a difference. The bride and bridegroom are not likely to be strangers to each other. The boys and girls have worked together in the fields and orchards, have played together along the banks of the jube. Only in the mosque and in the school have they been separated. After the age of eleven or twelve their freedom has been curbed and girls have sought the company of girls, boys of boys. But when Madar-i-Kadkhoda mentions a name there is always a response of memory and the desires of the boys and girls are taken into consideration.

Since it would not do for either the bride's family or the bridegroom's to seem too eager, it takes five months or more of talk before the arrangements can be completed. Finally the boy's mother sends a tray with henna, a silk scarf, sugar, cookies, candy. Her messenger is her husband, who not only carries the tray but helps to eat the good things as he discusses the marriage with the father of the girl. If this discussion is fruitful, after two days the boy's mother sends another tray. This time the materials on it—yogurt, milk and cheese—are symbolic of the basic meaning of life.

After this tray is received there is high excitement in the home of the girl. If the family is well off there will be shopping in Teheran; but even if the family is very poor there will be important preparations to be completed. In Sarbandan a little brown man comes with his antiquated Singer sewing machine and his eleven-year-old grandson to make the wedding dress, the new chador, and to complete the dowry. The boy, like a little gnome, cuts and sews along with his grandfather. The old man has but one model and one size, but he makes all the wedding dresses in the village. This dress differs from the usual village costume in that the skirt is to the ankles. The bride must have two chadors, two pairs of trousers, and two pink dresses, one of which should be silk.

After a week of frenzied preparations the girl's mother sends a tray of rice, meat, henna and sweets to the home of the boy, signifying that the bride's preparations are completed. The bridegroom and his father bring the money gift to the mother of the bride, a gift that shows the appreciation of the young man and his family for all the mother has done to bring the girl to maturity. This money gift is known as shir barka, and is usually used to help toward the preliminary expenses of the marriage ceremony.

When the contract is signed the bridegroom's family agrees to pay, when asked for, another sum of money equal to the girl's dowry. This sum of money is known as mahr, a marriage portion, payable at the time of divorce or upon the death of the husband or at any other time that it is asked for. This is the bride's safeguard in a country where the law allows the man to "divorce his wife any time he desires to."

In Sarbandan the bride's mother usually turns over the shir barka to the bride and with it she buys the things that are necessary to begin her married life; always a samovar, sometimes other things—a rug, a kettle, a quilt, a tray.

Four evenings before the marriage is the ceremony of bringing in the wood. A dinner for the boy and his men friends is given at his home. At midnight each of the men takes a donkey up the mountain into the timber land. Under the early-morning sun the procession returns to Sarbandan, each donkey loaded with wood, and carrying a red flag.

Hail to this blessed day!
The lane is narrow,
The bride is tall;
Don't touch her hair,
It is arranged in curls.
Oh, blessedness and happiness!

Then everyone shouts, "Yes," and claps. "Congratulations!"

There are many stanzas and those who do not know all the words can at least join in with:

Oh, blessedness and happiness!
Yes!! (Clap) Congratulations!

The men, and sometimes the donkeys, step to the beating of the donbak (the marriage drum). The bringing in of the wood is a custom I had not seen before I went to Sarbandan.

The procession of the girl's friends moves through the town the following day. Each woman, not wrapped in her chador—her chador is tied about her waist, and in her own way she is beautiful

—but dressed in her brightest, best clothing, carries a gift. Some may have trays on their heads on which there may be henna, or rice, or sugar. One woman leads a living lamb whose white wool has been died with henna. Around its neck is a string of blue beads to which is fastened a tinkling bell. Singing, the women move toward the house of the bride. Here there is the ceremony of the henna, each woman putting a gift of henna into the hand of the bride.

The next day begins the ritual of the cleansing of the bride. She is taken to the bathhouse, she and her friends marching to the dum-dum-di-dum of the donbak. Here her friends assist her to become beautiful. The unwanted hairs on her face are taken off with a special thread, her eyebrows are plucked, her face is cleansed, her nails are colored with henna. Each girl's mother has sent a tray of food. There is sherbet—a sort of acid drink made with either fruit juice or vinegar and sugar—melon, dried fruit, cookies, candies. They have entered the bathhouse early but it is three in the afternoon before they have finished.

When the bride leaves, the bridegroom and his friends go into the bathhouse. What they do there I do not know, but the donbak is beaten all of the time he stays; from three until, perhaps, midnight.

On the afternoon of the next day a decorated horse is brought for the bride. The bride, wrapped in a white chador, and wearing a white veil held by a crown of many-colored feathers, mounts it and rides toward the bathhouse. Her friends, on foot, sing and dance as they go. Now the bride is truly a queen and her friends are her subjects. At the bathhouse she dismounts and enters.

The bridegroom does not ride a horse nor wear a crown, but no matter how hot the weather is he wears an overcoat to prove that he is very rich. He enters the bathhouse, going to a different room, of course.

Constantly the donbak beats-beats-and-beats.

But still these two are not prepared for the final ceremony. The girl rides back to her own home, the boy goes to his. With a chosen friend at each side, he sits on a chair, often borrowed for this one occasion, which has been draped with some bright material. The friends with him count the money that has been sent as wedding gifts, and pack the other gifts. They are very busy.

The girl, at home, is putting on make-up. Her hair must be beautiful, her eyebrows drawn with just the right quirk, her finger-nails perfect. She is too nervous to do these things for herself, and her friends help her.

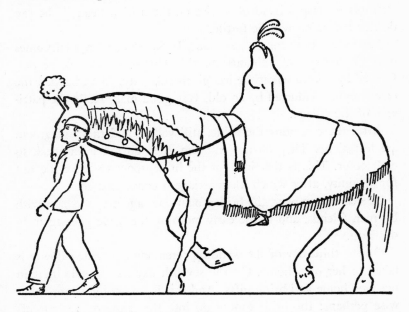

Now the boy moves toward the girl's house, his friends with him, dancing and singing all the way. With them is the decorated horse for the bride to ride. She comes out of her home, her family and friends with her. Now she mounts the horse and again the procession begins. Even though the journey may be less than a mile, it may take an hour. The bride's family, her father, her brothers, pretend that they are reluctant to have her leave them. "The horse wishes to go this way," they say, and lead it off in another direction. Or, "The horse wishes to cross the jube," and the procession waits with laughter and singing while a makeshift bridge is built of wood. Once across, the men may decide that the horse wishes to go back. The longer this bridal trip takes the more seriously will the bridegroom regard his marriage; that is their superstition. Sometimes the horse is stopped. "This donbak is no good. We must find another." Or, "We are weary of walking, let us dance."

Finally the bridegroom's home is reached and the girl and her friends go into the room. The boy climbs up on the roof and attempts to drop a handful of rice on the bride's head. If he can do this the union will be fertile.

Now is the time for the ceremony. In Sarbandan a mullah comes only for the special religious months. This marriage will be performed by one to whom he has given authority. In Sarbandan the ceremony is conducted by an old, very good man, really the patriarch of the village.

After the ceremony the bride, still veiled, and the bridegroom are left alone. They do not embrace, they do not even speak to each other. This is the time for the bridegroom to make the test for virginity, after which the marriage is consummated.

The ceremony over, the bridegroom goes again to the bath with his men friends, and in the early morning the bride goes again to the bath.

On the third day of the wedding ceremony the bride's dowry is taken to her own home. On the seventh day her friends meet in her new home and bring gifts. And this is something strange, but wise perhaps: the bride cannot go into the home of her parents for a year unless she becomes pregnant. In this year she learns how to live with her man, her particular man.

This wedding, celebrated by four or five hundred people even if the participants are poor, is the beginning of a marriage so important that it will never be endangered by cruelty or infidelity. The wife is the man's most costly possession. Why shouldn't he cherish her?

I often stood at my door and watched the processions; the bringing in of the wood, the procession of gifts, the bride on the decorated horse. It made my heart sing to hear a young girl cry out from her perch, "The whole world, the whole world is at my feet!" Often I heard the celebrations going on in homes not far from mine; the applause when each gift was displayed, a gift of money counted. "May God bless Mashdi Mokhtar!" "May God keep his children safe!" "May God bless Lady Najafi!"

For, though I never attended the celebrations—I would have been an intruder—I always sent a gift.

There were several marriages, and only one was different from the others.

As I saw patient after patient in the clinic the gossip of those who waited their turns flowed in and out of my ears like radio music—heard but seldom listened to. And just as an often-played record will abruptly make a conscious impression on one's mind, some words or phrases, spoken again and again, would cut through my concern over the work under my hands, and reach my conscious mind. Such a phrase was "Sima is coming back to marry her cousin, Buzar."

I did not know Sima, but by listening I soon pieced out her story. She had been engaged for two years, but the family had needed food and clothing and Sima had gone to work in Teheran. There she had taken a fine job with a family and had been able to send home enough money to get her family through the winter. It was clear that her parents were counting on her to continue to do this, but now she had sent word that she was coming home to be married.

Even in Sarbandan, where famine sits at every door opening, there must be happiness at a new marriage. There was some pride that all the charms of the city of Teheran couldn't keep Sima away from Sarbandan and love any longer.

I began to listen for word of Sima. She was home. She had arrived by charcoal truck. Next there was the exchange of preliminary gifts. It was some days before I saw the child—a girl of sixteen, perhaps, when she came into the clinic to have me look at a slight reddening of her finger under a brass ring she wore. The rash wasn't serious, but there was something about Sima that worried me. She was a lovely-looking girl, small-boned, dainty, with expressive very dark eyes and surprising dimples that appeared only now and then at the corners of her mouth. She was laughing, she was gay, but both her laughter and gaiety had in them desperation. Or was that my thought and not reality?

I reassured her about the slight rash and advised her to leave off wearing the ring for a while. I gave her a vitamin B shot because I thought it would help to make her less excited about her coming marriage.

I saw the trays from the home of Buzar carried to Sima's home; from Sima's home carried to the home of Buzar. I heard the dong-dong-de-dong of the donbak as she was taken to the bath. I stood outside my door as she finally rode the gaily caparisoned horse on the last journey to the home of the bridegroom.

As the procession drew near me she fell from the horse. They carried her, robed in the white chador, the gaily colored feather crown, the white veil, into my home and I motioned for them to put her upon the cot that was my bed. I asked the wedding party to wait outside. I could see the pulse beating rapidly in her neck and I knew that she had not fainted, as members of the party thought. Quietly I lifted the veil and looked into the most anguished eyes I have ever seen. "My lady," she whispered, "I am not a virgin."

She looked beyond me fearfully at the wedding party waiting outside. I asked quietly, "Why did you accept this marriage then, Sima?"

The words tumbled out and her eyes swam with tears. "I went to this home to work. There were two children. The wife was very cold, very proper, very beautiful. She kept every cupboard locked because she feared that I would steal. But she did not keep her husband locked in her tight cupboard. He came to me, first with small gifts, then with sympathy, finally with affection. I gave trust."

"He was your lover."

"Not many times, Lady Najafi. I do not know why I did it, except that the wife was so cold—and she kept her cupboards locked."

"But why did you return for this marriage?"

"Because I truly love Buzar. I've loved him all my life. And what

was there in Teheran but work, and shame? This husband tired
of my weeping and worry. He took me to a doctor who—"

"I know." I had heard of the few unethical doctors in Teheran
who passed the word from mouth to mouth that the hymen could
be replaced so that any girl could seem to be a virgin. It was a
treatment that lasted only a few hours and Sima had been back
in Sarbandan more than two weeks.

"But now I am afraid. How can I know that this is so?"

I thought of the long, long wedding ritual and of how happy
a boy and girl could be these days leading up to the most important
event of the life. I thought of Sima, sick with fear and yet not
knowing where to turn.

I went to the door of my home. "Friends of Sima, she is ill.
She must stay with me for several days while I care for her. You
must go home now."

"But the food is prepared. The gifts have been received." There
were protests in the crowd.

Somebody led the horse away. A rash of parties broke out through
the village, but Sima lay on my cot.

I had no advice to give this child, and yet she had turned to me
in the only way that she knew how. Finally we called in her parents, then Buzar and his parents.

"You are not of my house," her father said, white with anger.
"Never enter it again." The mother wept, turned away and followed her husband down the lane toward her home without a
tender word to the girl.

"I'll marry her anyway," Buzar said bravely. His face was a
battleground for shock and love.

"That you will not!" His father's voice was loud and determined.

When all five had left Sima sat on the floor, her back against
the cot, and seemed to shrink into herself. She was an old woman,
lost and miserable.

I do not know which of the parents carried the news but soon
the kadkhoda brought a gendarme to my door. They had come for
Sima to take her to the jail in Damavand. I could not believe it. I
argued that she was helpless in this situation, but they took her.

I left my work in Sarbandan and went to Damavand. I visited all of the people of importance that I knew. I would never have done this for myself but I would do it for one of my people. After several days they released her and she disappeared. I have never heard from her. She is no doubt a vagrant somewhere, perhaps a prostitute.

Such a reason for moving into sin! "She kept her cupboards locked." And yet as long as society keeps its cupboards locked, giving confused girls like Sima a sense of being denied the valued things in life, just so long will sin be an easy step.

I resolved that somehow, sometime, and that time as soon as possible, the women of Sarbandan would not have to go away in order to remain alive in the winter. I could do no more for Sima. I could only help those others who were like her.

There were other weddings. Through the night I heard the dong-dong-de-dong of the donbak as the bride was taken to the bath. If the family is too poor to employ a donbak drummer, someone beats the rhythm with his fingers upon a metal tray. The drumbeat is solemn, as marriage is solemn. The bride, through the acceptance of old traditions, must go seven times to the bath to perform her ablutions. She will stay each time long in the bath while the solemn beat goes on outside the walls of the bathhouse.

And as I heard the dong-dong-de-dong, the bathhouse, with its dark and broken corridors, its ancient pool, came into my mind.

The bath. Perhaps a new bath should have come even before the schoolroom or the clinic.

"Mashdi Mokhtar, tomorrow is Thursday," I told him one Wednesday morning as I stopped into the teahouse for a glass of tea.

"My lady, tomorrow is Thursday."

"I would like to speak to the council."

His eyes stayed on my face for a minute, then he smiled and his gold teeth glittered. "My lady, you are a persistent woman."

I sent Asghar to the homes of each of the council members with a reminder that tomorrow there would be a meeting of the council. I was not a member. Officially I could not call a meeting. But there was need for a meeting, so—

"Gentlemen," I told them when they were assembled at my home, "I have something of importance to discuss with you."

I spoke of the cure of the scald-headed boys and they nodded. This they had seen for themselves. I spoke of the need to prevent reinfection. I spoke of how that reinfection might be accomplished. I spoke of the need for a new bathhouse.

They listened until I mentioned the bathhouse; then a murmur, not traceable to any one man, but to the throats of all, began to cover my words. Abruptly one, Haji Agha, spoke louder than the others. "This takes money," he said. "Do you have money?"

Even if I had had the money, which I hadn't, I wouldn't have given it for the bath. People do not appreciate what comes so easily. If they had to worry about the financing of the bath they would take pride in its upkeep, pleasure in its use.

"Has the village no money?" I asked.

Then there arose a babble of voices in which only a few phrases were distinguishable. "It was not our fault—" "I say, if you had —" "You can blame no one but yourself—"

I knew what the argument was about only because I had heard the story previously from Mash'hadi Mokhtar.

In the spring, the nomadic tribes move up from the southern grasslands and rent grazing lands on the high slopes of the mountains. For several years a tribe called "The Black Tents" had rented unused grazing land from Sarbandan, but the past spring the members of the council had divided sharply on what should be charged for the land, what land should be put to such use. When they finally had agreed, the black tents of the herdsmen had been set up elsewhere and another village was collecting the rent. Sarbandan had lost its chief source of extra income. Now each faction blamed the other for this disagreement and no one thought further of the bathhouse.

Just as I had before, I walked out and stood looking at the stars above the dark mountains. The wrangling ceased and I returned. Finally it was agreed that I would draw the plans for the bathhouse and find out what assistance we could get for the building.

In Persia, especially among people who have not been touched too closely with Western ways, the bath is the center of both religious and racial tradition. The bath is not a quick private thing for the purpose of cleansing one's body as it is in America. Rather it is a rite, a ceremony, that cleanses the spirit as it cleanses the body. One spends several hours at the bath, sitting on a clean tray and washing, washing, washing, from a clean bowl. Finally one dips briefly into the general pool. There is conversation, sometimes sherbet as the bathers relax in the pleasure of each other's company and sink themselves into the security of old traditions.

Philanthropists coming in from the West seldom appreciate this function of the bath. They see the pools as sinks of filthy water— which they sometimes are—and look about for some way to replace them with sanitary methods. One foundation built in a village a modern shower bath. The people were delighted. So the girls went to the bath and stood under the spray hour after hour with conversation and music, and perhaps trays of food.

But who is going to bring wood from the mountain to heat all of this water? In fact, where is the water itself going to come from? Especially in the winter.

I made a rough drawing of the new bathhouse. It should have one room with a bench running around its wall just as in the old bathhouses. But there would be this difference. In the bench at regular intervals would be set bowls, each with a faucet. Now the girls—or men—could sit hour after hour on the bench and wash in the bowls without use of so much water. In an adjoining room would be a small shower under which they could stand for a moment just as they formerly had dipped into the pool.

Shapoor Mozaffari and another construction engineer from the Damavand Development Bongha, Monechehr Sharif, took me to see bathhouses that the Bongha had helped to construct. When I met with the village council I told them about these baths, showed my own plans, and urged them to do something!

But still the dong-dong-de-dong of the wedding march to the ancient, broken-down bath continued. It takes so long to do things in Sarbandan!

Eight ⌘ SHAHRIVAR

Shahrivar, September, is the golden month. In the fields below the Mazandaran road the wheat is as high as a man's shoulders, and as golden as the sun. Now it is time for the harvesting. Part of me is sorry. I have loved standing in my doorway, or high on the mountain trail above the village, and watching the mountain breezes pass over these heavy heads and stir them in waves like winds on golden water. But I feel happiness, too, for this wheat will become the winter's bread.

Before the harvest there is one magical night. On the evening of the full moon, generally near the fifteenth of the month, visitors come from Teheran to enjoy the beauty. The wind on the fields seems to make the wheat dance and clap hands; the sky is clear and close enough to touch; the moon sends a liquid white cloak of light that makes the village seem enchanted. There are laughter and shouting and dancing. The village people, who usually go to bed with the coming of darkness, watch for a time, then retire to their little houses. It seems to them very foolish to frolic in the moonlit fields.

Dr. Kasemi and Dr. Emami with Miss Emamverdy, the secretary of the Imperial Organization of Social Services, are my guests. For a time we join in the merrymaking, then we sit in my home, tea glasses in our hands, and talk and talk through the night.

96

The next day the harvesters appear in the fields with scythes and sickles. From my little home, the men's arms, swinging these bright blades, seem tireless.

Behind the men come the women, tying the grain into sheaves and standing the sheaves like sentinels row upon row. And standing there, under the sun in the bright blue sky, the straw dries and grows ready to give up the precious wheat. Sometimes the threshing floor is of hard clean earth, the flails are of wood, made by hand. Beating the wheat is strenuous work and the sweat, like bright beads, stands out on the straining bodies of the men.

More often the wheat is threshed by machine. In Sarbandan the only threshing machine is owned and operated by an old man who sometimes brings his eleven-year-old grandson, whom he entrusts with driving it. The machine itself is very simple. It resembles a two-wheeled cart, but the wheels do not turn on an axle. They are fastened to a pole which turns when they do. To this pole, evenly spaced, is attached a series of knives. It is these turning knives that cut the grain into small pieces. The driver sits on a seat above the knives and guides the ox that pulls the machine around a great wheat stack. The wheat is thrown by pitchfork into the path of the machine.

One day, just before noon, the little grandson of the thresher was carried to the clinic and Asghar came running to find me. The child, driving the machine, had dozed in the heat of the sun and had fallen from his perch behind the oxen, directly into the busy knives. Someone had seized the oxen and stopped the knives, but already he was cut and bleeding. Strangely enough, one side of his body was badly sliced, the other was without injury. I cleansed and bandaged his whole body and gave him a tetanus shot to keep him from developing lockjaw. He stayed with me for many days and when it was time to go home his great black eyes, which had followed me on all the errands in my home, filled with tears.

After the threshing the straw is packed away for the braiding of mats and man begins his wait for nature to assist in the next step. While the wheat was standing tall and golden and uncut in the field, while it was standing in sheaves, the prayer had been, "Please, God, no rain." Rain at harvest time can mean famine and death to an entire village. Now the prayer is, "Please, God, send wind."

When finally the wind does arise the men hurry to the stacks of threshed wheat. With great forks they throw the wheat into the air and the wind carries away the chaff in a dull yellow cloud, and the heavy golden grain falls to the waiting earth.

Now is the harvest completed. At once the grain is ground in every home with mortar and pestle and the people celebrate as they eat the first life-sustaining bread. Sometimes a farmer's entire crop belongs to the landlord who has loaned money during the year or to the shopkeeper who has furnished, on credit, sugar and tea and other staples during the long winter and waiting summer. Now there will be more credit; a new term of bondage.

Now that the villagers' work was ended mine had just begun, really, though the summer had been a busy one. The children had been my first concern. As I won their love and trust the parents had come to trust me, too. They had listened to my instructions about sanitation, they had co-operated with me in all my attempts

to make things cleaner, safer. Now my work-study room was finished and soon classes for the village women and girls would begin.
Sarbandan had been kind to me.

But there was my dream of starting a school for teachers still
unfulfilled. I had felt that someday I should start such a school
when I first studied the villages of the Varamin area; when I
worked in the school for teachers in Ghaleh Nou. Now I needed to
do something about the dream.

I had neither facilities nor money to start a real school, so I
decided to satisfy myself with the training of three girls. These
girls would live in my home and I would instruct and guide them.

Because living conditions in Iranian villages like Sarbandan are
very primitive, most young women from the cities are not interested
in village work. I decided to choose my first three students from
young women who were accustomed to less than I had to offer. I
first considered selecting three girls from Sarbandan or from near-
by villages, but this plan I discarded because girls are not respected
as persons in their own villages.

I turned to the Imperial Organization for Social Services for
advice and they allowed me to choose girls from their work center
—really a home for orphaned boys and girls. Over a hundred girls
applied for an interview. Again I felt the hurt of giving opportunity to so few when so many are reaching for it.

I talked with each of the girls. I did not hold out a promise of an
easy life, a free life, of a high salary when the training was completed. I told, instead, of poverty, of ignorance, of need, and of the
happiness that comes from work and weariness. I told them that
the girls I chose must be quick to learn, able to read and write
well, interested in handicrafts, gracious, pleasant, sunny, strong.
Some were discouraged by my picture of village life; but most were
eager, willing to try.

Finally I chose three beautiful girls: Effat, Farkhondeh and
Ashraf.

Effat, already a helper in the work center, was twenty-two. She
had no parents, and an older married sister had taken their four
little brothers into her home. Effat was tall, fine-boned, exceed-

ingly white-skinned. Already she was skillful in many things and in Sarbandan these skills would mean much.

Farkhondeh was just seventeen. Her very long brown hair she wore in a braid thicker than a man's wrist. As she talked her face was strangely illuminated, as if something deeper than beauty was shining through it and setting it alight. Farkhondeh's mother, she told me, was in an institution for the insane; and her father, a tailor, had tried to keep his large family together in the back room of his shop. But grief and worry and poverty and hopelessness had made him give up, and now the children were cared for in the work center and the father sat alone in his shop, his sewing held close to his failing eyes.

Ashraf, timid, soft spoken, was the prettiest of the three; that is, she would be pretty when good food, sunshine and happiness had had a chance to fill out her thin face and body. Only recently had she left her mother, a poor Teheran washwoman, to go to the center, and I could tell from the tears that came often to her eyes that the cord which bound her to her mother was still strong.

One girl who begged to come with me I left at the work center. She was a little thing with a pitiful curve in her back from a childhood illness. Nearly all of her life had been spent in a hospital. "Choose Pooran," Effat and Farkhondeh begged, but I thought that village work demanded more physical strength than Pooran could possibly have.

While I was interviewing the girls and making my selection, I made preparations for them in Sarbandan. The tiny room at the end of the newly built work-study room would do for me. The three girls could share the clinic room in which I had lived since my coming to Sarbandan. When I had first come to the village the people, even the children, had let me settle into my one room as well as I could. Now, as I moved my things out of the general room, I had many willing helpers. Little Rabbit, with a pot covering his head, ran smash into a rock wall while everybody laughed.

Next I made three beds of medicine boxes and covered them with smooth sheets and warm jajims. I bought, at cost, material for dresses, chadors, trousers, pajamas. I also bought wool so that each

r first center. The small window is in the room I rented from the
khoda, the large windows are in the workroom and the rough adobe
m is my bedroom. A bell hangs from the roof and the chairs and
es are made from sections of logs.

An old man feeds charcoal to the fire that heats water for the bath.

UNICEF (*United Nations International Children's Emergency Fund*)
furnished us with much-needed dried whole milk.

The old bath.

The new bath.

Bathhouse for the dead.

Harvest time, and men and women are busy in the fields.

These chickens are Americans. I received them from Varami

Winter.

*All the world
is white.*

*See the anxious look on the face of the woman in the light figur[ed]
chador. She knitted the piece I am checking. Effat is at my elbo[w].*

Carpetmaking is a natural industry for the people of the villag[e.]

Effat and Pooran (The Little One).

Pooran comes home for a meeting.

Farkhondeh and I on our way to Khosravan.
The donkey is loaded with medicine.

Farkhondeh and the dog are weary.

...metimes it seems a long way between villages.

...ghar and the "sheep boy."

*Many officials visit Roodehen to celebrate the com
tion of the bath.*

*We are planting a door-yard garden. This is b.
planting.*

The new center.

The clinic.

Our chicken house, made with our own hands.

A chicken makes a fine gift for one who is establishing a new ho

is the boys' school.

*Imperial Highness
Princess Ashraf.*

Shapoor and I at the "Old Palace" at a state function.

might knit a heavy sweater for the cold winter.

When all was in readiness I was so excited that I jumped around like a child. My friend Mr. Farshchi took me in his car to call for the girls and bring them home.

Farkhondeh was dressed in sleazy blue silk and all of her possessions were tied in one square of cloth. She was radiant with excitement. "My lady, my lady. All my life I have dreamed of mountain air!"

Effat took me aside, her beautiful face serious and tears standing in her eyes. "Lady Najafi, I cannot come."

"But why?"

"Today I went to say good-by to my sister and my four little brothers. . . ."

"Yes?"

"She says, that is my sister says, that I am of age and that I must help her to care for the boys. Now she expects a child of her own and her husband says it is not good to have four other children in his house."

"How old are your brothers?"

"Five, seven, eleven and thirteen."

I hesitated. The tears that had gathered in her eyes began to roll down her cheeks. She brushed at them with the back of her hand as she turned away. "I am sorry, my lady."

"Effat," I asked, "would you like to bring them with you? The five- and seven-year-old, perhaps?"

She dropped to her knees. "Oh, Lady Najafi, could I? I would take such good care of them. They would be so quiet and well behaved. You will see!"

"We will tell your sister to have them ready next time I come to Teheran."

Ashraf was in the car, looking out of the window. When she turned to me her face was tear-streaked. "Teheran is so beautiful," she said.

The first evening the girls, even Ashraf, were ecstatic over the village, over their beds, over the fact that there were just three in a room when they were accustomed to fifty. They laughed and chattered and ate and drank tea, and Farkhondeh smiled so warmly on Asghar that he tried to go through the wall instead of through the door when at length I sent him on an errand in order to have one less under my feet.

Every woman in the village found some errand to take her by my door. All the men, too, seemed to be on their way to the village center or to the home of a friend. At last it was dark, the parade ceased to pass my door, and the girls were in bed. I was tired, more tired than I usually was after a day of work in the clinic. Oh well, I reminded myself as I stretched myself in my bed, the girls are used to the discipline of the work center. They will settle down very fast. This is only the first day.

There was a tapping at my door, the tapping of Asghar. "What is it?" I asked, lifting myself on my elbow.

"I hear crying," he said. "One of the girls is crying."

Quickly I dressed and hurried back to the girls. It was Ashraf who was crying. By my lantern I could see that she had buried her head in her covers to stifle the sound, but she was shaking with sobs.

"What is it? Are you ill?"

"It is too quiet here, my lady. I cannot stand it!"

I thought of the homesick girls at Ghaleh Nou as I sat on the floor between the beds and told the girls a story. How could I blame Ashraf tonight? Sarbandan and Teheran are so different.

The next morning Asghar was ready to make breakfast before the girls were awake; but he seemed willing to wait. When I wakened them, tousled, rosy and beautiful from sleep, I gave each a very special gift: a copper basin, a sajjadah (prayer rug), a mohr (the piece of clay from the fields of Kerbela on which the forehead is placed in prayer), a tasbih (a string of prayer beads), and a Koran. The girls thanked me for the gifts but still they stood about awkwardly as if they did not know quite what to do.

"First we must fill the basins with water," I told them, "then I will show you how my mother taught me to perform my ablutions." And so I taught them to wash first the face, then the right arm, then the left. Next the head is bowed and the water is passed over the part in the hair. The right foot and leg are washed, then the left. Over each part of the body the water is passed three times. Finally a white band, covering the hair, is placed around the head and the chador covers the head and body. Now it is time to kneel and put the forehead to the clay of which man is made, and offer the morning prayer.

Of course in this one morning the girls did not learn the smoothness of motion, the rhythm of the ablutions. But they were cleaner and nearer to God.

While we were praying I heard someone's stomach growling with hunger.

"Why must we do this each morning?" Ashraf asked when their prayer was finished. "I'm starving!"

I knew the question was one many people might ask.

"It is hard to answer, Ashraf; only this I know. Compassion for others flows most easily from a feeling that God has compassion for us. It is easier to be patient with those who make mistakes when we realize before we begin the day that God will be patient with us."

I invited Asghar in to prepare breakfast and he was so excited over Farkhondeh's half-glances and small laughter that he was completely useless.

When Asghar had first come to be my servant I had invited him to sit with me and eat. There were just two of us and we were both human beings. When my mother and Fakhri had come to visit me, Asghar had placed a plate for himself in the usual way. "Get up from the table," Mother had said quietly, and Asghar, embarrassed, had taken his plate to the porch to eat.

For a moment I had been angry. Only the thought that it was my mother who had spoken kept me from saying, "Why did you treat him like that in my home?"

Mother turned her quiet eyes on me and read my anger. "Najmeh-jun, Asghar is a good boy, a fine boy. But he will always be a servant and he will not always work for you. It is your responsibility to him to train him to be a perfect servant. You are spoiling him—spoiling his life."

So after that Asghar had eaten alone, and so had I. But now I had another problem.

As soon as the breakfast was over Effat set herself to clean the classroom; Ashraf started a long, competent job with her hair; Farkhondeh hurried through the making of the three beds, then went outside to do some task that was not there to be done. How she showed herself!

Finally I called her in. "Farkhondeh, you were showing yourself before the man who lives in the house above us on the hill."

"Yes? If you do not wish me to, I won't."

"Listen. He has a wife all tired out from bearing nine children for him, from cooking for him, and cleaning and putting up with him. No wonder that he looks at you!"

"I am sorry, but—"

"I want you to be happy, Farkhondeh, and I want the people to love you, but you must not show yourself like that. I cannot have it here."

Her head dropped. I knew men would look at her again and again even if she did not show herself. I knew that this freedom after the institutional life would be difficult for any girl to use wisely.

"I am trusting you, Farkhondeh."

But often Farkhondeh did not remember, or else she did not know all that I meant when I said "show yourself," because wives came to me with angry words.

Every night Ashraf cried for Teheran and for her mother and I had to comfort her with stories, with my arms around her long after the others were asleep. With Effat there was little trouble except that learning good grooming and cleanliness came hard to her. That is, there was little trouble until, ten days later, her two little brothers, Hosein and Ali, came to live with us. They were round-headed, snappy-eyed little boys, all appetite and reaching hands and big voices. They spilled out of the car and over to the home of the kadkhoda, where they at once began to challenge the kadkhoda's children to show their strength. Oh, the quarreling and the fighting!

Effat screamed at them, spanked them, and they set up a howling all out of proportion to the strength of her blows. As soon as she had set them again on their feet they were over to the home of the kadkhoda and had picked up the quarrel where it had been interrupted.

Of course the whole disturbance bothered me, but what bothered me most was Effat's method of handling it. I talked to her about children and about how to handle them. Neither the Sarbandan boys nor her two little brothers would be willing to settle quietly to a friendly bickering companionship until they had tested their strength. It was her duty to keep out of their fighting until they made their own adjustment. And this I told her again and again: "Effat, this is our opportunity to teach the villagers a better way of handling their children. You are spoiling everything and you are spoiling yourself."

So with Farkhondeh's flirting ways, Ashraf's crying, and Effat's screaming at her two rowdy little brothers I began to wish that I had never thought of this plan for training village workers. All I needed, however, was my sister's criticism to strengthen me.

My sister Fakhri, visiting me, said, "Najmeh, I should think you would go crazy with those girls."

"No," I answered, "I love them. They will learn."

Fakhri made a little sound of disbelief in her throat.

"A mother has a little baby," I explained. "She bathes the baby. She makes him entirely clean and then—Well, she has the same thing to do all over again. Does she throw the baby out?"

"That is different," my sister insisted. "A baby doesn't know better."

"And that is the answer," I told her. "Farkhondeh and Effat and Ashraf do not know better. When they know better they will do better."

I was talking fast to convince myself.

But the girls did learn. I taught them sewing, and they made their clothing; first their pajamas, later their trousers and skirts and blouses. I taught them to knit, and they sat in the sun and knitted on the big needles the heavy yarn that would make warm winter jackets. I taught them to use ashes for washing, how to purify dishes in the sun, how to clean the room. Again and again I pointed out mistakes and helped them to correct them. I bridled myself with the leather of patience. And finally I allowed them to make home visits with me.

They did not understand, at first, the importance of these visits. "But we are going to be teachers," they said. "When are we going to learn how to teach reading?"

One afternoon I took out the first literacy book prepared by the Near East Foundation. The first picture was of a snake. Beside the picture was the word: Snake. Beside that the separated letters: S N A K E, but in our language of course.

They were stimulated and excited. They called Hosein and Ali in and insisted on teaching them to read. Even after I had gone to bed they held the open book in front of the kerosene lantern and imagined themselves teaching those who knew nothing of these symbols though they had spoken the language all their lives.

When I felt that the girls were well enough adjusted to leave them in charge of my home, I went to Teheran to spend Friday with my family and to attend a wedding. At a meeting of the specialists of the Damavand Development Bongha, Shapoor Mozaffari, speaking for his parents, had given me an invitation to the wedding of his sister.

Instead of the elaborate floral piece that it is customary to send to a wedding, my girls and I gathered wild flowers in a high mountain valley and made an arrangement of our own. Accompanied by my nephew, Ali, I went to the wedding, and Shapoor, who attached himself to me at once, introduced me as "A young woman who works in the same department as I do." Ali, who seemed to know all of the young people wherever he went, took care of himself.

I returned to Sarbandan rested, feeling at peace with everybody. The girls met me, bursting with big news. "My lady," they said, stumbling over each other's words to be the first to tell me. "Last night Masoomeh stole some sugar." "She put it in her chador." "We saw her do it!"

I sighed, all the happiness draining out of me. "If Masoomeh had sugar for her family she would not have taken mine," I told them wearily.

Their faces dropped. They had expected to follow me to Masoomeh's home and demand the return of the sugar. They were waiting for the excitement.

How could I explain to these girls that while they should hold themselves to the strictest standards of honesty they must not judge others without compassion? I sat with them for a long time. "I could do without for myself," I told them. "But I do not know, certainly, that I could see my baby without food. What do you think?"

"But it was sugar, my lady. Not necessary."

"She will learn," I told them. "I will take her sugar as a gift when I again have some. We will see what happens."

One day a messenger came from Damavand. He delivered to Mash'hadi Mokhtar a telegram from the Governor General of Teheran Ostan. Teheran is not only the name of the capital of Iran but also the name of one of Iran's most important provinces. According to the telegram the Governor General, with Mr. Masoudi, member of parliament from Damavand, would visit Sarbandan.

At once the whole village was thrown into a fever of excitement. It is a custom in Iran to honor special visitors by butchering some animal in their presence. Sarbandan must butcher a sheep or preferably a cow. Already the kadkhoda had been down to the teahouse to talk about the matter with Mash'hadi Mokhtar. Together they decided that the animal ought to be a cow to do "big honor." When they came to tell me of their decision I asked, "Who will pay for this animal?"

"Who always pays?" Mash'hadi Mokhtar asked. "The people."

"I am going from house to house to make a collection," the kadkhoda explained to me. He waited for my donation.

"This is wrong," I said. "The people have not money for such things."

"But we must," they said, eyeing me with greater disfavor than usual. "This we must do. It is good. It is right. It is necessary."

"Look," I finally said, seeing that my protest would get nowhere. "Nearly every day it is necessary to butcher at least one animal in Sarbandan so that the people may have meat. What time is this done?"

"In the morning."

"On the day of the visit do not do it until afternoon."

We said no more. The animal would be butchered in the usual ceremony, then eaten in Sarbandan in the usual way.

I was glad that these two men had not decided to butcher a camel!

I missed the butchering part of the greeting ceremony but I did show the visitors the makeshift clinic, the work-study room. Both said, "How is it that Sarbandan is so clean?" And Mr. Masoudi, because he is a very perceptive man, said, "These people have hope in their faces."

The girls served them melon which my family had brought up from Teheran and we talked about the things that I had done in Sarbandan; the help that I had received from the different agencies; the things that the people had done for themselves. Then I asked for some of the things that were most needed: a physician each week with pay and transportation, help with the construction of the clinic for which we had the land, and the plans and the interest of the people.

Out of this conversation grew my request to the Ministry of Health for 120,000 rials each for the construction of three clinics.

For some time I had been visiting the neighboring villages. This had all come about most naturally. By the traveling of words people in other villages had heard of the clinic in my home and had come to me for help. They had gone home and reported their visit to others. These others had come to Sarbandan. They had eaten the free lunch which I tried to serve people far from their homes, and had invited me to their villages.

I had taken Saturday as a visiting day, and I always walked even though the distance was several miles. If you wish people who must walk to trust you, go among them walking.

Now as I talked with the Governor (the Ostandar), and with Mr. Masoudi I showed my maps of seven villages in the general area and explained the needs of these villages. Perhaps an assistant physician could come to Sarbandan when a clinic was completed. Two physicians might take care of three clinics. When my visitors left I felt more hopeful than ever before about the health work in the villages.

But shortly after this visit the Ostandar requested that I come to Teheran. There I faced three hours of questioning.

"Are you a Persian?

"Are you in the employ of any foreign country?

"Where do you get the money you use?"

These intelligent men, like the simple villagers, feared me, thought that I might be a spy.

I went home shaken and unhappy.

When I got out of the government jeep early in the afternoon a group of angry villagers met me in front of Mash'hadi Mokhtar's teahouse. "Those girls locked us out of the clinic. They closed the doors against us," they accused. They had grown accustomed to entering at any time. The girls had evidently wanted some privacy for their studying.

When I reached home I didn't speak to the girls about closing the door against the villagers. I simply began to take the door from its hinges. "Why are you doing that, my lady?" they asked.

"If this door is to be closed against the people we will not have a door."

The girls looked at each other, then they said to me, "My lady, the neighbors come often. Sometimes they take the things that belong to you. They don't respect us when we speak to them."

Again we sat together, glasses of tea in our hands to make the lesson friendlier. "Just as soon as you learn to serve these people they will respect you. When the school opens and you can guide the woman in her reading, the girl in her sewing, they will know that your words are really my words."

"You mean we must *earn* their respect?" Farkhondeh asked.

"Yes, that is right."

A group of village women waited outside my door hoping to hear me scold the girls. I went out to them.

"You are always welcome in my home," I told them. "I have told the girls always to make you welcome."

"When I look out of my door at night and see your light burning, my lady," one of the women told me, "I can go back to bed in peace, knowing that all will be well with us for this night at least."

"Always we will leave the light burning," I promised.

But after the villagers had gone away I still felt sick and shaken, reluctant to face the chatter of the girls, the rough playing of the rowdy little boys. I said good-by to the girls, serious-faced and repentent, and walked out into the fields alone. Alone. Those in the government with whom I must work had no trust in me; the girls would never learn.

It was just dusk. I sat on the ground with my back against a rock wall, my eyes on the jube. For a long time I sat before I took a paper from my pocket and began to write:

Oh, God, I thank Thee for permitting me to be in the field at dusk once more.

The tiny birds are dipping their beaks into the water to sip it for the last time before they fly to the Mecca of their hopes.

The streams are murmuring, pulsating, singing as they run toward Thee.

The blood-red sun has totally disappeared and given its place to the dark of night.

Everything is suddenly still.

I wish that I might borrow wings from the birds and fly toward Thee.

But now I am lame and I am grieving.

Oh, God, please open my heart so that the rays of Thy affection may penetrate my soul.

Then I shall be able to fly to Thee buoyant through enlightenment.

My heart throbs with ecstasy at Thy nearness.

Tears rush from my eyes like turbulent streams and I feel a great lifting of my soul.

Oh, God, what is this fascination in Thy Love which makes everyone fly to Thee with eagerness and bow down before Thy grandeur?

Surely this is a sweet hour.

I thank Thee, for not letting me return to my cottage

Empty.

Nine MEHR

The beauty of the mountains in the month of Mehr (October) is so shining that the heart cannot encompass it. The memory stores it away, color by color, and later, when the world is white, the mind pieces together these flashes, painting a broad canvas with fabulous color. The canvas is not painted with a fine brush but with a palette knife in great patches of golden-brown, amber, rust, scarlet and tangerine of the mountain slopes and the jewel-like blue of the Persian sky. Sarbandan, lying at the edge of this beauty, is invaded by fingers of brightness wherever rows of trees, called tongue-of-a-bird, hold a thousand bright gold coins against the sky.

On the lower side of the Mazandaran road blocks of earth, in which the yellow-tan stubble still stands, contrast with the rich red-black of the earth which has been turned so that the winter snow may lie soft on the bare breast of the land.

There is sound in Mehr, too; the sound of whispering, rustling, silk-swishing, as the growing autumn breezes pass through the Persian carpet of fallen leaves. When I walk early toward the top of the lowest hill, I turn and look down upon this carpet. The early sun on the dew makes millions of flashing jewels—diamonds, amethysts, sapphires.

Summer is over in Shahrivar, but now it is again summer—a summer that is deceitful, like a beautiful woman enticing with charms that are only transitory.

I must have time to absorb this beauty because it is beauty upon which I live; but I have work to do. Much work.

From the time that I had come to Sarbandan I had tried to get the council to take responsibility for the improvement of the village. They had met around my samovar nearly every Thursday afternoon. In October they voted me the secretary of the council. They would have made me chairman but I was not an actual member, and besides, a woman in that position is unheard of in the villages.

Our membership differed from the usual village council in that we had many small landlords and these ordinarily represented themselves on the council. When they voted that something needed to be done I encouraged them to vote also that they would do it, as far as possible, by themselves. An example of this was Mash'hadi Mokhtar's gift of the land for the clinic.

As secretary I could make application to any agency of the government, in the name of the council. Of course, having lived all my life in Teheran except for my school years in America, I ordinarily made such applications through personal friends. A much easier way to do things in Iran as well as in other places.

I took my position as secretary seriously and tried to get the council members to take their positions seriously, too. They voted that if a member were absent without cause for three times he no longer belonged to the council. And now belonging to the council was of real importance. It gave status and dignity to both the individuals and the group.

The council voted to invite a representative of Point Four to Sarbandan. I forwarded this invitation. The council presided at the turning of the first earth for the bath.

The trouble I had with that bath! The council members wanted to build the bath themselves according to the traditional pattern. I wanted the council to assist in the building of the bath and build it according to my own plans—a combination of the Point Four plans and the traditional bath. Point Four was willing to assist but wanted to build according to their plans. Finally a compromise was reached; Point Four would allow the modification I had suggested.

Then came another quarrel.

I was making my home neat one morning when Mash'hadi Mokhtar appeared at my door.

"Lady Najafi, it is terrible, terrible."

"What is terrible?"

"Point Four will destroy our bath before the new one is built. We will have no bath!"

I remembered his telling me the first day I talked to him that the old bath was not usable. He had forgotten this.

"Why will they do this?"

"They say we will never co-operate in building the new one as long as we have the old one."

"Perhaps they are right."

"No, they are wrong. Really wrong!"

"What are you going to do about it, Mashdi Mokhtar?"

"Me? I thought you would do something, Lady Najafi."

"What can I do? I am not really a member of the council. My word does not have weight with Point Four," I said. "Call a meeting of the council at the teahouse. Invite representatives from Point Four to be there. Then explain that we cannot be without a bath and tell them why. They do not understand, perhaps, that a bath is a religious necessity."

"But, my lady, you know how to say these things."

"So do you, Mashdi Mokhtar. So do the others."

"I think you do not know what this means, my lady. Elsewhere they—"

I had heard the story that was going around Iran of one agency that found the latrines unsanitary and sent a demolition crew with a bulldozer to knock these down and fill in the latrine pits. Six months later, according to the story, a construction crew arrived in the village to build new latrines. We could not have this happen with the baths.

"Believe me, I do understand, Mashdi Mokhtar. You will have to fight for what you want."

I knew that I must not "mix in." I would not be in the village always, perhaps not for very long, and the people must have practice in fighting their own battles.

But while they fought, I prayed, "Oh, God, you know how to move the heart of every man. Guide us now." Anything that I have deeply wanted for my people I have got through prayer. God has not always answered my prayers for myself, perhaps because at times I have prayed selfishly, but for the people, yes.

And so the old bath was left while work on the new bath was begun.

The council also voted to ask the Development Bongha of Damavand for help with transportation. We were taking ten patients a month to the hospitals in Teheran in addition to the scald-headed boys, and girls, too, who were being taken in for radiotherapy. I forwarded this request and we were granted the use of the jeep of the development specialist once every fifteen days.

At first this jeep was driven by a burly, handsome young man called Akbar Agha. He was slangy, easygoing, happy, but very religious. Constantly he talked in a loud voice about his children, five of them, about his wife, about the other people whom he drove for the Development Bongha. When he grew tired of telling he used his loud voice for asking: "Why are you doing this work? . . . Is not the smell of this bus horrible? . . . Why do you not live in the city?"

Often as I rode I closed my ears to the constant talking. Sometimes when we returned to Sarbandan late and were both tired I asked him to come into my home and join me for a tea. Even though my servant, Asghar, and always one or two of the girls were there he never came in. "You are not married, my lady. It would not be proper," he explained.

Once when Akbar Agha had other duties, the jeep was brought by Shapoor Mozaffari. Since we planned to get a half dozen patients to Teheran for the opening of the clinic he had to arrive in Sarbandan before dawn. A thief, seeing him leave his room at midnight, watched until he drove away, then entered his room. When he returned nothing movable was left. He had lost all of his clothing, his blankets, his gold cuff links, everything. The thief was caught when he tried to sell the things in the bazaar and was placed in jail at Damavand. There Shapoor went to visit him and found him a hungry, pitiful youth without education or opportunity. All who worked for the Bongha laughed when they heard that Shapoor was sending gifts of fruit and other special food to the thief who had stolen everything from him.

But I did not laugh, and when more and more often Akbar Agha could not come and the young engineer took his place, I enjoyed talking to one who felt as I did about all unfortunate people.

It was in one of these discussions, as we bumped over a deeply rutted road, that Shapoor said, "I wish that more landlords would pay their special taxes. Villages don't have to have roads like these!"

I had heard of the Farmers' Share Increase Act but Shapoor's words set me to studying it. The Act provided that the landlord increase his tenant farmers' income by giving an additional 10 per cent of the farm's earnings to the men who tilled the soil, and in addition that he pay another 10 per cent for village improvements.

After I had studied this act I read and explained it to the Sarbandan village council. The men discussed it quietly—they no longer wrangled, at least not much—and they decided to collect this tax which had never been collected in Sarbandan. This meant not that they were planning to collect from others so much as they were consenting to pay the tax themselves.

In the village of Sarbandan there was one wealthy landlord who had ignored the council. After we talked about the Farmers' Share Increase Act, I suggested that this landlord be invited to visit the council. He was invited but he ignored the invitation. He was again invited and the second time he came. The moment that he walked in, silence fell on the meeting. Everyone was too awed to speak. They were afraid even to begin the discussion of our planned projects. I waited for the chairman to speak until the silence grew frightening, then I spoke. I said in a few words that we had been studying the Share Increase Act and since we were trying to make many improvements in the village we wondered if he wouldn't like to pay his share.

"I have paid my share!" His voice was firm.

I knew that he had not paid this tax because I had investigated.

"I am sorry," I told him. "That payment is not on the records."

"Of course it is not on the records. I pay my tax directly where I can see how it is used. I whitewashed the mosque last year."

"That is your duty to God. That is not a payment of tax."

The council members eyed me incredulously. How can you speak to this man of importance in that manner, those eyes said.

"Another year I served food at all the celebrations to honor my dead father."

"That is your duty to your father."

He was getting nervous. I could see the dew coming out on his forehead; his tongue ran around his lips, his hands shook. He had not expected to meet someone who was informed.

"I have nothing more to say, Lady Najafi," he said stiffly, and left.

The men had been afraid to speak in his presence. Now their voices rose in a wave of astonishment and chagrin. I knew they could see me banished to some remote corner of Iran.

The next day this man sent me an enormous basket of eggs, and eggs in Sarbandan are a luxury. This was a bribe, I knew, so I sent Asghar back with them. The next day he again sent the basket of eggs. I sent the Rabbit to round up his little friends. Every little child in Sarbandan had an egg to eat that day.

When the council met again I told them about the eggs. "I'm not going to work with you if you can't be men. Stand up and speak out, or I'm leaving the council."

They shook their heads miserably, but they couldn't be pushed. "Lady Najafi," Mash'hadi Mokhtar said, "it is impossible to be perfect."

"Well, it isn't impossible to try," I told him.

A few days later I was surprised to receive a call from this landlord. He had come to pay his tax. I knew the amount he offered me was just a fraction of what he owed. "I am not a tax collector," I told him. "You must pay to the kadkhoda."

Later the kadkhoda told me that the members of the council had come to him to pay the tax. For the first time I felt the progress of

Sarbandan rested not upon my shoulders alone. These men were learning quickly. I felt a great singing inside me. I had not thought to be so happy so soon.

Probably the project that interested my neighbors most, however, was the building of a chicken house. This I built myself in my spare (?) time following the excellent plans furnished by the American Point Four. The walls were built of mud and straw, with window openings all along one side closed with slats of wood. Often in the evening, as my girls sat knitting on their winter sweaters, I whittled away at this wood. It was a pleasure working with my hands, a relief from the consideration of problems that confronted me during the days.

With Asghar's help I put in a roost for the chickens to stand on at night and a shelf where they could lay their eggs. But they never liked this shelf.

From Varamin I got fifteen beautiful American chickens, the gift of the Near East Foundation, and for all of the villagers who wished them, fertile eggs. The fact that the chickens would hatch in the cold of the winter did not bother the villagers. These people would be lonely without a sheep, a donkey, a cow, maybe a few hens, living in their tiny houses with them. Besides, they often told me, the presence of the animals kept the house warmer. No doubt. And smellier!

I soon found out something about American chickens. Although they grow to half the size of a boy they have more than a boy's appetite. How these chickens did eat! The Iranian chickens are scrawny and not so beautiful, but they are hunters and find their own food in the fields and dooryards. Any egg that the Iranian chicken gives you is a gift. The egg of the American chicken is merely in trade for food.

When Asghar went into the yard to feed the chickens and called, "Pew, pew, pew, pew, pew," the dogs, birds and all the neighbor chickens came running.

The chickens, with their American background, should have recognized the American nests on the American shelf, but they didn't. They put their eggs down anywhere. Little Rabbit, finding the eggs, would break the bottom and suck the egg in one gulp. Hosein and Ali, seeing this, would come screaming to Effat, since they felt themselves to be guardians of the hens. The older children would, I think, take home the eggs they found. At any rate, when I lacked eggs in spite of my beautiful flock I could always buy American eggs from a neighbor who had only Iranian hens.

Perhaps the greatest blessing that October brought was the opening of the fall term at the school for boys. Hosein and Ali, now chummy with the sons of the kadkhoda, strutted off to school dressed in new outfits from head to toe. How blessed is silence!

Effat, freed from the worry of the boys, put her mind and strength to cleaning the study room which had just been finished. Farkhondeh, the novelty of freedom worn off, was conducting herself with decorum. Only Ashraf cried every night and moped through the day.

On October 18, the work-study room was clean and ready for the women's classes to begin. I had brought a bell from Teheran and this I struck; its resounding voice echoed through the valley. Asghar took the megaphone from its nail in the bathhouse and called, "School today. School today!"

We, the girls and I, had been talking quietly about this school as we went on our calls through the village. Now from the little houses the girls and women came in a broken stream. In the first hour there were sixty-eight who had registered. Sixty-eight! I had planned on thirty, or thirty-five at the most. I had not read the real hunger for learning that was behind the women's noncommittal comments whenever the school had been mentioned.

Working in Sarbandan was like climbing Mt. Damavand. Every time I reached the top of the "last" hill, another rose before me.

The answer to my overcrowded classroom was to find and furnish a school for the little girls so that in my school I could teach the mothers and the older girls. I put this problem to the back of my mind for further consideration while I began that first difficult day.

The smell in the little room grew to be an all-pervading stench. Sixty-eight unwashed bodies, sixty-eight pairs of unwashed bare feet.

Again, with all my high plans for the school, I had to begin at the very bottom. "Look at your feet. Are they clean?" So after all, the first lesson that was taught in the new schoolroom was one in simple cleanliness. "You must wash your feet each day before you come to school."

"We shall have two sessions of school," I told them. "In the morning the children and the younger girls; in the afternoon the women and the older girls."

I didn't want the women and children together because the conversation of the women was not appropriate for the children to hear. Morning would be the best time for the women to clean their houses, bring in their water and wood, take care of their few animals. In the afternoon the children could mind the babies while the mother was gone.

The women and the older girls left, the younger girls and the children stayed. From my school supplies I took out unusual materials—combs and kerosene. With the help of Farkhondeh and Effat I began the lesson. There was not a girl in the room whose hair was not peopled with tiny lice—lice love to live in clay houses. We dipped a comb in kerosene, combed out the lice, wiped the comb on paper, dipped it again, combed again, dipped again. It seemed an endless job with the forty girls wiggling protestingly under the scraping combs. As we worked I explained about the lice, showed them what the lice were like, how to recognize the nits. Then I talked with them about being clean. We would learn many things in the school, I promised, but first we must be clean.

I did not give the girls the combs to take home. Instead I sterilized them and kept them for future use—perhaps use in the afternoon. The workroom, now serving as a schoolroom, was going to be thought of as a place for cleanliness.

After the torture by comb I told the girls a story and showed them the books we were going to read. On the first page was that arresting snake. Reading was indeed something to look forward to.

We would also learn sewing, I promised. For the present we would have school twice each week.

It might seem strange that school should be held just twice a week, but I had reasons. As I had made my visits to the home of Sarbandan I had discovered that a daily school would disrupt the lives of the villagers and they would give up coming entirely. A twice-weekly school could be managed by nearly anybody who was really interested. Later, when a school for little girls was arranged, that school could meet daily as the boys' school did.

In the afternoon the mothers came back. I gave them the combs and the kerosene and taught them to work on each other. I also gave them D.D.T. to take home to eradicate the lice on the mud walls and floors and in the bedding. There were many other simple things they needed to learn. How to cut the nails, for example, many other things about good grooming. They learned to wash their teeth with salt. Sometime I could get toothbrushes for them, but for the present they worked with a clean finger. Always I tried to save their pride when I was teaching them these simple things.

I had not expected Eshrat to come to the school, but she came, her face closed and insolent. Every time I explained something she said, "I know." I made no reply, just went on working with the others. Then, later, when everyone was busy I told this story:

Once upon a time a young bride went to live at the home of her husband. Her mother-in-law became her teacher because she was young and needed much knowledge. First she must learn to cook.

"Go put the rice in the water and soak it."

"I know, I always have done," the girl answered.

"Put salt in the water."

"I know. I always have done."

"Boil the water."

"I know, I always have done."

"Put the rice in the boiling water."

"I know."

"Now put it in the sieve and wash."

"I know. I always have done."

"Now put some oil with the rice."

"I know. I always have done that."

"Go get a sun-dried brick and put it in the rice."

"I know. I always have done."

All the women laughed. Eshrat turned with energy to her nails.

"We never know everything," I explained. "Only God does not need someone to teach Him."

As I taught them how to be clean I tied cleanliness in with prayer. Moslems cannot offer prayers correctly if they are unclean.

Of course, they were eager to learn to read and they wanted to sew—on a machine! As a student in the United States I had dreamed of teaching the village women to sew on machines, had even hoped to introduce power machines, but now with my experience in the village I found that there were more basic things that must be taught at first. There were not more than two families in the village of Sarbandan, including the small landlords, who would ever be able to buy a sewing machine. I explained that first we must learn to sew very beautifully by hand. And in order to interest them I showed them some of the beautiful things that we would make.

Visiting the homes, I had seen the food supplies sitting uncovered on floors or on rude shelves, the flies crawling in and out over them. I had had my friends in Teheran save boxes for me: candy boxes, cracker boxes, any sort of boxes. I had also asked them to save materials for me so that I had a large box of attractive pieces. We would cover boxes with material, decorate them, use them in the homes as objects of beauty. I showed them that many different stitches were needed in covering a box and they agreed that learning the stitches would be a good start.

That is why we started on the sampler, which had each stitch carefully done until it became a tool of the worker. These samplers could be hung from a willow rod for wall decoration. Some of them were very beautiful. It was my idea to teach the women how to make all the stitches, give them some idea of the application of these stitches and then allow their own creative instincts to find expression from the point of the needle.

After each woman had made a box—and some of them, faster

than the others, had made several—we would go on to other needful things. I showed them the sewing bags to hold needles, pins
and scissors which could be hung from the ceiling to keep things of
danger out of the reach of the children. I showed them the pin
cushions we would sew, stuff with wool, fill with bright pins and
keep in the bags.

And last, I gave each woman a large square of extremely fine
muslin, almost like linen in its appearance, which I had brought
from Teheran. When the owner had enough skill she could make
her piece of muslin into a tablecloth for celebrating feast occasions.
The finished cloth I showed them had a border of wide drawn work
and festoons of mountain flowers done in soft colors. I watched
the faces of these women as they wrote their names to be pinned
to their muslin; as they studied the beautiful tablecloth I had
spread before them. The glowing look on these thin, usually tired
faces paid me for my effort. These women were happy, and happiness comes so seldom to older people in my villages.

Seeing the models had excited the women to effort. Many days
when there were not classes they came to the workroom and Farkhondeh or Effat, who were much cleverer with a needle than
Ashraf, would give them the help they needed. This feeling of
"belonging" in the schoolroom was important. It made the more
formal learning easier.

One day I brought wool yarn, very fine, from the Imperial
Organization of Social Services. This we crocheted into, lacy head
scarfs. The girls were delighted. The women, looking at themselves in my mirror, watched the delight grow in their own eyes,
at how enchanting the right head scarf can make even a woman
of thirty! Later we used cotton thread and crocheted table linens
which someday might prove a profitable export item from Sarbandan.

I had hoped for carpet looms. While they had been ordered
for me they were all bound up in red tape and when it was time
to use them they were not available. I happened on the next best
substitute—knitting. The people in the village had the wool from
their few sheep. The sheep that were killed for winter meat gave

up both hide and hair. Other sheep were sheared. Wool was even picked from the shrubs where the sheep had passed in their grazing. The villagers knew how to card it, and even spin it, though they had no spinning wheels such as were once used in Europe and the United States. They knew how to dye the wool with native materials. All of these things that I myself didn't know I kept my hand out of entirely. My success depended upon my being expert—at least more expert than they—in anything that I worked with them on. In the United States a teacher can afford to say, "I'm sorry, I don't know the answer to that question. Why don't you look it up and report back to the class?" But in Iran such an answer would destroy the confidence of the students. A teacher must be infallible and all-wise.

After the women had made their own yarn, heavy and uneven, they brought it to school and learned to knit. I furnished the needles, and the girls and I were patient in giving instruction. We made sweaters, gloves, but the most challenging article was socks.

We made some things that might be of use only in Sarbandan: long padded gloves that reached to the elbow for stirring the pot over the outside open fires, clothesline for drying clothes that had formerly been stretched on the bushes. But the funniest thing was "operation sheep lingerie."

In Sarbandan, as in other mountain villages, as soon as the harvest is over the animals are sent out to find their own food, and this they do until the growing season begins again. At lambing season the villagers sent the sheep and lambs out together to forage, and to keep the lambs from nursing the sheep's milk, which the people were planning to feed to their own children, they tied some old rag around the sheep to cover the udder. These filthy rags were certain to make the milk unsanitary, I thought, so in the classes we made sheep brassières. Oh, those sheep looked definitely feminine cropping the grass in their brightly flowered finery!

The second semester we would make, still by hand, a chador, a pair of women's trousers, a blouse. Since the part of the chador that covers the head wears out first, I would teach the girls to reinforce this part with a square of cloth folded into a triangle.

This would make three thicknesses of material that would be worn through before the chador was used for something else.

When I was working with the Near East Foundation, and I do not know whether or not they still do this, they gave free cloth to the women in the sewing classes. I had seen women waste this cloth, or go home and put it to their uses and not return to the class. I purchased cloth for my students from the Imperial Organization of Social Services, which procured it at cost. I planned to give it to the women at cost and those who could not afford to pay even this amount could be given tasks to do in the school-room, the clinic room, or in my own room. This would make the cloth have value.

"How can you be so hard?" my sister Fakhri asked me. "When a chador must last for two years, a pair of shoes for three, trousers and blouse even longer, you could get your friends to—"

"To teach any people that something can be had for nothing is not good."

"Oh, you philosopher!" Fakhri said impatiently.

Soon the day's work fell into a regular pattern. We began the class with a prayer, followed it with an inspection for cleanliness, talked about such problems as a recognition that some things belong to us, other things to our neighbors. At first the complaints that someone had taken someone else's pencil, or book, or paper, or knitting needle made me depressed for hours. How was I going to help these women when they were unwilling to learn the funda-mental rules of decent living?

Over and over again I told myself, and the girls, "If they had, they would not take"—but I wondered. I wondered if the habit of taking might not persist beyond the point of need. But as the days went by the reports became fewer and fewer and finally I handed the complaints over for the class officers to handle. These officers had been nominated from the floor and elected by secret ballot so that the women, too, could learn democratic procedures.

After the prayer I told a story, usually with a moral point, as often as possible from our great literature or history. Then while part of the class worked on handiwork under the direction of

Farkhondeh, Ashrat and Effat, I taught the others slowly, day by day, to read. Sometimes when there was a new problem in handi-work one of the girls would take the reading class while I taught the manual skills. After the reading lesson was over we changed and those who had been working now read. As an extra incentive the quickest students were allowed to go when they had finished the day's lesson. I did not trouble myself with time-killing seat work.

Now my week fell into a routine: Saturday, classes; Sunday, visit-ing the homes in the village; Monday I saved for office work, for taking the patients to Teheran to the hospital or clinic; Tuesday, clinic; Wednesday, classes again; Thursday, clinic with council meeting in the afternoon; Friday, the clinic again.

It seemed that we would never cut down the calls on the clinic. We did find, however, that much of the illness was due to hunger— just plain starvation. I talked with the officials of UNICEF (United Nations International Children's Emergency Fund), who gave me powdered milk and vitamins. Every child who went to school, both boys and girls, was given a glass of reconstituted milk on Wednesday and on Saturday, and mothers and little children who specially needed it received it even more frequently.

But often as I lay upon my cot at night, listening to the deep night silence, broken only by the bell on some wandering animal, I thought about the work that I was doing. I accepted my clock-tight schedule without question. All that I was doing needed to be done. But what was I leaving undone? Was I building a structure upon the foundation of my own personality or was I building on foundations of wisdom, and right thinking, and correct doing?

I wanted my work in Sarbandan to last beyond my lifetime there, and to spread to other villages whose need was just as great.

October was coming to an end. Soon it would be winter, and the things that I had done would meet a strenuous test, not set by visiting officials, but by the hand of cold and poverty and famine.

Ten ABAN

Winter does not come stealthily to Sarbandan. In the month of Aban (November) it comes with fierce determination. Under my eyes it turns the brown stubbled fields to dead gray and the plants and shrubs to shrunken, broken stalks. It freezes the edge of the jube to rippled glass and with its gusty breath sweeps from the orchard trees their last dry leaves. Now as I look up toward the mountains the branches of the apricot trees make black iron lace against the harsh azurite sky.

People who are fortunate enough to have a change of clothing put the fresh ones on over the ones they have been wearing with the hope of keeping the cold out of their thin bodies.

Neighbor calls to neighbor, brother to brother, father to sons, and all of the men and boys who are old enough to help go up into the mountain timber carrying their axes over their shoulders and leading the donkeys burdened with quilts and with food. The expedition to bring wood for the winter will take three or maybe four days.

A moonlight week is chosen. Nights are very cold, and to keep warm the men will work through the night under the light of the moon and sleep during the day when the sun gives some heat. In spite of the hard work this is one of the best times of the year for the men. They tell jokes, much like American tall tales, they sing, they laugh and are merry.

A large pit is dug and in it the men pile small shrubs and twigs. These they burn and into the fire they put fresh logs. The wood is made lighter for carrying by burning it in this way. It is now half charcoal, half wood, and it is charcoal that will keep the fire under the korsee through the long, long winter.

From Sarbandan the women look up toward the timber area and watch the smoke curl toward the sky. The smoke, smelling exquisitely sweet even in the village, means to the women warmth for the winter. It symbolizes to them, too, though they do not say so, the love of their men for the wife, the child, the mother. There is tenderness in these curls of wood smoke.

After three or four days the men return to the village, the donkeys burdened with the charcoal.

When the wood is brought in and the charcoal put away, a feeling of sorrow settles over Sarbandan. It is time for the men and older boys to go to Mazandaran. There is no longer work in

Sarbandan but in the rice fields of Mazandaran there is always work with pittance pay. The season of working in Mazandaran is not a holiday for the men; it is a miserable time. The food is inadequate, the living accommodations indescribably poor, the hours from sunrise to after dusk, and the work arduous. Many who say goodby to their families may not return. It is almost as if they were going away to war.

In just a few days the village changes its appearance. It is a village of women and children and old men.

And now the women come to visit me; not for medicine or lessons, but to say good-by.

"Lady Najafi, I will no longer be in the class," Zahra, a young woman who had been doing unusually well, told me. "I shall be grateful to you for the rest of my life, and I'm sorry that I cannot stay in the village."

"I am sorry, too. You have been a good student."

"I cannot stay in the village because I must earn my living. I am going to Teheran."

A middle-aged woman, the mother of eight children, spoke. "I am sending my daughter to Teheran, too. She must help with what money she can earn."

"But away from home—" I began.

The woman's words came in a rush as if she had tried to dam them and the dam had given away. "Oh, my lady, if we could just earn a few rials a day during the winter. Just a few rials. We would be able to keep our families together. If you only had some work for us to do—"

I turned to Zahra. "Are you going to be near friends or relatives?"

"I will find work. In a home perhaps."

"Zahra, how is your cousin, Sima? I have not heard of her since she went away."

Zahra's face became closed to me. "I know nothing of Sima." Then she burst out, "But, Lady Najafi, I must go. The body must have food. I cannot eat at my father's almost empty table when there are younger children who are hungry!"

"I know, Zahra, I know."

"I will not do as Sima did. You will see."

I spoke gently. "Zahra, there is not one of us who knows what we would do in Sima's place. Not one."

The tears came to Zahra's eyes and her face was again open. "I loved my cousin. We have been more than sisters since we were born."

"Sit down, Zahra. Let us have tea together." I turned to the older woman. "Please join us for a tea." I bustled about my samovar and it was not until we sat with glasses of tea in our hands that I spoke again. "If you will wait until I have had time to go to Teheran I will speak with my mother, my sisters, with my friends, and find a place where your employer will teach you, be kind to you, feel responsible for you, and keep you in happiness and safety."

"We will wait," the older woman said at once. Zahra was thoughtful. "I will ask my mother. We will see."

It was late afternoon when she came back to tell me that she also would wait.

Each time that we had discovered a problem in Sarbandan I had been able to turn to some social service, either philanthropic or governmental, for aid. Now there was no place to turn.

When I first returned from America I had been granted an audience by the queen. We had talked about many things, for at that time my head was filled with enormous dreams. One of the charities we had talked of was the government-sponsored food kitchens where the poor were given enough food to keep them alive. I suggested at that time that those who were fed should be tested for aptitudes. Surely if they had eaten they could not refuse to answer a few questions. Many who were weak in body might prove to be strong in intelligence. Many who were intelligent might be lacking in physical strength.

At least, I suggested, this screening would prepare the way for trade training which, in the long run, would be far superior to the gift of food for which nothing was expected in return.

"That is not our pattern," the queen told me.

Later the Princess Ashraf invited me to lunch with her. Again we talked of a screening or testing program that would eventually take the poor from the bread lines. She seemed interested and said she hoped to talk with me again. She invited me to be a member of the women's council of the Imperial Organization of Social Services, an invitation that I gratefully accepted.

But nothing had been done about state employment bureaus, about in-service trade training, so I added a new service to my work in the village: that of employment counselor and labor agent outside of Sarbandan. "You will wish that you never knew Najmeh," I told one of my friends. She put her arms around me. "I can do a little," she said.

Now when the girls must earn outside of the village I placed them with my family or friends, visited them, carried word of them to their families and word of their families to them.

But this was only a temporary answer. Even I could see that. I would not have solved the women's employment problem until every girl and woman could find work in Sarbandan for the long winter months. The sixteen carpet looms that had been promised me had not been delivered and when I investigated I was informed that the matter was still under consideration.

With my own money I purchased knitting yarn and in the classes I distributed it. This yarn was not for the use of the villagers, I explained. It was my yarn. The expert knitters could take it home and knit socks. These I would sell. After I had kept the money the yarn cost, the rest of the sale price would go to the knitter.

"We are to be paid?" one woman asked incredulously.

"Yes, paid!" I assured them.

Each woman and girl went to work making a trial swatch. These I inspected carefully for evenness, for springiness. Then I gave out the yarn and we cast on our first socks. Such enthusiasm! Only Eshrat looked at me from sullen eyes. "When do we receive these rials?" she asked.

I held my voice to an evenness I didn't feel. "When you have satisfactorily completed a pair of stockings."

"May we make more when these are done?" another asked.

"Of course."

Now the needles clicked and clicked and the song of the needles was a song of hope.

After dusk an old man came to my door. "Lady Najafi, may I come in?"

"Certainly, come in and have a glass of tea."

He laid by his pipe and accepted the tea. He sat silent for a long time as I watched him without staring openly into his face. Finally he said, "I can knit."

More than this he was incapable of saying to a woman. I got the yarn and needles, showed him the pattern. Soon on the sunny side of many of the little mud houses, their frail bodies sheltered from the cold winds by the thick mud walls, many of the old men of the village sat knitting, knitting, knitting. When I stopped to

say good morning to one such old man he gave me a toothless smile. "I was good only to sit. Now I am good to knit!"

Next year, next year, I kept saying to myself. Surely small industry, since the stocking knitting had been received with such zeal, is the answer not only in Sarbandan but in the other villages of the long winters.

As if winter were not hard enough without complications, an epidemic of illness struck the sheep of our section. Waiting one day in front of Mash'hadi Mokhtar's teahouse for transportation to Teheran I saw an old man bargaining with the grocer in the next little shop.

"Write it well," the old man was saying. "Write it better than that."

The grocer, a perspiring, worried little man, was writing with black ink upon a slip of paper. His face was so near the paper that his nose almost touched it and his tongue worked in and out of his mouth in concentration.

"Write it well," the old man insisted again.

Thinking that I might be of help I walked over to them, but though I greeted them pleasantly the grocer went on with the painstaking writing.

"What is this?" I asked.

The old man looked away from the paper and gave me a quick smile of recognition. "He is writing an amulet for me, to cure my sheep." Then he turned back and watched the slow progress of the pen.

"Father," I said, "I have heard of this sickness of the sheep. I have sent word to Damavand and the animal doctor will be over to see the sheep in our village and make them well."

"There is nothing wrong with my sheep except that some evil eye has glanced on them," he said stubbornly.

"You don't really think that this piece of paper will help them, do you?"

He looked at me from under fierce knitted brows. "It will help them certainly!"

"You could have the amulet for the sheep and have the doctor see them, too," I suggested.

"A doctor does not understand the evil eye," he told me sagely.

Then the grocer, afraid of losing his fees for writing such amulets, put in craftily, "Besides, the doctor never comes. You know that, my lady."

"He comes," I said.

"Not until the sheep have died. It is always too late with the animal doctors from Damavand."

I walked away. The grocer was right. To call a doctor did not mean that one would come. For me it was different. I had a wide acquaintanceship and I usually put my call through to a friend, who spoke to a friend. This is not a fair way, but perhaps it is the way over the whole world. I have heard my American friends speak of "pull." The old man, who was well thought of in the village, might, I reasoned, represent wide village opinion. I made a special effort to get the veterinarian to Sarbandan very soon.

When the veterinarian came there was no reluctance to have him look at the animals. The disease, fortunately, was something that medicine could handle, and shortly all of the sheep in the village except the old man's were well.

I sought him out one day as I went through the village checking on the reasons why some of the girls and women were not attending the classes. "How are your sheep?" I asked him.

"They died."

"I am sorry." I thought perhaps he might blame the death of these animals on my "eye."

I waited for him to tell me that he was sorry that he had not taken my advice. He didn't, of course. Village people are too proud ever to admit that they have been wrong. Too proud, and not wise enough.

He did say something that is true of all village people. "When I see I believe. But I must see."

"Then you will believe next time?" I said lightly.

He didn't respond to my light tone. "I wish that I could, my lady, but I am—" He shrugged, then repeated again, "I believe what I see. I am made that way."

With life in the village fallen into winter quiet, Ashraf was more unhappy than before.

I watched the smiling faces of Farkhondeh and Effat as they bent over a village woman's shoulder showing her the meaning of a letter in the book, or how to use the needle. I watched Ashraf, too; now much prettier since good food had put some flesh under the transparent skin. But there was no joy in the big dark eyes nor on the smooth, ivory-toned face.

At night I heard sobbing as I stopped at the door of the original room of my home which the girls now shared.

Quietly I went in and sat down by the bed. I wiped the girl's tear-swollen face. "What is the matter? Ashraf, why do you cry?"

"I hate Sarbandan. I want to go home."

I thought of the miserable cave that the Imperial Organization of Social Services had rescued her from when they first took her to the work center. I thought of her mother, struggling over other people's soiled clothes to keep her own body alive.

"Ashraf, you may not like Sarbandan now, but you will learn."

"I have tried, my lady. You know how hard I have tried."

There was a muffled snort from one of the other beds. It had long bothered both the other girls that Ashraf was so unwilling to carry her part of the work. "She is so lazy. Send her back," the girls had complained. But I had said, "No one is really lazy. Some people just do not see a good reason for working." And I had wondered how to help Ashraf to look ahead.

"You must be honest with yourself, Ashraf. You must not stop now and give up this opportunity without thinking very seriously." I told her that the preparation she was receiving would make it possible for her to get a position with the Development Bongha, where she would receive a good salary. I told her that in this work she would meet men of the finest character and with opportunities for advancement. This, briefly, was her chance to lift herself into a position of security and happiness. But still she cried.

"I am hungry for the city. I hate this poky little village."

"I signed for you, you know. The Imperial Organization of Social Services will not let just any person take a girl away. They trust me to train you and to love you."

"I love you, Lady Najafi, but I hate the village."

"I cannot return you to your mother. You must go back to the work center."

"But the work center is in Teheran!"

I thought of how I had worked with this girl. I had tried to love her and do for her as for the others. But it was not enough. She was still city-sick.

"Besides," she said, "I do not like to tell you this. Asghar comes in to the room after I am—"

The other girls raised on their elbows.

"That is not true," Farkhondeh said.

"That's a lie," Effat agreed.

"Tomorrow you will go back to Teheran, Ashraf," I said. "You do not need to speak untruthfully of Asghar. I know him. But remember this. If you go back now there will never be a second chance for you. Never."

"I do not want a second chance. I want to go back to Teheran."

After I had gone to bed I could not sleep. I had had difficulties before. But this was different. In the months I had had Ashraf in my home I had been unable to change her or help her at all. At times I had felt her pulling against me with the other two girls. She was a girl of high ideals, a beautiful girl. Sadly I recognized that people are not clay in the hands of a potter. No matter how eager the hands, a vessel cannot be shaped against its own design. This I had been told before, but like the old man with the amulet I had not believed it until I had seen it.

It was two days before I could get transportation into Teheran; then I took Ashraf back to the work center and brought home Pooran. Pooran, who would never be able to do heavy work. Pooran, whose bent spine pushed her head forward in an unnatural line. I had thought that my students should be normal, not handicapped in any way, and beautiful. But the day that I took Ashraf, normal and beautiful, back to Teheran, Pooran caught my hand and held it. "My lady," she begged. "Please, please take me with you."

Standing there in the crowded general room of the work center I said a silent prayer, "God help me to know." And abruptly I knew. "Yes, Pooran. Today I will take you back."

When Effat and Farkhondeh saw me coming with Pooran they set up a shouting and laughing that were almost hysterical. "Koochek, koochek (little one)," they cried, as they hurried to make her comfortable.

Pooran learned more quickly than any other student I ever

had, save Moneer, and in less than a week she was carrying her full teaching load of sewing and reading. She was a gifted reader —one of those who make the page come to life and move like a play before the eyes—and a very fine needlewoman. She could not take her turn at sweeping and cleaning and scrubbing, that is true, but the other girls gladly relieved her of that load. In Pooran a bent body had purified the fire of the spirit.

And then, as if every good thing was happening at once, the government sent me three looms, one of which was a carpet loom. Of course I knew nothing about looms, not even how to thread them, but I was joyful. This, at last, was a tangible move toward the employment of women during the long waiting months of winter.

Both Farkhondeh and Effat had learned so quickly and were now so patient with the women in the classes that I felt I could leave for a few days without being met by a group of angry villagers. This time my journey took me to Ghom. In Ghom the most beautiful carpets in all the world are made.

At Ghom I walked about as if I had nothing on my mind except, perhaps, the purchase of a carpet. I looked at the wool, I talked with weavers about the dyes that were used in the wools, I watched the weavers work. Finally I purchased wool for the first carpet. I would have some of it dyed in Teheran and some in Sarbandan, for in the villages many of the old people, like Madar-i-Kadkhoda, for example, know how to make everlasting dyes from the jackets of nuts, from leaves, from berries.

I had watched one old man, Mash'hadi Ali Reza, work at threading a carpet loom. I spoke to him. "Mashdi Ali Reza," I said, "you are fine at weaving carpets. Very fine."

"Yes," he agreed. "I am sixty-five and I have been making carpets since I was eight. That is a long time."

"Would you teach me how to make carpets, Mashdi Ali Reza?"

"You, my lady?"

And then I told him about the workroom in Sarbandan, about

the new looms, about the women eager to learn how to make carpets. I watched his face, and his expression changed not at all. Later we began to bargain on a price that would be suitable for Ghom's best weaver of carpets should he desire to come to Sar-bandan. That settled, I made arrangements for Mash'hadi Ali Reza's journey to Sarbandan.

The looms were set up in the workroom, and after we had decided on the design for the rug he began to thread the loom. This the girls watched with such absorbed interest that they forgot even to eat. When the threading was completed it was time for instruction to begin. The three girls and two of the quickest village women sat down at the loom.

"Lady Najafi, I am tired," Mash'hadi Ali Reza complained. "I want to die with my children, not in this cold land."

In sixty-five years one could grow very accustomed to the heat of Ghom.

"Be content, old one," I told him. "I will make a surprise for you."

To make him happy and willing to stay in Sarbandan I arranged to have his wife join him. I made beds side by side for them in the work-study room. The night she arrived I heard them whispering together all night. Now he will be content, I thought.

The next morning they both brought smiling faces to the breakfast table. "Today we will return to Ghom," Mash'hadi Ali Reza told me. "It is good."

"It is not good," I said, too astonished to do things in the slow, patient way that is more apt to insure success.

He pointed to his wife. "She says it is good. It is good," the old man said. Directly after breakfast the wife got his things together and they left. Yet Westerners think that in my country women have no power!

The loom which I had been so eager to procure stood threaded but quiet. A friend from Teheran came up and threaded one of the small looms and taught the girls to weave narrow lengths of material. But still I wanted to get busy on the carpet and sought for some expert carpet weaver to act as teacher.

While I chafed at having the loom stand unused, work on the bath was suspended. The ground, the contractor said, was frozen so hard that excavation was impossible. In the old bath the dirty water, when the pool was drained, ran into the jube, later to be used for household purposes by people who lived lower on the stream. In the new bath the water was to be drained into a modern cesspool where it would filter out slowly into the deep soil. But now it was impossible to excavate for this cesspool or even for the bath.

One morning we awakened to a strangely silent world. The wind which had whistled for days had died down and the air was clean, sharp and very still! Over everything—every house, every field, every tree—was a heavy blanket of snow. I stood in my doorway and looked at this entirely white world with a response to the beauty that shook me and held me. After a time the snow began to fall again. Faster and faster and faster. It was a curtain that cut the rest of the village from my sight. We made a fire in the workroom, scarcely expecting any students, but at schooltime a few girls came struggling through the snow. Some had shoes, others had their feet bound in many rags. One girl, smaller than the others, came wrapped only in a cotton chador. (I must spend some time in Teheran begging warm clothing from my friends.)

Teaching was light, however, and visiting was impossible. I sat with my three girls and reviewed them for the work ahead. From the first I had planned to send each of these girls to a separate village, allowing them to start as I had started, to find out whether my methods were dependent upon my own personality or if they would work whenever a dedicated person walked among those in need.

My girls now had the skills for their work. I would take the rest of this frozen month to teach them the philosophy. This I tried to do by telling them many stories.

When you stand on a corner in Sarbandan, or Teheran, or New York, or London, and watch the people stream by it is hard to realize that under the worn chador, the cashmere coat, the ragged jacket, beat hearts that are all alike. It is hard to understand that the same motives that move us move them, too. We want to live long and be healthy, we want to belong, to love and be loved, to be secure, to feel that we are worth while, to have the commendation of our peers, to have something to look forward to. So do they. In each human heart one of these urges tops all the others. In the villages of Iran people do love and are loved, they do feel that they belong—perhaps to the ages—but they want fiercely to live and be healthy. They need something to look forward to. These homely truths I taught my girls and they nodded because they were intelligent enough to look inside their own hearts and see these things.

When we go into the villages we find the people living the lives of their fathers, I told the girls, believing as their fathers believed, content with possessing what their fathers possessed. We may grow impatient. But to them this link with the past offers security, a sense of belonging; in it is nurtured the seed of their family relationships which give them the love without which life would be impossible. How can we overthrow their way of life because they are unenlightened? their practices unsanitary? their methods obsolete?

We must work slowly, with patience, perseverance, understanding and love. I have a personal theory that no matter what you do for a person for whom you feel contempt you have not done a good thing, for the contempt poisons the gift.

I told my three girls many stories about the people in our village who had been cheated so often, given so many empty promises that at first I could not reach them at all. When they themselves went into other villages they would face this same problem. Villagers fear three things: hunger, disease, and the government agent.

Hunger, which is no more than a word in progressive countries and which, if it should be prevalent, would be met by most strenuous government measures, is common in the Middle East. In the villages of Persia it sits like a howling dog at every doorstep. The villagers, knowing that it follows crop failure and crop failure is due to natural causes, ascribe their hunger to God and curse those who they feel have displeased Him. They regard disease with awe and feel that it is a punishment sent from heaven, as is famine. And the government agent! The only government agent with which the people are familiar is the gendarme—the rural police—and they fear him as they fear the evil eye or a ghost.

Once I had suggested to the council that we ask the government for a gendarme post to protect the village. Suddenly it seemed that the group had been struck by lightning. With a loud "no" they unanimously vetoed the proposal. I asked for a reason and they gave several. "A gendarme post needs a building." . . . "A building needs rent." . . . "There are other expenses." . . . "The government does not have a budget." . . . "We do not have disputes." . . . "Even when we have disputes the kadkhoda or the council." . . . And then the most ingenious reason of all: "My lady, it is good to have the gendarme in the next village. If we do have a dispute it has cooled before we travel that far. We kiss and again we are friends."

I put my hands over my ears to shut out the loud phrases. These were words. But even in the eyes of these more intelligent and wealthy villagers there was a strong, old story of fear. Perhaps that fear went back to the time when it was necessary for the Shah to subjugate the tribes in order to build a nation. I do not know. But the fear of government was there.

Now I asked my girls to walk softly wherever they went so as not to increase the fear of the people.

After we had talked, I brought out a great box and opened it. I had bought each of the girls a beautiful handkerchief, nylon stockings, gloves, lipstick, dainty shoes, nicely fitting brassières (which they had never had in their lives), a luxurious silk flower, and yardage for each to make two new blouses, two long full skirts, two pairs of slacks to wear under the skirts. I next brought out the coats I had had in America. They were not the coats I would have purchased for the girls, but they were the coats I had. To Pooran went a short coat of soft pink wool, to Farkhondeh my gold-colored velvet party coat, to Effat my all-purpose wool fleece. They tried them on, the artificial flowers pinned near the shoulder. They put on their nylons and their shoes which actually fitted them, and swayed across the room on the unaccustomed heels. They embraced each other and exclaimed, "How beautiful you are!" and while they laughed the tears rolled down their faces.

It was Farkhondeh who asked, "But, my lady, what coat do you have now?"

"Sometime I will have a coat," I said. "But now I will use a shawl. A very warm shawl."

I helped each girl pack her own special belongings into a suitcase. When an opportunity came to work in a village she would be ready.

"When we go to the village we must go walking or riding upon a donkey. We do not wear nylon stockings, nor high-heeled shoes. Over our heads we wear a neat kerchief; our dress is clean and simple. We wear nothing that the villagers themselves cannot look forward to wearing."

Then I shooed them away from me with a gesture. "But when you go to Teheran to talk with the agencies, you are ladies."

"We are ladies," Farkhondeh cried in an excess of good spirits, and swept Effat off her feet in a big embrace. But she kissed me quietly, and though she tried to say something it was only her eyes that spoke.

Eleven ❧ AZAR

In Sarbandan in the month of Azar (December) there are three colors: the gray-brown of the shivering trees and of the mud houses, the gray-blue of the distant winter sky, the eternal whiteness of the snow. The snow, which in Aban was broken by footpaths, now lies in a continuous sparkling blanket. The women and girls, coming to school, walk on its frozen crust.

Attendance has picked up in the school. I have been able to beg shoes and other clothing from my friends for the most needy, and all the village has learned that the schoolroom is always warm and dry and comfortable.

The room, which in the warmer months had seemed almost large enough, now seemed very small. Every woman and girl bathed weekly at the decrepit old bath. The women of Sarbandan are neat and clean! But the clothing could not be spared for washing and for drying. Besides, what great work it is to break the ice on the jube to obtain water, or to melt snow enough for even the necessary household use. After each bath the people put back on the clothes they have been wearing. This they do from the first day of winter until the first day of spring.

Oh, the smell that filled that schoolroom! After the class had gone in the evening, heedless of the cold, we opened the doors and windows, but the smell never completely left the room. And it was growing heavier every day.

Now is the time, I thought, to work again on a separate school for the little girls. Perhaps grades one to four.

At the next council meeting we discussed this school. All the members of the council favored it. They were growing more and more progress-minded. Their donation of land and their promise of assistance in building the clinic had filled them with pride in their civic-mindedness. Praise had done these men much good.

"We must have a school for the girls but it is too cold to build now, Lady Najafi," they told me. "Where is the mud? Where is the straw? Where is the summer sun to dry the bricks?"

"Where is some bare earth to put the building on?" I laughed, looking out over the unbroken fields of snow.

"What then shall we do?"

"Many are away at Mazandaran," I said.

Mash'hadi Mokhtar smiled and his gold teeth gleamed. "Let us repair a house that now stands," he suggested. "We can find a suitable house, perhaps."

So the whole council set out to find a house. The one they found was occupied by a lone woman who was willing to move in with her daughter, whose husband was also away at work. I myself would not have selected this house. It had two rooms, the larger of which was about ten by thirteen feet. Into this larger room we would have to crowd more than thirty girls. The tiny lean-to room would be the home of the teacher.

Next, the council planned the improvements. Looking around my little room they decided on gypsum plaster for the inside, doors, windows, shelves in one or two of the alcoves. Immediately the improvements were got underway, the doors and windows being brought out from Teheran.

When the building was finished I, as the secretary of the council, wrote to the Ministry of Education offering the building for a school for primary-grade girls. It was accepted and the whole town was out in spite of the cold and snow to see the school desks and benches unloaded.

There were dozens of willing hands to carry the furniture into the schoolroom. But what furniture! We had been given the discarded furniture from some other school. Many of the desks and benches had broken legs when they were unloaded. Others were broken as they were carried in. Others gave way under the weight of the villagers, eager to sit at the desks and try them out. I had expected good furniture when we had made the effort to prepare the room and I was so angry that I couldn't speak. But the villagers laughed. It was a good joke, it seemed. Soon old men, even mem-

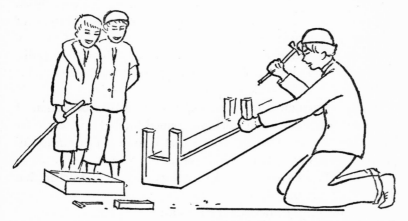

bers of the council, were sitting on the floor, their mouths full of nails and a hammer in their hands, mending the broken-down equipment.

One of the councilmen spoke to Mash'hadi Mokhtar: "Lady Najafi is angry."

Mash'hadi flashed me a look and the shrewd brown eyes under the overhanging eaves of his brows were twinkling. "That cannot be. Anger is for the ignorant!"

I laughed, too. Laughing is better than crying.

Now the school was ready. Where was the teacher? The Ministry of Education had placed the school in the charge of the principal of the boys' school. The council visited him and received a great bag of promises. Even they could see that this overworked young man did not know what to do next.

The kadkhoda called a special council meeting. The council insisted that I write urgently to the Ministry of Education asking for a teacher.

I waited, we all waited, for an answer to the letter.

Mail delivery in Iranian villages is unique in the world, perhaps. The mail is sent out of Teheran to the nearest city or large village. There it is held until somebody happens to be going in the direction of the village to which the mail is addressed. It is held at the teahouse in that village until somebody is going further in the right direction and then it is sent on. Sometimes a letter will have a dozen such stops and be carried by a dozen men-of-good-will, none of whom is responsible to anybody.

The strange thing is that the villagers themselves are not dissatisfied with this service. Indeed, they'd rather trust these strangers than the government officials.

At first I thought that I was simply waiting for notification of a teacher's appointment to reach the council through me. Later the council grew impatient and insisted that I go into Teheran to call upon the Ministry of Education myself.

I was informed that they had not yet found a teacher, but they were working on it.

I said nothing. I knew their problem:

A young boy or girl who is just graduated from high school looks around for a teaching position. If he can find one in a town he is happy. If he must go to a village he promises himself that this will not be for long and goes unwillingly. The wages are very low so there is no incentive to work hard at the teaching. Frequently he does as little as he can and still hold the school together, all the time praying that the year will sometime end and he can get back to the city.

After several days a friend came out with the word for the council that a teacher had been found. A likely young man—

I gave the information to the council. There was a howl of protest, a flurry of arguments. A boy to teach our girls! Never. For a girls' school we must have a woman teacher. I did not take part in the discussion.

After the meeting had broken up and the word had gone with the speed of light around the village, several mothers came to me. I knew them all. I had visited in their homes and some of them attended my classes. "Lady Najafi, we do not want this thing. You must do something."

"I am not of the Ministry of Education," I told them. "You can do something if you wish." Then I talked with them about a petition to the Ministry of Education. I did not call it a petition— I said a letter—but I told them how strong is the request of many and how weak is the request of one. I waited for them to ask me to write the letter for them. I wrote the few lines asking for a girl teacher instead of boy; then I showed them where to sign.

How proud the women were who had been in the classes and could sign their names! I showed the others that even a mark made by different people is different and can pass for a signature. I watched the excitement burn on their cheeks as they put their marks on the petition. After these women left others came to sign the paper. Later the fathers of the girls—those who were not in Mazandaran for the winter—came and signed, too.

In this matter, which did not seem of great importance to me, the villagers were for the first time acting in a body. I was excited, stimulated. I prayed that the Ministry of Education would respond favorably to the petition.

It was almost the end of the month before the new teacher arrived, brought out by one of the development specialists from Damavand. She was a woman. Frail-looking, but a woman! In spite of her loose clothing I could see that she was pregnant. I knew by her eyes that she was sick with loneliness, and the first confidence she gave me was that her husband was in the army serving in the south and would not be back for many months.

I sent Asghar over at once with one of our wooden beds and a chair made from a section of a felled tree. To her own bedding I added a quilt, and to her supplies a luxury or two to welcome her to her new home. Would she be like Effat and Farkhondeh—or like Ashraf?

The schoolroom was finished, the teacher installed, but still the room stood empty, the benches and desks unused.

The council wanted me to do something about the problem; but the registering of the students for the school was the work of the principal of the boys' school since he had been put in charge of both schools. The council visited him. He lifted his shoulders in a shrug and said that his burden was already too great to be borne by any one person. They came back to me.

I had hoped that they would be able to take care of each problem as it presented itself. They had handled well the keeping of the old bath open until the new one was completed. But here they were stopped by an obstacle they could neither see nor understand.

One day Farkhondeh and Effat visited every home in Sarbandan where there was a girl of elementary-school age.

"Why have you not gone to the new school?" they asked the little girls.

"Lady Najafi did not give us permission," came the answer in almost every home.

The women had thought that the new school would compete with my workroom and they were being loyal to me!

"Lady Najafi sends me to give you her permission," the girls answered. "She wishes you to come, if you would like, to her home in the morning at eight."

Thirty-two girls, ranging in age from six to fourteen, came the next morning. I gave each a glass of reconstituted milk and a cookie. I talked to them of the new school and the door to the world that is opened when a schoolroom opens its doors. Then I led them single-file across the frozen snow, under a surprisingly bright blue sky, to the new school. The whole line sang as it snaked across the glittering field. The songs were old folk songs, sung with the special intonation of the old-fashioned singers in Persia—a sound most heartbreakingly beautiful.

Heads came out of doorways to watch the procession. There were clapping and laughter and tear-filled eyes. The opening of the school was now a big event!

There were thirty-two students in the schoolroom. There were

forty benches. How long would it take the village to outgrow its
school?

As I walked from the school to my workroom I felt an unusual
lightness, a sort of intoxication of relief that is hard to describe but
wonderful to feel. Someone else was bearing a burden which I had
found heavy. Someone specially equipped was doing the work
that I had tried to do with my mind and strength concentrated in
other channels.

Almost a month had gone by and still the carpet loom stood
accusingly in the work-study room. With the problem of the girls'
school settled, I took a trip to Zanjan, where excellent carpets are
made. There I found a young woman who had been a carpet
weaver since childhood and who was willing to return with me.
"There is only this," she said, after the bargain had been completed. "I have a child that must come with me."

I took a deep breath. There had been Hosein and Ali, who
were to have been so quiet and well-behaved and who had almost
driven us insane until they were conquered by the eight-year-old
son of the kadkhoda. "How old is this child?"

"Not a child, really. He is an infant. A baby."

"That is good," I said. "Bring him. Yes."

So Masoomeh came, and with her her little boy of just the best
age to toddle around and pull table covers off over his head, to
overturn candles, to take things from the lower shelves. He was of
the age, too, to be toilet trained, and Masoomeh's way of training
him was to take his lower clothes off entirely, so toddling about he
left a trail of puddles—and other things—behind him.

If I had wondered about Farkhondeh's advancement in the three
months she had been with me I would wonder no longer. She
took the child in her care: bathed him, fed him, trained him, put
him to bed.

Both the baby and the mother grew fat and beautiful.

"How is it, Najmeh-jun," my mother asked, "that everybody
that is fed here grows fat except yourself?"

The carpet was progressing, too. So carefully we made it! Every
small mistake was taken out and the work put in again.

Then one evening Effat came to me with a serious face. "Lady Najafi, Masoomeh says that she is leaving."

"Leaving?" I could not believe this.

"She says she has word that her husband is back in Zanjan from the army. He wants her to return."

"But not now. It is winter, even colder in Zanjan than in Sarbandan."

"Winter does not change her husband, Masoomeh says. If she does not return he will marry another wife in the village."

"Well, she must go then," I agreed. For to marry another is not just an empty threat in Iran, where polygamy is still allowed and sometimes practiced in the villages.

But now the loom did not stand still. The girls went on with the work. However, I could see that their skill was not great enough to work without instruction, so I sent them back to the small looms.

One cold morning I felt an uneasiness. At first I did not know just what I was uneasy about; but the thought of the girls' school kept coming to my mind.

"I must go to the girls' school," I told the three girls as we drank our morning tea.

Pooran raised her shining eyes to my face. "But my lady, it is snowing."

Farkhondeh shivered. "And it is cold."

"But I must go," I told them, bundling myself into Farkhondeh's coat and putting my own heavy shawl over my head.

Outside, the wind blasted the snow against my face and I covered all but my eyes with the shawl. As I stumbled through the snow I tried to argue away my feeling of worry. The children were in a warm room (I wished that I were). They were being taught things that I had had no time to teach them.

Never had the way to the school seemed so long. My hand, holding my shawl across my face, was numb in spite of my knitted glove when I pushed against the schoolroom door, eager for its warmth and comfort.

There was little more warmth in it than there was outside. The only warmth came from the bodies of the children huddled in the seats.

"Good morning, my lady," they said as I entered, struggling to their feet to greet me.

"But where is your teacher?" I asked.

"She's sick. She stays in bed this morning."

"Where is the fire to warm you?"

"There is no fire."

"Why don't you sit two together on a bench until I return? You will be warmer that way."

I went into the mean little room that housed the teacher. She was lying on the bed, her face folded tight with pain. She needed care more than did the children.

"Oh, my lady," she said. "The children—"

"Yes, I will see that they are cared for," I told her. "But why is there no fire?"

"There will be no more fuel this month. The Ministry of Education gives so much fuel each month for each classroom. When that is gone there is no more."

"But what of the school in the south where there is no cold weather?"

"Their fuel is the same as ours, my lady."

I resolved to take up this matter with the Ministry of Education. How much better to bring these children into the school in the spring, summer and fall and allow them to remain home in the winter if there was to be a problem of keeping them warm.

Again there was an emergency meeting of the council. Eventually the Ministry of Education would take care of our problem but its load was heavy. Temporarily the problem was ours. We discussed the cold schoolroom and Mash'hadi Mohktar, with a generosity that astonished me, said, "I will give kerosene for one day each week."

"I will also," I offered.

Before the meeting was over enough fuel had been promised to keep the room warm six days out of seven.

Meanwhile there was the problem of the sick young teacher to be taken care of. I did not want her to lose her position, because I knew that she would eventually feel better. The principal had his time fully taken at the boys' school.

"I will send one of my girls over to teach the children and care for the teacher until she is better," I promised.

Both Effat and Farkhondeh struggled through the wind-driven snow, carrying food and kerosene and other supplies.

For each child and for the teacher Effat made a glass of warm milk. Farkhondeh lighted the kerosene in the heater and began the lessons. After a time Effat came back and I heard her talking with Pooran. "Farkhondeh would make a perfect teacher for young children. She pours love over them in a stream."

Sweet Farkhondeh. She poured love over everyone in a stream, but I had bigger plans for her than mornings spent in an elementary school. There was my plan to extend my work to other villages and let these girls whom I had trained fill the role I had filled in Sarbandan.

Many days during the long winter one of the girls or I went to the school in the morning and conducted the classes and cared for the teacher. We did this without pay, without entering our names on the report. We did not wish the Ministry of Education to say at once, "See, a woman will not do as a teacher for our schools. A woman is sick, a poor thing, undependable!"

Besides, the experience was good for the girls, and for me.

Now the weather grew colder. The temperature dropped to thirty below, then to forty. There were no animals left outside; all had moved into the little homes with the families. Blizzards kept the women from coming to the workroom to learn reading or needlework. The doctor got through the snow-blocked roads only once. That day he arrived at eleven and had to leave at three to get back to the city before dark.

Effat and Farkhondeh and I worked with the doctor. He looked at a patient and prescribed treatment. I took down his instructions as fast as I could write. Farkhondeh kept an unbroken line of patients traveling under the doctor's eyes; Effat gave emergency treatment as it was indicated.

Two hundred patients the doctor saw in four hours! But for four days after his departure the three of us worked from morning until night completing the treatments he had ordered. I, like the other women of Sarbandan, began to look toward summer with a hunger greater than the hunger for food.

After the four busy days in the clinic we again settled down to a quiet life in our snowbound village.

These days I spent with Farkhondeh, Effat and Pooran. It would not be long, if my plans were realized, before we would no longer be together, and we made these snowbound days a happy time. Sometimes we made ourselves soup, sometimes cookies and sweets, often we sat with glasses of tea cupped in our hands and talked together of those things necessary to a good life. It was warming to me to feel the idealism of the girls, their dedication.

We were sitting this way one afternoon when my door flew open, letting in a sudden drift of snow. "Lady Najafi." The man who spoke was blue with cold and his face was seamed with worry. "You must come at once. Our daughter bleeds from the mouth and nothing will stay the blood."

"I will come with you, but you must go into Damavand and bring a doctor. There is little that I can do." And again those words, "I am not a doctor."

"But Damavand!"

"Asghar will find you a donkey. You must hurry." Then I turned to Asghar, reading by the korsee. "Find a donkey and go with the man."

Having learned where he lived, I bundled up, with the girls' help, and started floundering along to the home where the girl lay sick. Before I reached the house I heard the sound of weeping. Someone was watching from the doorway, one brown hand holding aside the rug that served as a door. The room I entered was lighted by a piece of rag dipped in grease which was burning in a flat dish. By this wavering light the patient's face seemed to be the color of tallow. She opened her eyes and said, "You have come." She smiled,

closed her eyes again. Then in a moment, "But where is my father?"
"He has gone to Damavand to bring a doctor."

"He will be lost in the snow," she said. Then she kept repeating
at intervals: "Lost . . . Lost . . . Lost."

I lifted her head on to my lap and tried to put a few drops of
warm broth between her cold lips but I was not successful. If I only
were a doctor! If Sarbandan had a resident doctor in the clean new
clinic! I sat in this way for hours, it seemed, before there was a
shout outside the door. The father, the doctor and a bus driver
were struggling toward the door.

The mother again held aside the rug and the three men entered.
The doctor knelt beside the mat on which the girl was resting. He
held her wrist, put his stethoscope to her chest. "I can do nothing,"
he told me. And then to the mother and father, standing with
their hands clasped tightly, "It is too late. Too late for a doctor."

But he stayed until she died, helpless as I had been. As soon
as he had closed her eyes he stood up. "I must return to Damavand."

And now in the room where the girl lay dead there arose an
argument. The father had rented a bus to bring the doctor out
because there was no other vehicle available. He had thought the
price the driver named was the price for bringing the doctor and
returning him to Damavand. The driver insisted the price agreed
upon was for one way. Finally the father went from door to door in
the cold and blizzard to borrow from his relatives all that they had
in money in order to pay for the bus. He would be in debt all his
life. And the girl lay dead.

The time of the deep snow is a time of tragedy. Another day
my door was opened by a woman so thin, so pallid, that I thought
for a moment she had come to my house to die.

"What is it?" I asked. Then I saw that her feet were bare and
that the shawl she had around her shoulders was nothing more
than a piece of worn-out cotton chador. "Come inside and warm
yourself. Let us rub your feet with snow to take out the frost."

"I cannot wait, my lady," she told me, lifting imploring eyes to my face. "I have waited too long already, perhaps. But my feet feared the snow."

I gave her stockings of wool but there were no shoes to fit her. I pulled on my overshoes and reached for my shawl. "I will go with you."

She ran ahead of me lightly. I followed, sometimes breaking through the crust on the snow because of my heavy overshoes. She waited for me at the doorway of her house. She pushed back the ragged rug that closed the opening. In the room I saw six children, all of them lying close like fish in a can. Over them was spread a heap of ragged quilts. Quickly I bent to put a hand on the forehead of the child nearest me. It was so hot that my hand involuntarily moved itself away.

"How long—?" I started to ask, but the woman had collapsed. With more strength than I thought I had I laid her beside the children—all boys, I noticed now—and pulled a part of the quilt over her.

I went next door and called. "Yooo-hooh! Who is there?"

In a moment the rug was pushed aside from the door and Eshrat's face appeared. Her expression turned from curiosity to sullenness.

"What do you want, my lady?" she asked politely enough.

"Will you go down to my home and—"

"I have no shoes, my lady."

"Wear my overshoes, then."

"I have no coat to wear against the wind—"

I could feel my patience leaving me and a hot tide of anger rising behind my eyes. "Eshrat, did you know this whole family was sick?"

She shrugged and was silent.

"You did, then."

"It was not my business."

"If you couldn't help them why didn't you come to me?"

She shrugged again. "I never do."

"Will you watch over these sick ones while I return to my home for medicine and food?"

"And carry the sickness to my child? Hmph! It is not my fault if evil has brought God's anger upon this household."

Leaving the sick family alone I hurried home, collected food, some simple medicines, some charcoal, and Farkhondeh and I, loaded like donkeys, returned to the house. Before dark, Farkhondeh left, but I stayed on.

I bathed the hot foreheads in cool water. I held warm broth to parched lips, I gave aspirin tablets and antibiotic shots. And it was not until I sat cramped in the only available corner in the tiny hut, listening to the sleeping of my seven patients, that I had time to evaluate Eshrat's words. "It was not my business. . . . I never do. . . . It was not my fault. . . ."

Eshrat angered me. She had always angered me. My emotions destroyed my ability to think. Now I was so tired that I was drained of emotions, but my mind went on. Perhaps if I fully understood Eshrat's problems I could understand why she didn't embrace someone else's. Perhaps when one never has enough to eat, enough of anything, really, she cannot help but think first of herself.

Before light Farkhondeh was at the door. "May I take your place here, my lady? I have slept."

I rose, stiff and bone-weary. I kissed her as I passed her in the doorway. There are Farkhondehs and Eshrats in every world.

Another day it was Mash'hadi Mokhtar's brother, Malek, who came to my door. "Will you come to the teahouse?" he asked.

There was not a meeting of the council at the teahouse, but several of the men were there. Mash'hadi Mokhtar told me at once the reason that I had been sent for.

"Did you know Afsaneh?" he asked me.

"Yes. She was a good student at the school."

"She is dead."

"And her husband? Is he in Mazandaran, Mashdi Mokhtar?"

"He is dead. The weather is too cold for those who have the lung sickness."

I nodded. This I knew. The men waited for me to ask another question. "And the children of Afsaneh?"

"The children are our problem. There are six children. Neither Afsaneh nor her husband, Majid, had relatives. We have no orphanage."

"You may bring the children to my home, Mashdi Mokhtar. Farkhondeh will mother them until we can do something better."

I turned to go. "And Mashdi Mokhtar, let me know when a bus will go by to Teheran. I must do business there."

When I had first come to Sarbandan there had been no bus service at all. The bus that ran between Teheran and the Mazandaran area always went by the new road. But recently, if there were passengers for the villages along the old road—passengers or freight—the bus came through Sarbandan. Sometimes there were two buses a week—sometimes none at all. Mash'hadi Mokhtar and I had talked of a better bus service and he had even made inquiries, but it seemed that such service would have to be operated by private capital.

The buses from Mazandaran were awful. They were always crowded with passengers, domestic animals, dairy products, almost anything. The rule was that donkeys, sheep, cows, goats and chickens must ride in the back of the bus. But sometimes they overflowed these quarters and a passenger was as apt as not to find a donkey sitting on his lap. (This is, of course, an exaggeration.) While it was supposed to take three hours to go from Sarbandan to Teheran it more frequently took six. With the roads covered with snow and ice the ancient machine often slipped and skidded on the mountain passes in a way that made the heart stop beating. Sometimes it glided into snow banks where it came to rest for minutes or hours or even days.

When Mash'hadi Mokhtar sent word that the bus was expected I dressed in my city clothes and went down to the teahouse to wait for it.

"You have business in Teheran," Mash'hadi Mokhtar said, not making his voice a question.

Because I could see that he was eaten by curiosity, I said, "My house is very crowded with six extra boys and the oldest of them nine."

Mash'hadi lifted his eyes. "May God give the best of good fortune to this visit," he said devoutly.

Finally the bus lurched into Sarbandan and I climbed on. It was not as bad as I had expected. People were not eager to travel over the icy roads in unheated buses. We reached Teheran without incident.

I went to the home of my sister, Fakhri. Together we visited the orphanage that is the special charity of Queen Soroya. Fakhri had visited before. It was new to me. Like many of the charities sponsored by important people, it was conducted by people high in Teheran society. We were greeted by a friend of Fakhri's who took us through the establishment. It was the most beautiful place I had ever been in. Beautiful! Clean and rich with luxury. The nursery where the younger children played was like heaven.

"What are the ages here?" I asked.

"Mostly under six."

"How many children are here?"

"Eighty."

"I came with the hope that you might be able to take six more."

"Not six!" Fakhri's friend was horrified. "We will talk to some others later about this thing."

Later when we talked, the decision was given me plainly. "We might make room for two. Perhaps for one only. Are these children beautiful? Are they healthy?"

"They are not beautiful. Even now Farkhondeh, my helper, is pulling the hairs from their heads one by one because we cannot at this time bring them into the clinic."

"Scald-headed?" she shuddered. "How awful."

I said no more about my orphans. We thanked our hostesses for taking us through this wonderful place. But outside I said to Fakhri, "Where do you suppose these children go when they are too old for this orphanage?"

"How can I know?"

"There are few homes in all of Iran that are as luxurious as that orphanage. How can you rear children in a place like this and turn them out into the world?"

"They will be adopted, no doubt."

"And why should eighty children be dressed in cashmere and fed upon imported fruit when thousands cry for bread?"

"Oh, Najmeh!" Fakhri was impatient. "You know very well that charity cannot take care of every orphan in need!"

"They are all children. All children of God."

I did not place even one child in this orphanage; but my oldest brother took the boy of nine and Mohsen, my brother nearest me in age, took the one that was seven. And I stayed in Teheran until I had found homes for the four smaller boys. It hurt me to break up this lively, loving family, but there was no other answer.

Twelve ✤ DAY

Day (January), and in Sarbandan the snow still falls. Shrubs and bushes are covered and only the homes of the villagers lift a portion of brown wall above the flat white plane that is the earth. Even the occasional bus from Teheran to Mazandaran does not run, and no cars make their way up the Mazandaran road.

A scattering of women still brave the sub-zero temperatures to come to the classes. When they arrive, soaked to the skin from plowing through the drifts, they dry their chadors and shoes beside my korsee. They sit, their bare feet toward the warmth, and read or sew. There is something about the intimacy of a room that must be lighted by a lantern even in the daytime that makes even the shyest woman open her heart and mind. As I teach the women a new stitch or a new word, I move quietly into their hearts and before long I have heard the deep life story of a silent one who, I thought, would always be a closed book to me.

As I listen to these stories the feeling grows that I must extend my work beyond Sarbandan. What am I doing? What must I be doing?

"That was the year my four little ones died," one woman says. "My boys are a different family entirely. Amir was not born until the others all were gone."

"Do you remember the summer that no child under two lived

160

through the summer sickness?" another asks.

In all of these stories there is a tone of resignation. Not yet are the villagers ready to fight for life and opportunity. Too long their role has been to accept what came.

When I chose Sarbandan as the center of my work I had thought to extend my activity into villages that were near by but more remote from the highway. Now I could see that there would be many problems in working these villages; that energy would be wasted which might be put to better use if I chose villages near the Mazandaran road. For this reason I thought of Roodehen, Sargorg, Ah, and Sadat Mahaleh.

Roodehen I had passed through many times. A village of perhaps thirteen hundred, it was a fifteen-minute stop for the buses that ran between Teheran and Mazandaran. Besides, since it lay between Teheran and the famous spa, Abe-ali, the government was planning to build a paved highway. I had stopped at the village several times and asked questions. It had once been a part of the Pahlavi Endowed Properties, lands which belonged personally to the Shah, but he had divided it among the farmers. Working in a village of this kind would be a new experience for me, since I had worked formerly with landlords and landholders.

Toward the middle of the month came a slight break in the terrific cold. The snow, which had been as hard as paving stones, grew transparent, almost like lace, and a person walking over it broke through knee deep at every step. The stone walls appeared as the snow shrank and man's boundaries on God's world were again apparent. The sun on the back of the neck was a caress and when it was reflected from the surface of the snow it set up a shimmering that dazzled the eyes while it made the heart dance. Of course it was not yet spring. This was just an oasis in the dreadful desert of winter.

Villagers began to venture out from their houses, which had been made airtight against the cold. There were more women in my classes, more children in both the boys' school and the girls' school, more old men talking politics over a glass of tea or a pipe in the teahouse.

When, after more than two weeks with no communication from the outside world, the first bus from Teheran stopped in front of Mash'hadi Mokhtar's teahouse, I resolved to go to Roodehen. The driver was on his way to Mazandaran, but promised to return by this same road.

I was ready when he returned, not dressed for the city, but in low-heeled, stout shoes, a bright kerchief over my head, a dress of figured cotton and a sheepskin jacket.

The driver looked at me curiously. "Where to, my lady?"

"To Roodehen."

"To Roodehen?"

I sat in the seat directly behind the driver as far away from the consignment of sheep going to market as I could.

"Have you been before to Roodehen?" the driver asked as he lurched away from the side of the road and hit the rutty highway, now half slush, half ice.

I shouted above the noise of the apathetic engine. "Yes. Many times."

"Have you noticed the mustaches on the men?"

"Yes." I wished that he would keep his mind on his steering wheel and on his coughing engine.

"Fabulous! They respect those mustaches very highly and when they make promises they swear by them."

Now that the engine was really pulling I could not have heard myself had I shouted.

"If you insult a man's mustache you insult his honor. You are really risking your life."

Still I was silent.

"Very religious people, those. My lady, are you by any chance an Ali-Allahi?"

"I respect them highly," I shouted.

"Eh?"

I let the conversation, one-sided as it had been, die.

A friend of mine was an Ali-Allahi and I knew something of the worship of these very religious people. Because of Ali's goodness and wisdom they have raised him to a place next to God. They do not worship as other Moslems do. They fast not for the month of Ramazan but for three days; and their prayers are in their own language, not in Arabic. At the beginning of a religious service, instead of the intoning of a prayer there is strumming on the taboor, a guitarlike instrument called "David's tar." At first everybody sits and listens to the taboor. Soon all the men present begin to chant, "Ali . . . Ali . . . Ali . . ." The excitement grows and some men rise and begin to move to the rhythm of the music and the chanting; the movement grows into a dance; the dance into an ecstasy of excitement. They are now drunk with the love of Ali and begin to do strange things: swallow fireballs, swallow swords, walk on burning coals. In their ecstasy they lose physical sensitivity as they give themselves to their emotion. For four hours this meeting lasts. And the strangest thing of all, according to my friend who followed this faith until he was fourteen, is that the men who have done these things and fallen exhausted to the ground, are unhurt by the experience.

The bus driver had spoken of the fabulous mustaches of the men. My friend had told me that his father, being an officer in the army, had trimmed his mustache. The grandfather, much respected as a Seyed in the sect, had cursed his son and driven him from his door.

Before starting for Roodehen I had reviewed everything I knew about the Ali-Allahis. In my classes in Sarbandan I had taught the girls how to perform their ablutions and how to pray. This I would not teach in Roodehen. Here I would try to build upon this strangely different background. I must not make a mistake. I sat in the swaying bus and planned and prayed.

We arrived at Roodehen safely and I went at once to the tea-house.

"Lady Najafi," the owner of the teahouse greeted me. "Is it not winter?"

"There is sickness in the winter," I told him. "There is hunger for education, too. This does not leave one in the winter."

He nodded gravely. "It is as you say."

"I would like to see the village council. I have something to say to them."

"That will not be hard." He brought me a glass of tea from his samovar. "Come near the korsee and be warm and I will send my nephew on this errand."

Soon, much sooner than it could have been managed in Sarbandan when I first went there, the nephew returned with an invitation to come to the home of the kadkhoda. He himself would show me the way.

In Roodehen the snow was even softer than in Sarbandan, and I slushed through the path to the kadkhoda's home, feeling the water enter my shoes at every seam.

The men rose to greet me. "Welcome, Lady Najafi. We had hoped that you would come."

"Then you knew of my questions in the village?"

"Of course. There is little news in Roodehen. What there is has wings and flies fast."

They made room for me beside the korsee and in a few minutes I was handed the chopogh to smoke. I took a puff that made me dizzy and passed it on. There was openness in these faces. I knew that the council had discussed me, that they knew about my workroom and my clinic and my classes.

"We have a school for the boys," they told me. "Now it has four grades. We are determined to have six grades next winter."

"A school for the girls?"

"No."

"A clinic?"

"A doctor who comes sometimes. Perhaps every three weeks. Something like that."

"Perhaps you do not need my help."

"There are other villages—Sargorg, Ah, and Sadat Mahaleh. These villages have nothing. The people can come with ease to Roodehen."

"There is a four-grade school in Ah," one of them put in.

The kadkhoda nodded. "I had forgotten that school. But still, Lady Najafi—"

"These are my plans," I told them, being as frank with them as they had been with me. "In my home I have trained three intelligent young women. I will send one of these young women to you. She will work in Roodehen as I have in Sarbandan. Every two weeks she will come to Sarbandan and discuss her work. At that time I will give her any help she needs."

They listened gravely. Nodded.

"But this you must do—" I expected the protest I had met in Sarbandan. "You must furnish a house for this girl and her two young brothers, a place large enough so that she can teach your girls and women, see your sick and dispense simple medicine."

I studied their faces but there was no protest. "This we have found already."

My feet had just begun to be warm and dry, but we pushed out into the slush again and half waded, half walked to the home they had selected.

"It is satisfactory," I said.

I stayed in Roodehen until a jeep from the Development Bongha in Damavand came up the road and gave me a ride to Sarbandan.

When I told the girls about my visit they were delighted. Farkhondeh caught my hand. "Let me go, my lady."

"I have other plans for you, Farkhondeh. Effat is older. She must have the first turn."

I took Effat into Teheran with me the next time the bus came through, leaving Pooran to take care of Hosein and Ali, and Farkhondeh in charge at Sarbandan. With Effat I made a very careful list of just the necessary items for beginning the work in Roodehen. "Now you go buy these things," I told her. "I will visit with my mother while you are in the bazaar."

I put the money that I figured she would need in her hands.

"But my lady!" She was more than astonished. "All of this money? How can I spend this money? It is yours!"

"You have a list. You know how you can spend it."

She counted it again. Never had a girl felt so very rich.

In the evening she returned. "My lady," she admitted sorrowfully. "The money is gone and the list not taken care of."

"Gone?"

"You should have purchased these things yourself, my lady. I have wasted your money, and yet I did my best."

I sat down with her. "You have not wasted the money, Effat. You have used it to learn how to spend money. In your work you will have to handle much money. Each rial that you waste would buy bread for the hungry. Now you know what it is to use money and you will learn."

When Effat, her little brothers and I went back to Roodehen we hired a car to carry our belongings. Effat now had the same equipment that I had had when I began my work in Sarbandan. She had other things besides. Simple drugs, for example, that I had learned were necessary.

The moment we arrived at the little house that the villagers had prepared, Hosein and Ali, in spite of the fact that it was almost suppertime, went searching for someone to quarrel with. They could not be happy until they had tried their strength against that of the boys of Roodehen. Effat started to arrange her home with enthusiasm. But when I kissed her I felt that her cheeks were wet. She seized my hand and kissed it and my hand was wet, too.

At the first opportunity, I went again to Roodehen.

My first look at Effat's face told me a deep story.

"The council has been wonderful, my lady. But the girls and women do not come. I have no one to teach. I sit alone."

"But you must begin your visits. It is cold, I know, but—"

"I visit but they do not talk to me. They do not have confidence in me."

My heart was heavy but I could not show her my concern. If the people of the village would not accept these girls, then every plan I had for reaching many instead of few would fail. I smiled at Effat, but all the time I was measuring her. She was sweet, she was efficient, she was simple, she was humble—Nowhere could I find a reason for her rejection.

"The people of Sarbandan did not accept me at once," I told her. "Effat, what do you think these people most deeply need?"

She was silent, a frown creasing her brow.

"Food? Clothing? Sanitation?" I remembered when I could find no answer for this question in Sarbandan. The answer really should be "All things."

"There are many with the scald head," she said at last, her voice curling up like a question. And in her words I found the path to the confidence of the people. It was the cure of the scald head which had seemed such a miracle to the mothers of Sarbandan.

We asked the teacher of the school for boys to look after Hosein and Ali until we called for them; then we began our house-to-house visits. In each home we took the names of children with scald head. That is, we took the name if they would give it. Some gave their names reluctantly; some ran and hid.

During the next week I arranged for the radiotherapy at the Teheran clinic and rented a jeep station wagon that would carry the ten boys whose parents had asked for treatment.

The night before our appointment at the clinic I spent in Roode-hen with Effat. Her two little brothers we took over to the home of the schoolmaster, together with a cone of sugar and some tea. They would spend the night and their sleep would not be disturbed when we arose at four in the morning to get the clinic-going group together.

It was amazingly cold the next morning as with lanterns in our hands we began our walk through the village to waken the boys. At five-thirty a large shuffling crowd had gathered. Now there were twenty who wanted to go, though their mothers, and sometimes their fathers too, hung to them as if they would never see them again. By six-thirty we still hadn't left. Parents were offering to pay their own fares if they could accompany their children. And the station wagon was built to hold ten!

We removed the seats, and into it we piled as many people as could be pushed in. Thirty-five people in a space meant for ten! We arrived at the clinic of the Imperial Organization for Social Services at half past eight.

Having gone through this same experience with the children of Sarbandan, I had thought that this experience would be just a repeat. It wasn't. The boys were terrified of the equipment. Besides, they were hungry. I played hide and seek with some of them to get them under the machines. Next I sent Effat hastily for bread and cookies and we held out a tempting morsel, always withdrawing it until the child had spent the proper number of minutes under the machine. Teaching them to accept bribes! A fine thing!

When they had all been treated we piled back into the same station wagon.

When we arrived in Roodehen we put the boys in the arms of their parents and I left Effat. Except for the meetings we would all have together to discuss the problems that rose in the villages, Effat would now stand on her own feet. She could make of Roodehen a model village or she could fail. I trusted her to succeed, and deeply—deeply I prayed.

Again the cold descended upon Sarbandan, even fiercer because of our short respite. The breath of the men made icicles on their mustaches. The ice on the jube was so thick that everyone melted snow to fill the domestic water jar. The faces of the women and girls coming into the classes were red with frost and with snow-burn, their hands and feet almost purple. The kerosene heaters and the korsee were kept burning day and night.

It was on a day like this that a landlord from the village of Khosravan came to call on me. It was midmorning when he arrived; midafternoon when he left. In spite of the cold I took him to see the clinic, the girls' school, my chicken house, and I served him tea in my own schoolroom where the women, with Pooran and Farkhondeh guilding them, went quietly on with their work.

"I have heard of these things. I myself wanted to see them," he told me. And I thought:

> They want but they fear;
> They love but they hate.

"If you will begin your work in Khosravan I will help you all that I can. I will even give you a room for the school."

"We shall see," I told him. "Our energy, now that our work is just beginning, must go where it will do the most good."

"Near us are Japon and Ainehvarzan. They, too, would profit by your work."

Again I said, "We shall see."

And so on another cold day, Farkhondeh and I set out on foot for Khosravan.

Seven kilometers does not seem a long distance unless one is walking. It seems an even longer distance when one's feet are like blocks of ice and the breath stings in the nose and throat. Farkhondeh began to cry. "It is too far, my lady."

I did not comfort her. "You are made of very soft stuff," I told her. "Too soft stuff for the work that we have to do."

She dried her eyes. She did not speak, but she quickened her step.

In Khosravan the sun was as bright as in July but it was unbelievably cold. Farkhondeh and I were forced to seek shelter in the home of one of the village leaders, Haji Esmail. We called at the door: "Whoo-oo, anybody at home?" and the door was opened by the old man himself. He had the thickest, longest beard I have ever seen, colored a remarkable shade of red with henna. He wore a tall fur hat and an ancient long robe.

"Come in, my lady. You are the teacher?"

"Yes, we are teachers," I said. Then I commented on the warmth of his korsee and the hospitality of his home. "Haji Esmail, I understand that you can both read and write."

A shine of pride brightened his eyes. "I learned at forty."

"And now you are—?"

"Eighty." There was satisfaction in his tone.

"I would never have thought that you were eighty. Sixty, perhaps, but not eighty."

"Yes, yes, my lady. I am eighty. I can remember when—" And like any other old man he launched into stories of his childhood, his young manhood, his middle years. But mostly his childhood.

Farkhondeh gave me a troubled glance and I broke into the story. "Are you the only man in this village who can read?"

"No. There is one other."

"Then there are no schools?"

"There are no schools but there are thirty students. I myself teach them when they come to me."

"Does the village have a bath?"

He called abruptly to a woman who had sat near the wall, her head bent, seemingly resting. "Heshmat, show my lady the bath."

The woman rose obediently, wrapping her chador more closely about her.

"That is not necessary, Haji Esmail."

The woman sat down gratefully. I noticed that her feet were bare.

"It is a small bath. Perhaps four or five can be accommodated. I myself built it. But now it needs repair. I built it many years ago." And he fell to counting, figuring by the ages of his sons and grandsons and great-grandsons.

Again I broke into his talking. "It is not necessary to know the day and the year," I told him. "But if it is ruined it should be repaired. I will talk with the Development Bank." I thought of the Farmers' Share Increase Act. "Do you have landlords in this village?"

"We have one very important landlord. He lives in Mazandaran but the three months in the summer he spends in Khosravan. Then there are several smaller landlords."

It must have been one of these "smaller landlords" who had visited me, I thought.

"Heshmat, where is Sadegh?" Haji Esmail called in a rather gruff voice.

Again the woman rose and, going to the door, called, in a voice much older and more tired than Haji Esmail's, for Sadegh. A boy of eleven or twelve, round-cheeked, bright-eyed, smiling, came at once. There were good heavy shoes on his feet and he wore a coat whose sleeves covered his hands except for the ends of his fingers. On his head was a woolen cap. "My grandson," Haji told us. "Go, Sadegh, to the home of the kadkhoda and say that Lady Najafi and her helper from Sarbandan are in my house."

Sadegh took a staff from beside the door. He must have seen me look at him curiously, because he grinned and said, "The kadkhoda lives not far, but his home is high on the hill. One must use a staff to keep from sliding back faster than one climbs forward."

After Sadegh had gone the old man's eyes veiled and he again told of the past—of the time a kerosene lantern was first introduced into the village, of the time—

After a while Sadegh returned with five men. I rose to greet them and was happy to recognize the man who had visited me and promised me a room for my school if I should care to come to Khosravan. For a time we talked about the weather, about the long winter, about my work in Sarbandan. Each of the five men offered a room for the school. Farkhondeh and I followed them on a tour through the frozen village. Women's faces peered at us curiously from the edges of the rugs hung at the doorways. Plainly none of the rooms we looked at would do except the one first offered. It was the only one with doors and windows.

When we all returned to Haji Esmail's home to discuss the equipment we would need for the new school, this landlord said, "Sometime you may use my room. But not this year, of course."

I was astonished, but I did not ask why. The word "why?" embarrasses all villagers. I let him offer his own explanation. "You see, this year I have no child nor grandchild of an age for school."

I kept my eyes upon him but still I did not speak. He finished with a flourish as if this final argument were unanswerable: "I myself have managed to live happily without any school."

"You may use a room here in my house," Haji Esmail said, covering a long silence. Heshmat, moving like a wraith before us, showed us the room. There were neither doors nor windows and the walls were damp and cold.

"You have offered us a very fine room," I told him. "In the summer it will be very good, especially when we put doors and windows in it. Perhaps for now the classes should meet right here in this room."

"My korsee must burn for me. It might as well burn for many," Haji Esmail agreed.

So Farkhondeh began her teaching in Haji Esmail's living room.

I got her a donkey and even in cold weather she was able to come back and forth from Sarbandan.

After the talk about the school was settled (Farkhondeh would go to Khosravan three days a week, teaching sanitation, crafts, child care, as well as reading and writing), we all climbed to the home of the kadkhoda high on the hill behind the home of Haji Esmail. I was glad of the stout stick that I had borrowed from beside the door of Haji Esmail's home.

The kadkhoda was a tribal chief who spent only the winters in this village. In the summer most of the people who were not employed by big landlords went with this man to follow sheep over the mountain grasslands. He looked at me with eyes narrowed to glittering black slits from a face of worn leather. I wondered how to greet him—what to say.

"Salaam," I ventured.

He spoke to his wife with a gesture of his strong-knuckled hand. She brought several beautiful blankets, called jajims, and silently unfolded them before us. Abruptly an idea struck me and exploded into tiny stars in my mind. These jajims! These narrow strips sewed together to make blankets we could make on our small hand looms, putting into them our own creative design.

"They are beautiful—beautiful," I said, and my words were inadequate.

"Touch them. Handle them," he invited. "They are very durable, and very refined."

I did touch them, my fingers telling my mind how they might be made. The making of jajims I could teach. I had asked for sixteen carpet looms and one had been given. That one stood unworked—a carpet just begun.

The kadkhoda smiled at my excitement. "Well, at least we have bread and cheese," he said. So we drank tea and ate bread and cheese while in my mind I threaded a loom for our first jajim.

Later I stopped in to bid good-by to Haji Esmail. I wondered if he would speak to me of the landlord who had invited me to come to the village then had refused a room for the school. I hoped that he would not, because I would not know what to answer.

Perhaps I could say, "But today I have learned something of value for myself and for Sarbandan."

But he did not mention this landlord. Instead he stood up, straightening his back slowly until his fur hat towered above me.

"God speed you, and God speed us all," he said. And then devoutly, "God be praised that I have lived to see this day."

Thirteen ✿ BAHMAN

Bahman (February), and still the cold weather wraps Sarbandan in a chador of ice and snow. Still the villagers melt snow to fill their tall household jugs or carry water from farther up the jube where the sound of ax against ice rings out from daylight until dark, as ice is cut into great squares and packed in sawdust for the use of the wealthy when summer comes. The carrying of the water and the cutting and storing of the ice are almost the only activities that are visible in Sarbandan. How distant the face of the cold sun seems; how short his journey across the narrow, white world.

Still the carpet loom stands accusingly in the work-study room, the carpet just begun. The long winter months in which I had hoped that the carpet would be completed are passing away.

Some time before, a friend, visiting me, had suggested that I employ a young widow from Kerman who had woven carpets all her life and came from a family of carpet weavers. She had two children, a girl five and a boy three. I had gestured toward Hosein and Ali chasing Little Rabbit in the door, around the room and out again. "Already this home looks like a kindergarten," I said. So instead of the widow from Kerman I had brought Masoomeh from Zanjan and that had been a mistake.

Now I thought of the widow from Kerman. Effat had taken her two rowdy little brothers with her to Roodehen. Our home needed

other children. I wrote a note to my friend in Teheran, sending
her the bus fare for the woman and her children. By the devious
way that letters travel, especially in the winter, my friend received
the letter and sent me a reply. At once the widow from Kerman
would leave for Teheran. There I should meet her.

There was a break in the awful cold and Shapoor Mozaffari
brought the jeep for my use. Three patients were waiting to be
taken to the hospital in Teheran and I could meet the new carpet
weaver and her children.

The light car slipped and slid over the ice-coated road. Half the
time I spent in reassuring the three patients we were taking to the
hospital in Teheran, the other half I chatted with my driver. I
enjoyed talking to him, watching the light come up into his dark
eyes, seeing the quick smile touch his sensitive lips. I learned that
he was quick to anger, but this anger was at things, not at people,
and he understood the hearts of the poor.

When we arrived in Teheran and had delivered our patients to
the hospital we found that the widow from Kerman had not yet
arrived, but my friend assured me that she was on her way. We
decided to stop over for a day on the chance that we could take her
to Sarbandan when we returned. Both Shapoor and I were glad to
have a few hours with our families.

The next morning Fakhri's servant announced a visitor. I thought
that it might be my friend with news about my carpet weaver. I
was surprised to see Mrs. Mozaffari, whose son had brought me to
town the day before. I called Fakhri to meet her and chatted as
amiably as I could, all the time wondering about the reason for this
visit. Soon Fakhri excused herself and left me alone with my guest.
She spoke quickly:

"Under other circumstances I would talk with your mother,"
she said, "but already you are a professional woman, a person
who accounts herself to herself. That is why I am coming to you.
My son Shapoor loves you and wishes to marry you."

I had not anticipated this request. Never. Yet I was not really
surprised.

"Well?" she asked.

There were no words in my mind to say. I could not say yes. I had not thought of the request seriously enough to say no.

"In America I turned my face away from love. I thought to come home and give my life to my people. I planned to—" My words trailed away before her frank eyes.

Then she said in a way that is Persian, not at all Western, "My son is not worthy of you, of course, but if you would marry him it would make us all very happy." And she finished with a smile that was both radiant and gentle. I thought with a start, *She loves me. She really believes this thing will make her happy.*

"I think I am married to my work."

"One can do more for others when one is fulfilled oneself."

I nodded. I had heard that in Russia—or was it Germany?—schoolteachers who do not marry at a reasonable age are not employed to teach children. Unmarried women are missing something, and their frustration and hunger are reflected in their attitude toward others. At least that is the theory. I had jeered at this theory when I first heard it, but now in this woman's face I saw happiness and fulfillment and her words gave me pause. Had I not grown tired, sometimes, of the voices of women, women, women? Had I not grown weary of "handling" the council so carefully? Did I not often long for someone more mature and understanding than Farkhondeh, Effat and Pooran to discuss my problems with, to comfort me when I was discouraged, to laugh with me when I felt merry?

"I must think about this."

"We do not need an answer today," she said. "Any day will do."

Fakhri came in to bid my guest good-by. As soon as she was gone my sister turned to me with a blunt question. "What did she want?"

"She came to honor me; to ask me to marry her son."

"What! Why, Najmeh, you could marry a senator!"

"Why should I want to marry a senator?"

"You said you had turned your face away from marriage. Have you changed your mind?"

"I must think about it."

Fakhri laughed. "You and your thinking! Why don't you try *feeling* about it?"

"First I must take the carpet weaver to Sarbandan, then I will take time to feel, perhaps."

She put her arms around me. "Najmeh-jun, you funny little pussy."

The next day the weaver came in on the bus from Kerman and with her were two half-frightened, hungry children. Shapoor brought the jeep to the station and we packed the little family into the back seat along with their meager belongings. Shapoor and I sat together in the front seat. We neither of us mentioned his mother's call; but I looked at him with different eyes.

Back in Sarbandan the woman went at once to the loom. I could see by the light in her face and the way she touched the loom that she knew rug weaving and loved it. "You will be happy here, Zahra," I said.

She turned toward me one of the warmest, sweetest faces I have ever seen. "I will be happy." And I knew that this carpet would be completed—this carpet and many others.

Since Farkhondeh was so much of the time in Khosravan, Pooran took over the care of the children, bathing them, dressing them, feeding them, teaching them. At first they were shy and quiet, but after a visit or two from Little Rabbit the three became a close trio and were apart only when they slept.

Now it was necessary for me to buy more wheat. I had estimated the amount of wheat I would need for a year and bought it at harvest time. Five months had gone and the bins were almost empty. There had been many extra mouths to feed, many emaciated bodies to build to strength and roundness, and in Sarbandan all bread must be made at home. There is never a loaf to be purchased in any shop of the bazaar. This needed wheat I bought from Garmsar, and Shapoor brought it to me on one of his official trips.

Things were going very well in Sarbandan, in Roodehen, in Khosravan, but still I could not rest. Very soon I wrote a note to Shapoor's mother and to mine. In Teheran we had a small engagement party. Only our closest friends knew that we had decided to marry.

When I was in Sarbandan working with my people, the whole thought of marriage left my mind for hours at a time. When I stopped briefly in Teheran my sisters and my mother talked of it constantly. Soon, very soon, we should have the wedding. What would I wear? What mullah would perform the ceremony? What would be the promises in the marriage contract? What would be the date of the wedding?

For a time I was a divided personality. I cannot say how such things can be. In Sarbandan I worked patiently, feeling that the problems of the village were the outside limits of my life. In Teheran I shopped for white satin, for handmade slippers. I watched Fakhri and my mother unpack the white silk chador embroidered with real gold and jewels that had been worn by the women in our family for at least three hundred years. Najmeh, the bride, I left in Teheran; Najmeh, the woman of Sarbandan, I left in the village. Between these two personalities I was torn!

But my sisters and my mother were not torn in this way, nor was Shapoor. In him there was a definite tenderness, a watchfulness for me that touched me even as I felt it to be unnecessary.

Only Akbar Agha was miserable. "You must not marry this woman," he advised Shapoor. "No man can ever know what is going on inside her head. This no man can endure!"

In Teheran there are old-fashioned people—people who do things as their parents and grandparents did them—and new-fashioned people who have adopted the quick ways of the West. And so my family and Shapoor's asked me, "Do you want an American wedding? Do you want a European wedding? Do you want a wedding that is exactly Persian?" I thought of the village wedding with the bride feeling for a time like the queen of the earth as she rides upon the gaily caparisoned horse, a crown of feathers on her head. But after all, I was not of the village and I could not steal its ways. We decided upon the old, deeply beautiful marriage ceremony of my own people. Our marraige would not be performed with a few hasty words.

There are two parts to the Persian marriage; the first is the actual ceremony, the second is the claiming of the bride by the bridegroom. Sometimes there are months between these two ceremonies. At both of these ceremonies there is solemnity embroidered with merriment, food, flowers, music.

My mother-in-law sent me her wedding gift on a great wooden tray covered with a square of the finest Persian material. Wrapped in a large piece of hand-loomed silk in the richest Persian pattern were an exquisite copy of the Koran, a sajjadeh (a prayer rug upon which one kneels) with a picture of Mecca woven into the carpet, and a mohr (the piece of clay upon which one places the forehead during prayer). On the tray, too, were perfume, candies, cookies, and roses. On another tray were the mirror and the candelabra that would be used in the ceremony. Shapoor himself had polished the candelabra so that they would be perfect for me.

The wedding was at the home of Fakhri in Shemiran, a modern home but furnished with ancient Persian carpets and tapestries of great beauty. In one room Shapoor sat with his male relatives, in another were the guests, and in a third, opening onto the room for the guests, I sat alone. Dressed in a white satin wedding gown, wrapped in the ancient chador of my family, I sat cross-legged in the Persian way on the beautiful cloth which Shapoor's mother had sent me. Before me was the sajjadeh and mohr and the Koran opened to the words the mullah would read. At one side was a great long loaf of bread decorated with a word that means "This is a blessed day." On the other side was a tray of incense which would later be burned to give the rooms the rich fragrance of the East. There were also ceremonial foods, symbolic of life and fertility: egg, cheese, milk, vegetables, and cereals. In a beautiful bowl floated one green leaf which symbolized the beginning of the life process with the marriage ceremony.

Quietly I sat, my head bowed so that I would not look into the mirror flanked by the lighted candles. During this time the mullah talked with Shapoor and he signed the book.

And then it was my turn. Into the room came two women friends. Often kinswomen take part in the ceremony, but my friends had asked me to allow them to be with me. One carried a cone of sugar which she crumbled. "May the bride always be as sweet as this sugar." Then came another with a needle and thread, sewing, sewing. "May this needle and thread close forever the lips of criticism of this bride."

It is an ancient custom, foolish perhaps. But still, sitting cross-legged upon the square of heirloom silk, I thought of the symbols and of the words and I was touched in my heart by their simplicity and meaning.

The mullah, an old man whose shrewd dark eyes were covered with shaded glasses, read from the Koran and I followed with my eyes. The words were in Arabic but the passage was familiar to me. He raised his eyes and asked:

"Do you take Abolhassan Mozaffari to be your husband?"

For a moment my ears seemed to play me tricks. Abolhassan? He was a stranger to me. I was silent.

"Do you take Abolhassan to be your husband?"

The young man in the development jeep. The young man showing me the bathhouses in the villages. The young man who carried food to a jailed thief who had injured him. Still a stranger. I was silent.

The mullah must ask this question three times.

"Do you take Abolhassan to be your husband?"

Shapoor, compassionate, loving me, promising me in our marriage contract that he would never object to my work coming first. Shapoor, so patient, so gentle. Still a stranger.

Then Shapoor's mother came with the marriage gift. This gift, always of gold, shows that the mother-in-law is happy with the wedding. Her gift was a gold bracelet. Slowly my divided, half-frightened thoughts came into focus. Shapoor is a good man. Always I will be a good wife to him. Always. As long as I live I will never cheat him. I raised my head and answered:

"Yes."

There were clapping and shouting, and the orchestra played a special song and my husband came in to me. His face was alight and there were a sweetness and deep joy there that I had never seen before. My heart leaped to him. Together we knelt and looked into the mirror.

In the old days this look into the mirror, with the bride's face unveiled, very often was the first look the husband and wife had of each other. Shapoor and I had seen each other often, but as we looked into the mirror our faces were different. We were transfigured, in some strange, inexplicable way. The pearly white chador covered my modern gown. Perhaps it was incongruous for me to kneel there beside a Western dinner jacket. But that is the way things are in Iran—no line between the old and the new.

Gold coins were showered upon us—coins which the children at the party were quick to run forward and collect. The orchestra played. People kissed us and congratulated us. And once again I was lifted out of my body. These things did not seem real to me. I looked at my mother, wrapped in her chador and wearing upon her feet the soft, flat, hand-sewed shoes of fine suède that once were worn by all Persians of station. My older sister, Fatemeh, also wore a chador over her evening gown. Everyone else was in modern Western dress. Somehow I felt safe with my eyes upon my mother and my angel sister, Fatemeh.

When I gained the courage to look away from these symbols of my sheltered, old life, my eyes caught in the crowd of guests the face of Farkhondeh. Abruptly the many Najmehs—the old-fashioned, the progressive, the social worker, the wife, the village woman, the woman of the city—merged again into one. I was a whole person again. In a moment my arms were around Farkhondeh's shoulders and my fingers pressed deep into the reality of her flesh.

In the old-fashioned wedding, the bride returns to the home of her mother to receive instructions on what is expected of a bride, how to keep a house, how to make a man happy. This, of course, I did not do. I returned instead to Sarbandan, to my work. Back in Sarbandan, the wedding night seemed fabulous, unreal. Occasionally Shapoor and I saw each other as before. On the outside our relationship was the same—two social workers. On the inside there was the special happiness mixed with strange pain that people who belong together feel when they are separated.

The celebration that ended this period of separation was held at the Teheran Officers' Club. Shapoor's father is a government official whose work gives him a special interest in this beautiful, enormous club. Thousands of guests can be entertained here. Shapoor's family contented itself with hundreds. Since Farkhondeh had been at the first party, I had Effat and Pooran with me. They helped me dress in my gown of fine pleated chiffon. What most people did not know was that under this new transparent gown I wore the white satin dress of my wedding. Working in the villages had taught me to stretch a rial even when my own wedding was concerned. On my head I wore a coronet of jewels—also belonging to my family—instead of the simple flowers I had worn for the marriage. The girls told each other that I was very beautiful. Shapoor, too, whispered that I was very beautiful and perhaps, at that time, I was, since all women are beautiful when they are loved.

The club was filled with flowers, gifts from friends, and Fakhri, excited, whispered that we should start a florist shop.

Abruptly the orchestra which had played through the evening stopped, and I heard roistering male voices singing:

> Hail to this blessed day!
> The lane is narrow,
> The bride is tall.
> Don't touch her hair;
> It is arranged in curls.
> Oh, blessedness and happiness!

Then there was a loud, loud shout of "Yes!" accompanied by stomping and clapping.

"Congratulations."

It was the village song. My eyes found the radiant faces of Effat and Pooran. My two worlds merged. I was both Mrs. Abolhassan Mozaffari and Lady Najafi. Perhaps, all my life, I would continue to be these two, but the two became one flesh.

We stopped at Shapoor's home only long enough to change

clothes; then the four of us, Shapoor, Effat, Pooran and I, wrapped ourselves in blankets and climbed into the jeep.

Before we reached Sarbandan, Shapoor pointed out to me a flickering of lights on the road. When we reached the edge of the village most of the people I had worked with were waiting, wrapped in anything they could find to shut out the winter cold, stamping their feet to keep them from becoming ice, and swinging their kerosene lanterns back and forth. When our jeep stopped the men began to sing:

Hail to this blessed day!——

and when it came time to shout, "Yes," and clap and cry, "Congratulations," we were picked up by the crowd and carried to my home.

Farkhondeh and Asghar had made the home spotless, and in it were many gifts. The third day after the celebration our friends in Teheran would call at Shapoor's home and leave crystal, silver candlesticks and spoons, tea glasses in silver holders, mirrors and rugs and carpets. But here in our simple room were a basket of eggs, a loaf of bread, a bowl of wheat, another of rice, fresh wool ready for weaving or knitting, a packet of mountain herbs—gifts that spoke of sacrifice and confidence and love.

That first night, after we had settled in bed, the sound of merrymaking went on in the village and Effat and Pooran in loud whispers told Farkhondeh every detail of the party. After a time a great shouting arose at a house behind mine and higher on the hill. At first I thought it was a continuation of the celebration the villagers had planned for us. Later I detected angry tones in the strident voices. Perhaps the affair had started out as a celebration, but had changed color. Now there were loud shouts of "Donkey," "Fool"—this is the way one swears in Iran—and then a howl of agony.

Silence.

"Shapoor," I said, sitting up in bed. "We must go!"

"Najmeh," he answered, "we must not go. Not tonight."

Abruptly there was a loud knocking on the door. "My lady. Hurry! A man will die!"

I jumped from bed. So did Shapoor. Hastily I dressed and putting a shawl over my head I ran through the snow, up the hill, to the now quiet, still crowded house. Shapoor hurried after me, holding high the lantern he had stopped to light.

I knelt on the floor beside the most gravely injured man I had even seen. Somebody in an excess of anger had sliced him deeply from breastbone the full length of his torso. Shapoor held the lantern while I looked at his intestines spilling out of the opened body onto the floor.

"Do something, my lady," the men who ringed us urged.

"I am not a doctor," I told them. But my conscience spoke: "Najmeh, you must do something. This man has seven children and a wife who trusts you." But still I did not know what to do. If I left him lying there while he died from loss of blood then the villagers might say, "It was her wedding night. She did nothing for this man." If I treated him and he died there were those who would say, "What business has she to touch a gravely injured man? Does she think she is a doctor?"

"Shapoor, go to our home and bring back a door."

"A door?"

"A door and a sheet."

When he returned I ripped the sheet in strips and, with clean scrubbed hands replacing as well as I could the contents of the body that had spilled through the wound, I wrapped the strips round and round the man. We laid him on the door and wrapped another sheet around both man and door. Then, because I knew that infection must have entered his body from the knife blade, the floor, my hands, the unboiled linen, I gave him a massive shot of antibiotics. We put a blanket over the man and the door, lashed the make-do stretcher across the top of the front and back seats of the development jeep, and with Shapoor driving and I, wedged into the side of the back seat, holding the door from slipping, we hurried toward the hospital in Teheran, down the ice-covered road, mile after interminable mile.

There we left him, and Shapoor and I rode back to Sarbandan almost in silence.

"Najmeh," he said as we drove past the area where the feet of those who had celebrated our wedding had tramped down the snow only a few hours before, "I wonder just what it is that I have married!"

I could not answer. I did not know.

Fourteen 🍀 ASFAND

In Sarbandan, spring comes reluctantly, almost fearfully. In Asfand, March, timidly she invades the lower skirts of the mountain. Like a mouse, creeping, creeping, creeping, she climbs upward, melting the snow only where her light feet touch.

Every day Asghar shovels the snow away from the path that leads to my door. When there is not a blizzard or new snow on the ground, Shapoor coaxes the too-cold development jeep into movement so that he can reach his work in Damavand. Most people in Sarbandan who go out at all trust to a single footpath trampled by many feet. I have asked that a way be opened to both the girls' school and the boys' school, and the council has discussed it. There is no equipment for doing this work. I explain that three logs, fastened together in the form of a triangle on which a heavy man could stand, might be pulled, point first, by oxen. Mash-hadi Mokhtar gives me a superior smile and tells me that winter is too nearly over to bother with anything like this. Looking out over the white world it is hard to believe that this is so.

One evening when Shapoor had been at home for two days because he had not been able to get the jeep to the Mazandaran road, a man and woman came floundering through the snow toward my house. The man came first, carrying a child. Behind him

186

came his wife, barefooted, but trying to stay in the tracks he had
tramped with his army-issue boots.

In Iran each man serves a conscripted army service unless his
family can convince the authorities that he is dead. (There are
many men who have "died" who are still walking around in my
country.) From his army service the village man brings home
with him a knowledge of other places, more facility in reading and
writing, since the army has an ever-improving literacy program,
and the strong army-issue clothing which will be in his family and
be used by many for years to come.

As the couple drew near I opened my door and waited their
coming. In the stillness of the white night I could hear the woman
screaming.

At the door I took the child from the father's arms. "She fell in
the fire, she fell in the fire," the mother continued to scream.

I lowered my voice to almost a whisper and automatically she
did the same. "How?"

"She is newly walking. She fell into the dung fire. I do not
know how she pushed aside—"

I unwrapped the child. Her little legs were burned, almost to
the bone, to a point above the knees. "I must take her to Teheran."

"No, Lady Najafi, no! Do something for her here in the home,"
the man begged.

And the mother cried, "She will miss us. She will be lonely.
Do not take her away."

"There is nothing I can do here. See, she is very sick." I turned
to Shapoor. "We must go to Teheran."

The look he gave me seemed to say, "Najmeh, you are exactly
crazy," but he began to put on his heavy clothing.

With the aid of the father, Asghar, the kadkhoda, and a half-
dozen other willing helpers, the men almost carried the jeep to
the Mazandaran road. The engine was started by pouring kettlefuls
of hot water over the car's hood. Every second seemed to me to be
many. Finally we left the mother and father standing beside the
road, his arm tenderly about her, as we pushed off toward Teheran.
I held the dreadfully injured baby against my body. She was in

shock and I felt her cold and damp, pressing against my heart.

At once they let us into the hospital and took the child to emergency. Blood plasma would help to bring her out of shock. They could not tell me what more would be needed. They promised they would do everything that they could for her. Silently Shapoor and I drove back to Sarbandan. Asghar was waiting up for us and had hot tea ready. "The little girl would be better off dead," he said in a matter-of-fact tone.

"Asghar! How can you say such a thing?"

"I am sorry. But I speak the truth." He was silent.

Mash'hadi Mokhtar had said that the winter was nearly over and three days later it looked as if he were right. We wakened one morning to bright sushine. The ice took on a grainy look that meant it was melting. The villagers at once began to move about their houses; and the women, lonely for companionship, hurried back to the classes.

Now I began to see in Sarbandan many whom I had never seen before. The landlords who had been represented in the village by the kadkhodas were in the village to discuss with purchasing agents the sale of the next harvest's crops. Mash'hadi Mokhtar sent his brother, Malek, to take me to the teahouse to meet some of these men. They were interested in the school, in the workroom, in the clinic, in the bath. All of these things had raised the value of their property. I couldn't help but hear some of the bargaining that was going on with the purchasing agents and I was shocked to hear that the big landlords were being offered more for the same produce than the small landlords were.

During the slow winter months Shapoor had been bringing me books from the development offices at Damavand. Many of these were on sanitation, nutrition, subjects that I understood through necessity; but others were on the co-operative movement in which many men do business as one.

"Shapoor," I said one evening, "Sarbandan must have a co-operative."

He smiled in the way a man has with his wife. "Najmeh-jun,

that is too big a thing for even you to attempt."

"Nothing that is necessary is too big," I told him.

Again he smiled.

Sarbandan has the best cherries and apricots in the world, really, and with co-operative selling—I could see the income of the landlords increasing, which would mean more rials in the peasants' share; I could see Sarbandan purchasing improved seeds, insecticides, farm machinery; I even saw a co-operative store with tea, sugar, cotton goods at a much more reasonable price. And finally I saw the co-operative buying the carpet looms we needed, and Zahra instructing many villagers in carpet-making, instead of just five at a time. Later Roodehen and Khosravan and all the other neighboring villages could join this co-operative. Oh, how rapidly and how big I dreamed!

I felt Shapoor's eyes on me and looked up.

"There are problems, Najmeh-jun," he said.

Of course there were problems. I didn't need anyone to point that out. All I knew about co-operatives was what I had read in the books, and I realized from my other work in Sarbandan that theory and practice are often many miles apart. We would need experts of many kinds to organize such a movement.

What was more important, the co-operative would go against the natural feelings of the people. Iranians are what Americans call "rugged individualists." Many are like the village woman, Eshrat, whose deep selfishness and inability to trust others had been one of the most troublesome thorns in my whole work in Sarbandan. Yet, had not Mash'hadi Mokhtar given land for the clinic and kerosene to heat the girls' school? Had not even the most ignorant villagers come to my house and put their names upon a petition for a woman teacher? Hadn't the council, with no aid from me, kept their old bath until a new one should be completed? Perhaps with more intelligence this feeling would not persist.

In my country it is difficult for people to trust one another. When I had first come to the village I had been asked a hundred questions: Are you from America? Are you a Communist? Are you from the Ministry of Education? Only after a year in the village did I have the feeling that the people really had confidence in me. Farkhondeh and Effat were having the same problems in the villages where they were working. Even in Teheran men spend so much time protecting the property they have that they have time for nothing else.

I had tried to teach my girls, even as my neighbor, Masoomeh, took sugar from under their eyes, that the door must never be closed to her. I felt that someday I would be able to leave my home standing open all day and night. I knew that the farmers who became members in a co-operative might spend a great deal of time wondering what those who organized the venture were getting out of it, where their profits were going. Only a perfect system of bookkeeping, and an intelligence in each member that would enable him to understand the books, would take care of this problem.

I talked with Shapoor about co-operatives. In Damavand I talked with experts. Finally when the council met I talked with the council and found most of the men as enthusiastic as I was. They voted unanimously to investigate the matter further. I invited an expert, Mr. Malak Mansoor, to come and talk to the council. He pointed out to us that such a co-operative could not go into effect until after harvest. The year, as far as co-operatives is concerned, is from harvest time to harvest time—a "crop year." This would give us time to talk with the councils of near-by villages; time to send one of our own young men to the training school for co-operative leaders which the Near East Foundation was conducting.

We began a search for the best young man to send. He must be intelligent, capable, and have the confidence of the people. "Why not the young kadkhoda?" someone suggested. The kadkhoda from whom I rented my house was called "Old Kadkhoda"; the one who lived in the mountains and seldom came into the village, even to attend council meetings, was called "Young Kadkhoda" or sometimes, because he was short, "Little Kadkhoda." He was intelligent, used to making decisions, already had

many who trusted him. The council asked me to visit him and
see if he would be willing to give up his position as kadkhoda
and go to this special training school.

But before I could carry out this errand, before I could get
back to Teheran to see how the little burned baby was doing in
the hospital there, it was again winter. One morning we wakened
to snow coming in thick flurries and between the flurries the sky
was black and forbidding. Shapoor left with the jeep between
flurries. By midmorning a wind rose that swept the drifts against
the rock fences which had stood bare above the snow, and covered
them in rolling mounds.

"We are prisoners of the snow," Pooran told me as she sat
by the kerosene heater working at thread lace.

"It is too dark for that work, Pooran. You'll ruin your eyes,"
I said automatically, but we were prisoners. I was sure that Shapoor
couldn't get back from Damavand. Effat was in Roodehen, Farkhondeh in Khosravan. In Sarbandan there were only Pooran,
Asghar and I; and in the workroom Zahra and her two little ones.
The snow swirled about our stout house. In all the village there
was silence. Asghar, touching the wall at every step so as not to
become lost, fed the chickens and found that they were huddled
together, but not frozen. Our little dog who lived under one
corner of the storeroom now came into the house to lie beside the
kerosene heater.

At last the wind died down and there was the darkness of
night in the house. The snow was banked against the windows and
the door was locked securely on the outside by the hand of the
storm.

No one came to the classes. No one came to the clinic. We
were in a world of our own. Pooran read from our books and I
began to teach her Arabic so that she could read the Koran. I did
not worry about Shapoor, though I knew he would worry about me.

The third day of our imprisonment Pooran and I began to
talk about New Year's. I told her how New Year's was always
celebrated in the home of my mother, with food for everyone, and
with gifts for every person in the household and even for strangers

who happened by. I told her of going as a very little girl to a village with a gift of barbecued lamb for the hungry, and how I had dreamed, even then, of giving my life to helping the poor. And now, this year, I had many who trusted me and I was snow-bound—unable to get the gifts I had planned.

Early in the month the council had talked about a New Year's celebration for Sarbandan with a gift of clothing for the most needy children. I had at first thought that I would take the money for this gift from my own dwindling account, but Shapoor had convinced me—my common sense would have anyway—that using my money for something perishable would be of less value in the long run than keeping it for my work. The council, without a suggestion from me, voted to buy clothing from the development fund. I studied the law and found that the resolution was in keeping with it. Then I wrote a letter to Mr. Nazemi, the Governor, asking for fifteen hundred rials.

Now I sat in my snow-chained home wondering what had happened to that request.

One morning we wakened to a dazzling world. The sun was so bright that it shot arrows back at our eyes. The snow melted as we watched it, and where there had been a long stretch of white we now could see rock walls, houses, the jube, and soon even the roads and familiar paths. By evening Shapoor came chugging up a clearing road from Damavand. Later Farkhondeh and the donkey also came in.

Now spring was really here—unless there was another snow-fall, another blizzard.

Shapoor brought me a letter from Mr. Nazemi. He was sympathetic; he favored the use of money in this way; he was unable, because of formalities, to do anything before New Year's, which, by then, was only a week away.

The next day I dressed in my city clothes and when Shapoor left I went with him. As we drove through Sarbandan we saw tremendous activity. Every doorway was open. At New Year's every house is cleaned. Red earth is brought from the mountains and a new coat of clean mud is smoothed onto the floor and walls of the houses. All the dishes are washed and dried in the sun. If there is a curtain it is brought out for the celebration and then put away for another year. The richer people—or should I say less poor—who have a change of bedding use it just for this period. The women bake, too, cookies and other sweets. They go to the village store, for everything that will be needed for a year is bought at this season; shoes, chadors, sugar cones, raisins, tea.

The activity in the village made my trip into the city seem even more urgent. I had the definite feeling that time was moving faster than I.

In Damavand I got one hundred and fifty suits of clothes from the credit granted by His Imperial Majesty the Shah. These would not be nearly enough, of course, for the needy in Sarbandan and the other villages in my area, so I determined that only orphans would receive these gifts.

Because I was worried about the baby who had been so badly burned, I went into Teheran to visit her in the hospital. When I asked for her the nurse in charge said, "She is ready for release, Lady Najafi," and I thought, *What a New Year's gift this will be to her parents!*

Together the nurse and I went to the child's bedside. Without a word the nurse turned back the covers. Both the baby's legs had been amputated just below the hips. I tried to keep the shock from my face as I played with her. To my soft cooing noises she responded with laughter and jabbering. She reached toward me with soft, satiny arms. I held her for a minute and nuzzled my head in her warm little neck while she shrieked with laughter. Then I put her back into her bed. I could not take her home, though she was ready for release. First I must tell her parents about this dreadful thing. I will not say anything until after New Year's, I told myself, and as soon as I reached home, Pooran, Farkhondeh and I got busy preparing the clothes for gifts.

"There are almost enough clothes for all the children in the school," Pooran said joyfully.

I shook my head. "These clothes are not for Sarbandan only," I told her. And so we allotted a part of the clothes to each of the villages.

Although the snow was gone from Sarbandan it was still deep and firmly packed in the mountains. Asghar, on a donkey, started for Sorkhdeh, a tiny village caught high between two mountains. A line of children, some with their parents, formed at my door to ask for gifts. I longed to give to all; I could give only to a few. I sent for the kadkhoda and when he came I told him that it was his responsibility to pass upon the need of each of the children. These gifts, I said again, were for orphans.

In a short time Asghar came back. "The donkey is not big enough," he said. "Only her head shows above the snow. She cannot pick up her feet to put them down in a different place."

Finally Shapoor, Asghar and I, mounted on large work mules, reached Sorkhdeh at about noon. We distributed the gifts, drank tea, warmed ourselves and started back. Now it was really cold. Ferociously cold. I covered my face with my shawl, only my eyes showed, but even then I could feel the cold reaching numbing fingers through my clothing into my body. The sky was black while it was still afternoon, and only the sure-footed plodding of the mules kept us on the unseen path. Farkhondeh had lighted a lantern for us and we journeyed toward the light.

The clinic room and workroom were both filled with villagers, crying aloud in the peculiar way that mourners do. "We feared that you would never return, my lady," one woman cried as she dropped to her knees and put my icy hand against her warm, wet face.

"God brought us," I told her. And when the woman got to her feet the face, half hidden by the chador, was—Eshrat's!

During the next two days Asghar and I, leading burdened donkeys, visited the neighboring villages. When we arrived at a village center Asghar lifted his megaphone. "New Year's gifts for the orphans!" he called, and people came from everywhere, crowding around the donkeys. For this one day every child wanted to be an orphan. There were many poor, of course, but in a Persian village to be an orphan or the child of a widow is to be poor indeed! To these destitute children we gave the clothing. How I wished that there were gifts for all!

While Asghar and I were away, Pooran and Farkhondeh had been busy over the fire making cookies for everyone. The children, even the older boys and girls in Persia, go out at New Year's as American children do at Halloween, asking from door to door for gifts. We would not turn any of these away.

On the last Wednesday of the year a big outdoor fire is built. It is an ancient custom to burn the old willow roofs at this time and to weave new roofs for the houses. Perhaps this is a tradition from the time of Zoroaster, who taught that fire is the symbol of all good.

There were two things that kept my heart from floating free of my body in happiness at this season. The first was that the gifts had been so limited and the needs of the villagers so great. The second was something truly personal. I must go to the home of the burned little girl and talk with her parents. I dreaded telling such bad news, and yet the child should be at home.

The day after New Year's I decided I would delay no longer.

The father vaulted a rock wall when he saw me coming. He held aside the rug from the doorway for me to go in.

"How is she?" the mother asked eagerly.

"It has been so long," the father said. "But we knew that you would come to us."

"She is well. . . . She is happy. . . . I think that the nurses have taught her to say a few words. . . . She reached toward me and I held her in my arms. . . ."

All of these short phrases were dropped into a pit of silence. The eagerness on their faces was washed away by the intangible feeling that emanated from me and darkened the room.

I sat down between them, near the korsee. "She is well, but—she is without legs," I said in a low voice.

The father's voice was equally low. "Then to us she is dead. We do not want her."

"You must want her. In all other ways she—"

Again the father's voice. "What good is a girl who has no legs?

She can never work. She can never marry."

I turned to the mother, her face pale in the darkness of the room. "My husband speaks for both of us. We do not want her." Impulsively she drew toward her a little boy who had been hiding behind her skirts and covered his astonished face with kisses.

"But she is yours. She wants you!" I insisted.

"My lady, you should have let her die. We would then have had a grave for our mourning." The father dropped his face between his hands.

"She is young," the mother said. "She will forget."

"But you will never forget."

The father's voice broke. "You are right, my lady. We never will forget. But we cannot bring her home. It is hard enough to feed those who can someday repay us."

That night I could not sleep. I thought of the old days—the very old days before the time of Mohammad, the prophet—when the people had practiced infanticide. I thought of how Mohammad had not only condemned this practice but had given girls some value by making legal the marriage of a man to four wives. And I thought how much like this desperate couple those parents of old times must have been as they put their living baby girls in the grave. Love fought then, too, with necessity, and necessity was the stronger warrior.

I sent word to the hospital that the child would have to be placed in an orphanage. I did not trust myself to see her for I knew if I did I would bring her home myself. One of my friends took the child from the hospital. Sometime, she says, when the child is old enough, she will have artificial limbs made for her in Germany. Since there are portions of both legs left below the hips she will someday walk.

But her father and mother will never see this walking.

Fifteen **AGAIN FARVARDIN**

How the heart leaps when the earth is freed from its prison of ice. From the melting mountain snow a hundred streams are born and dash headlong into the jube, watering as they go thousands of varicolored flowers that spread like a rainbow carpet over all the land. Only where the slopes are in perpetual shadow do the snow banks, now gray and porous, still cover the awakening earth. The sky, always blue, is bright and clean in the day and sharply dark at night. The stars and moon are close enough to touch with a long pole, and the sun rides slowly from the east to the west.

From the cities many people come to see the mountain flowers. My home is crowded, and my table is always spread for guests. I am intoxicated with the delight of being alive. My head spins with the thought of many tasks that I can do now that the winter is ended. In Sarbandan there is a new glow in the faces of the women. Their men are home from Mazandaran!

In each home the mother has been making a strange cake. This is not an ordinary cake for eating. It is uncooked and in it are many whole grains of wheat. The cake is kept moist and the wheat sprouts and soon the cake becomes a beautiful green thing. In many homes there is a layer of the cake for each member of the family and the children watch this sprouting of wheat on their own layer. On the thirteenth day of the New Year the family takes the cake

197

out into the fields and throws it away. With it go all the bad feelings, all the fussing and fighting and quarreling.

Everybody is in the fields on this day; it is bad luck to stay in the home, so the village is empty. The girls swing in rope swings hung from the old cherry trees. They play singing games—"Uncle, Who Keeps the Bread?"—hop tag, and a dozen others. The boys, from five to fifty, play the rowdy game of alak-do-lak.

Alak-do-lak is played with sticks about four feet in length, used somewhat like a bat. A short stick, perhaps six inches long, is placed across two bricks which are placed about five inches apart. The short stick is tossed up with the end of the long stick and batted into the field. If it is caught by the team in the field, the team to which the player belongs is out. If it is not caught, but picked up, it must be thrown toward the bricks where the player has laid his long stick. If the short stick strikes the long one the player is "dead" and the next teammate plays. If the next player is neither out nor dead, the "dead" player comes alive again. Thus this game can go on forever. It is a wonderful game and I wonder why it is not played in America. Ambitious boys sometimes send the stick with such force that it causes injury to the boys in the fields. But it is truly a boy's game. Girls never, never play.

Then, abruptly, the short, happy day is over. Now begins the month for fasting and for prayer—Ramazan. There are no longer guests coming and making picnics on the flowering hillside. The swing ropes and the sticks for alak-do-lak are put away. It is time for spiritual things. Time to read the Koran in the classes and to discover the meaning which is buried in the Arabic words or stated briefly in commonplace Farsi between the Arabic lines. Often I wish for a literary translation of these words into our own language so that the women in my classes who have done so well with reading might enjoy the beautiful scriptures for themselves. I know of one man who has spent his adult life in making such a translation. In it he has preserved the meaning, the rhythm, the poetic quality of the original Arabic. But this translation will not be published— at least not now. The learned men of the Faith, the mullahs, will for many years to come, I think, be the interpreters of the Koran to the people.

But as we read the Koran in Arabic we explain in Farsi the meaning of each phrase. Mohammad's teachings were direct and simple; succeeding generations have added many of the elaborate conventions that are now a part of Islam. The women with their sweet, glowing faces watch us as we read and talk. We tell them that Mohammad had four daughters whom he loved deeply, and to him women were important. Our listeners realize that their own improving position in their little world would please the Prophet. It is what he would have hoped for.

This year my nephew Ali comes again to my home to sing the special prayers and the call to prayer. Next year he will be away attending university somewhere in Europe, so he spends the day teaching these bits of ritual to others so that in Sarbandan each year Ramazan may be correctly celebrated. Again, too, my mother comes with delicacies from Teheran and together we prepare the tray of sweetmeats and fruit for the closing day of the fast.

For the first time in my life I am eager for the month to end. I enjoy the serenity and tranquillity, but there is so much to do!

Visitors in Sarbandan, Ali, my mother, others, are constantly saying, "You have done so much!" I look about me. It seems that I must say, "Yet we have not begun!" Instead I laugh. "It appears that a new village should be built upon the ruins of this one. Anything that we start here uncovers another defect that needs a remedy!"

The first day after the month of Ramazan had ended, everyone in the village who could walk, ride or be carried came to the land which Mash'hadi Mokhtar had presented to Sarbandan for a clinic. There in the autumn we had built a small one-room structure which would eventually serve as a storeroom; this was necessary since we could get a loan only upon "improved" land. All winter the snow had covered the ground and the lonely little building with an impenetrable blanket. Now was the day for turning the first shovelful of earth. The real building was actually to begin.

For months, whenever transportation would permit it, I had been visiting the health and financial authorities in Damavand. Only now had the necessary credit been established and the funds made available.

We held a ceremony, with the members of the council each taking an important part. Mash'hadi Mokhtar had a new suit from Teheran and a new pair of glasses, not ground for vision, which gave his shrewd face the look of a scholar. The clinic was to contain four examination rooms, a large reception hall, a kitchen, a washroom, and the already constructed storeroom for supplies. It, like the other buildings in the village, would be of sun-dried brick, whitewashed inside and out with gypsum plaster. It would be beautiful and clean and prophetic, really, of the awakening of Sarbandan. And by the time that it was completed there would be two more clinics finished in the area.

There was no ceremony the next day, but still there was a crowd watching those who were working. This was not a silent crowd; every person in it had an opinion as to how the work should be done and everyone wanted the head mason to listen to him. Men who had never put up a wall in their lives knew exactly how such a wall should be built. Men who had never had a saw in their hands knew all about carpentry. But this is so everywhere, I am told. Only in Sarbandan the head mason did not know this. To every volunteer superintendent and supervisor of work he gave his ear. After a few days of all talk and no work I grew disgusted. No one but the workers could be on the site unless they were bringing food or tea.

Now life picked up for the masons. They were regaled with numerous glasses of tea, with fresh bread, with confectionery. Work seemed to me, who had waited all winter for the coming of the working season, to progress very slowly. One afternoon I stopped to talk to the head mason. He indicated the fringe of food bearers with a careless hand. "My men work very well," he told me. "With eyes upon them they are actors carrying a role and they must not disappoint the audience. We will complete the building by the end of Khordad as promised."

"I do hope so," I said, rather shortly.

He smiled again, disarmingly. "Already the people feel that this is their clinic."

"It is," I agreed. "Of course they are interested."

One afternoon Mash'hadi Mokhtar stopped me as I passed his teahouse. "It is accomplished, Lady Najafi," he said, with a wide, glittering smile under his carefully turned mustache.

I looked at him inquiringly.

"The transportation," he said grandly. "The daily transportation. Each day there will be a bus. You will see."

"Impossible!"

"No. It is possible, my lady. With Mashdi Mokhtar anything is possible." Again that wide and gold-punctuated smile.

"But how?" I asked.

"I have made the arrangements. That is enough."

As I went on up to my home I found myself singing—not words but a pleasant tune. Sarbandan had its businessmen. They might see advantage to themselves in providing service for others, but at least they recognized the need of such services. In this way do the blessings of capitalism come.

And Mash'hadi Mokhtar had not spoken idle words. Evidently he had made a business investment and was probably collecting a part of every fare for himself, but the bus did come once a day. On it came visitors from Teheran to enjoy spring in the village. On it I began almost twice-weekly trips to Teheran to pursue the projects that were nearest to my heart.

Ever since my first interview with Her Imperial Highness Princess Ashraf Pahlavi, I had been working on my plans for a small boarding school for the training of teachers in the villages. This, I planned, would be different from any other training school in the world. It would leave the girls really village girls, really Moslems, but it would give them the skills and develop in them the compassion necessary for working with others. The Princess had asked me to draw up a complete program and this I had done. Taking the girls into my home, loving them, teaching them, helping them to recognize their responsibilities had given me the practical illustrations of what would and would not work in such a school. Now my plan was finished and I was ready again to see Princess Ashraf.

In my report I had included the cost of such a training school and the salary of supervisors and teachers. The second part of the program was the course of study and in-service training.

My first success was the approval of the transfer of land for the building of the school by both her Imperial Highness and the Board of Directors. But on the amount needed for maintenance and salary there was great division of opinion. Of course, this figure was much less than that needed by such an organization as the Near East Foundation for similar work, because we would not employ any Americans. Still the sum was large and I could understand the reluctance of the board to approve the whole plan.

I was invited to meet in private with the Minister of Education and discuss my work with him. I told him of the three girls with whom I had succeeded, and of my failure with a city girl who could not stand the simple life of the village. He asked to see the program and we talked about it point by point. Next I met with a representative from both the Ministry of Education and the Imperial Organization of Social Services. It was decided that the Organization would pay for the building and land and the Ministry of Education would bear the cost of salaries and maintenance.

After this decision I went back to Sarbandan with a heart light as a summer cloud. But abruptly I was called back to Teheran. There was another problem. Since the two agencies were jointly putting the program into effect, who should have control of it? For this I had no answer. No one could have an answer without making a deep study of the whole problem. "It is not important to make a decision now," I was told. "The Minister of Education is to be replaced. Any agreement now could be voided by the new minister."

I climbed onto the bus which Mash'hadi Mokhtar had put in operation at such an auspicious time for me. I did not hear the people around me. It did not make any difference to me that my seatmate smelled of sheep's wool. All I could think of was the unfortunate fact that in my country the removal of a minister is usually followed by the dismissal of everyone who has worked with him and the junking of any plans or projects that he had in mind. All of my work toward the training school had come to naught. A year of work and planning gone, all gone.

Shapoor was in Damavand that night, in the middle of a four-day project. Shortly after supper, which Pooran prepared for me, there was a knock at my door and a group of women filed in. These were not women like my very first callers. They were the more progressive, more intelligent women of the village; not the wives of small landlords, nor the poorest villagers, but rather a middle section of Sarbandan society.

Perhaps they did not read the discouragement, despair, that were written on my face and that Pooran had already felt. At once one of them said, "Lady Najafi, the men in this village have a council. The women should have a council, too. There is much to be done that women can do that would never enter the minds of men."

"That is a fine idea," I told them. Already I felt some of the weight of disappointment dropping from my shoulders. "What should women do?"

I looked around the circle and saw the women's eyes on me. They thought I had the answer for my own question, but I waited. Finally one, Fatemeh, spoke. "When you first came to Sarbandan you saved the life of my baby. Do you remember?"

"I remember."

"It is soon planting time. Many women will be working in the fields. With them they will carry their babies, the tiny heads baking in the sun."

"Yes?"

"Why don't we women organize a nursery? One of us could care for several babies. Perhaps someone who cannot work in the fields is specially gifted to care for little ones."

"Farkhondeh could help," I offered.

And so the women's council was organized and already a project was under consideration. And only the month before I had been fearing the introduction of co-operatives because the people could not work together!

During the month of Ramazan everybody had spent many hours sitting in the mosque. The women's first activity was the direct result of this sitting.

Early one morning there came a hallooing at my door. "Lady Najafi, come out!"

I was already dressed and studying my schedule for the day. I went out, putting on my sleeveless sheepskin jacket as I went. For a moment I closed my eyes and then opened them again, expecting to see an apparition disappear. There was the women's council. Each had over her shoulder a shovel or spade.

"What is all this about?" I asked, wanting to laugh, but warned by the serious expression of their faces.

"We go today to build a latrine at the mosque," one said.

"For the men," another added.

"We are tired of seeing them go around the corner from the

men's door only to stand before ours," a third one explained.

I, too, had seen the men leave the mosque for a private errand that they did not complete privately.

I clapped my hands. "A good idea. If you can dig the pit and build the walls, I myself will bring the sanitary latrine slab from the sanitation school at Palasht."

I went with them to the mosque and watched while they measured the size for the pit. As some threw up the soil others mixed it with straw and water and shaped it into bricks to dry in the sun. There was still deep concern with the project but a spirit of frivolity struck the women. They chatted, they laughed, they sang. They had brought food and tea and as they tired they stopped to drink and to eat. They had a wonderful time. And the pit grew and the rows of brick, standing on end to dry, lengthened. The day was one long picnic.

The next day I went to Palasht for the sanitary slab. Palasht is in the Varamin area south of Teheran. I looked longingly at the development jeep and Shapoor, but there were rules concerning that jeep. I could use it one day out of every fifteen, but only one. Even if Shapoor and I were going to the same place at the same time, he was supposed to take the jeep empty while I found other transportation. Of course things did not work out in that way. If I were going to Damavand I rode, getting out before I reached the town. Along the way we picked up everyone we saw walking. Why not? The road was so rough that an empty jeep bounced like a ball over the ruts. With six or ten people in the back it traveled quite smoothly. Sometimes if we did not see walkers going in our direction we put great rocks in the back to make the ride smoother.

I took the bus to Teheran, and went on to Palasht by another bus. The trip was tiring but the slab was important.

These sanitary slabs are hard to describe without a diagram. To begin with you must know that the ordinary latrine in a village is nothing more than an open pit. One puts a foot on each side of the pit. That is all. Because the opening is large there is always a cloud of flies buzzing upward, there is an odor, a feeling of being close to filth. The sanitary latrines are cement slabs which cover these pits except for a small area. Over this open area is a cement bowl open at the bottom. There is no cleansing stream of water as in the American water closet, but it is easily kept clean with water from the aftabeh and since little light reaches the pit the number of flies is tremendously reduced. On each side of the opening there is a raised footrest. The entire slab could be bought at cost from the Near East Foundation. When I finally got my slab back to Sarbandan the total expense was about fourteen tomans (about three dollars in American money).

The women worked faithfully at the latrine. They even installed the sanitary slab and built a roof, something that many thought was unnecessary.

What a simple thing is the building of a latrine! What a great advance in thinking about sanitation, about culture, and what an advance in co-operation was evidenced by this building!

Each day I visited the slow-rising clinic. Each day I carried on my regular work. I tried to put out of my mind my disappointment regarding the plans for a training school. This I could not do. The only way that I could cease worrying about this project was to introduce a new one that would challenge me and keep my mind at work. It was natural that I should think of a village center.

My home was at present the center of the village—the little home rented from the kadkhoda and made larger by the addition of a schoolroom, a sleeping room, a small storeroom and a hen house. In this little room I treated all my patients and entertained the doctors when they came to Sarbandan. Council meetings were held here, of both men and women. All adult classes in literacy and handicraft met in the workroom. In addition, now that it was again warm and there was bus service, we had constant visitors, some for a day only, some for several days. Whenever there was a complaint the accusers and defendants came to my home. Besides, there were the twice-monthly meetings when Effat, Farkhondeh, Pooran and I met to discuss problems of village work.

The walls were fairly pushed out to hold all of this activity, and

I was never alone. Shapoor complained and I could see that he had reason.

One night at council meeting I said, "I feel that we have long outgrown this little house as a village center. We must have more room."

There were half a dozen protests. "But soon, Lady Najafi, we will have our clinic."

Soon? I thought, but I did not reply to this remark. "I myself will buy the land for this center and in it I will build my own home."

Immediately there were smiles. The magic words, "I will buy," had made this great change. "We will find what land is available," they promised me.

Much land was available, I soon discovered. And at three times the usual selling price. The people did not seem to understand that my residence in Sarbandan had brought about an improvement in conditions. They did not seem to connect my work there with the sale of their land at all. Here was somebody richer than they, and who were they to bow to a bad bargain?

"If you sell," I asked one of the farmers who was offering me a parcel of land at an unreasonable figure, "what will you do with the money?"

"Why, go to the city, of course," he answered. "Life in the village is very hard for me and my family!"

This I most certainly did not wish to encourage. "I'll tell you," I said to him and to others who offered land at such prices, "I will put this matter into the hands of the council and let them decide what price is just."

I was eager to have work on the new center begin, but when I told the council that they were to find a good bargain for me I acted as if I had all summer to choose this ground. In this way is business transacted in Persia.

So often had I gone to the mountains for strength that I would have loved to build a home high above the village. This I could not do since I planned to make it a village center. It should be near the schools, near the bath, near the mosque, next door to the people it was designed to serve. So I instructed the council to study land that was located centrally but still undeveloped, so that I might have room not just for the building, but for gardens and orchards and animal sheds.

Their slow, cautious inquiries set me to itching with impatience so I turned to other projects.

There was the post box. Ever since I had come to Sarbandan I had been impatient with the mail service. Friends who were coming from America or Europe to visit Iran wrote to tell me that they would be in Teheran. The date had long since passed by the time the letter would reach me. I had taken to having my sister hold my mail for me, but of course this was slow delivery, too. Now through the efforts of Dr. Birjandi, Sarbandan got a post box! Anyone with mail to leave the village could take it to Mash'hadi Mokhtar's tea-house, where the post office was located. At this place the government left the mail. It was only right that Mash'hadi Mokhtar be given this responsibility. Had he not got bus service for the town through his own initiative?

Then there was the matter of moving forward with a co-opera-tive. We were still thinking, talking, arguing in the council, and Shapoor and I were still thinking, talking and debating at home. Mr. Malek Mansoor visited us in Sarbandan again. We talked to landlords and small landowners. There were advantages in co-operatives that everybody could see. But deep in the eyes of these men one could read distrust, even fear. The whole venture depended upon finding someone to head the co-operative whom these men knew, in whom they had confidence. Again we spoke of the young kadkhoda and one morning I started on foot to his hillside resi-dence.

I found him examining his sheep as he freed them from their enclosure. His hands were gentle. I liked that. In fact, I liked this short, slight young man with the intelligent eyes and the quiet speech. He invited me into his cottage, but instead we stood leaning against the rock wall of the sheep's enclosure. I told him all that I knew about the co-operative movement. I told him that the council had thought of him as the one person in Sarbandan who could take the training and head the co-operative. His eyes turned wary as he listened, but he consented to come down and meet with the council and discuss the matter. What worried him most was that he might resign from his position as kadkhoda and then the plan for the co-operative might die. He asked rather plaintively, "What can a man do in Sarbandan after he has been a kadkhoda?"

"You can be a co-operative director," I told him. "That is better than being a kadkhoda."

Another project that the winter had halted was the building of the new bath. Often my walks took me past the site of the new bathhouse. Work had begun again with the frost leaving the earth. And I thought: How slowly things are accomplished! The pit is being dug for the cesspool; but it is as if it were being cleared with a tablespoon. There is more credit needed. More capital. The council must stop its discussions of co-operatives and land prices long enough to do something active about this bath. Surely another marriage season will be upon us before the bath is completed.

One morning as I walked up a winding path that ended high above the village, one of the kadkhoda's little boys came running and seized my skirt. "Come, my lady," he said. "My grandmother needs you."

Madar-i-Kadkhoda! I had stayed away from this wise old woman as much as I could. There was need for her in the village and the neighboring villages because there were many illnesses for which she had the remedy. She was a skillful midwife. I admired her while I feared her. And I feared her because, like other people with a little knowledge, she felt it was sufficient to take care of any eventuality. Patients could die of blood-poisoning while she poulticed an open wound with the web of a spider. She had not yet learned that my "medicine" was stronger for strong illnesses. But now she was sending for me.

I hurried to the home of the kadkhoda, expecting to see the old woman. Instead a mountain man stood before the open doorway.

"Madar-i-Kadkhoda wants you to come at once. With me."

I ran next door to tell Pooran that I was going to the mountains and picked up my bag of simple drugs, hypodermic supplies, bandages and such things.

It took me only a few minutes, but when I was ready Asghar stood in the front of my house holding a donkey for me. I mounted, and with the mountain man leading the way on foot we started up the mountainside.

I tried to find out from the gloomy-faced young man just what was the matter. Finally he said, "My baby will not be born. First it will kill its mother and then it will die."

"I do not think things are that bad," I said, trying to sound cheerful.

"Madar-i-Kadkhoda knows all. That is what she says."

"Then why does she send for me?"

"If she does not, there will be those who say that if you had been there things would have been different." Abruptly he stopped and turned to me, and the donkey, plodding with his head down, almost walked over him. "Tell me that you can save my wife. Tell me that, my lady."

There was such misery in the deep-set dark eyes, in the boyish face now drawn and gray with fatigue and worry, that I felt my body trembling. "I am not a doctor," I said.

We got to the end of the path, then to the end of the area where I could ride the donkey. I dismounted and followed up the mountainside, breathing hard and feeling a wearing pain at my side. Behind me, carrying my supplies, came the donkey, putting his feet down daintily on the precarious shale.

Finally we reached the home, a cave dug out of the side of the hill. It had but one wall, the front one, and that was made of sun-dried brick and had an open hole for a door. The man stood aside for me to enter. There on a bed of clean rags lay a girl of fifteen or sixteen. Her face was so contorted by pain that she scarcely looked human. Her knees were drawn up and Madar-i-Kadkhoda had put a chador over them like a tent.

The old woman looked up as I entered. "The child gave a hand,"

she said. "I touched it with snow and it withdrew it." I nodded.
The old woman knew so much more about these things than I did.
"But now he wants to give a shoulder, I think. He will surely
break his neck but first he will kill his mother."

I did not know what to do. Desperately I wished that there were
a doctor in Sarbandan. Yet even if there were, we could not take
this girl to Sarbandan.

"God, tell me what to do. Give me wisdom. Give me knowledge
now hidden to me!"

Suddenly I felt a warmth come over me, a feeling of comfort. I
got out my hypodermic kit and gave the girl a shot that would ease
the pain, bring relaxation. We watched as the pain faded from
her face, her eyes closed. While she slept I prayed. Perhaps there
is not room for prayer in the textbook theories of social service,
but prayer was the only path to wisdom that was open to me.

We spoke not a word in the room. I was praying. The girl was
sleeping. I do not know what Madar-i-Kadkhoda was thinking.
The young husband sat outside the door, tears dropping onto his
folded hands.

The girl's eyelids lifted. She bore down. Madar-i-Kadkhoda
lifted the chador. The top of a black-haired little head presented. In
a few minutes there was the lusty cry of the newborn boy. The
young father cried and cried, with relief perhaps. Madar-i-Kadkhoda cared for the baby. I gave the mother the usual large shot
of antibiotics and one of vitamin B. She slept and I waited beside
her.

What did it matter that the council would that very night report
on land and prices for the new center, talk about obtaining more
money for the bath construction, again discuss the co-operatives?

God, and only God, had brought the young girl through this
black, near-closing gate. I stayed beside her until I was certain that
she would live to rear this child that had been so miraculously
saved for her.

Sixteen 🝔 AGAIN ORDIBEHESHT

"It is spring, it is spring, it is spring!" my heart sings as Shapoor and I stand, arms linked, at the intersection of the Mazandaran road and the narrower road that runs up into the village of Sarbandan. At the side of the road the development jeep waits while Shapoor and I enjoy together the dream of living in a home of our own. Here in a smooth rolling green field, close to the village but not of it, we have purchased the land for our home. Construction has not begun but I have marked the shape and size of the rooms on the earth to make sure that from each window of my home I will be able to see the things that bring me inspiration and comfort. I smile when I think that I am "building for the view," a phrase I heard often in Southern California. With the eyes of hope I look out over the field and see the dream building there. Of course, our home will also be the village center—as you say in America, "Grand Central Station," with everybody coming with his problems, the council meeting there, the work of the clinic being carried on until the new clinic is completed and a doctor assigned to it by the government—but it will be ours.

I squeeze Shapoor's arm a little tighter against me. He has been patient living in the crowded room in the house rented from the kadkhoda. There is talk of using this home for an advanced school for boys, perhaps grades nine and ten. This will not be for a time, of course, until some of the boys now in the upper grades at the elementary school are ready for high school, but still I am in a hurry to have my new home built and move into it. Whenever there is a problem between Shapoor and me and his temper flares I have thought: When we have a home of our own, things will be different.

I take my kerchief off and shake my shoulder-length hair loose so that the breeze can blow through it. Shapoor ruffles it with a loving, playful hand. I know that he has been thinking, too . . . *things will be different*. For a moment I expect him to put this thing we are both thinking into words. Instead he gives a lock of hair at my neck a playful tweak, climbs into the jeep, and is off with a wave of the hand.

I watch him out of sight, then I turn and look toward the mountain. "Spring, spring, spring!" I sing to my own tune. No one can know the joy of this word who has not been imprisoned by a long, hopeless, white winter. I can see the women, sometimes the children, filling their household water jars at the jube. Carrying the water for domestic animals, for a family, can be a back-breaking chore, but from where I stand the motion looks like liquid poetry moving slowly over a screen of beauty. I take my eyes from the jube and rest them on the fragile white and pink of the apricot and cherry orchards, on the green and yellow of the flowering fields. Very soon, when the frost is gone from the deep soil, these fields will be broken for planting. Now, between the rock fences, stretch God's carpets.

Spring is mine, Sarbandan is mine. And the people—"God," I pray, lifting my eyes for a moment to the sapphire sky, "help me to remember that these people are yours, not mine. Help me to remember that they belong to themselves."

All at once I am stirred with impatience. There is so much that needs to be done. The slow pace of village life suddenly agitates me. I want to push, to drive, to force, but I know that this is not the way to work with these people. Time, to them, means very little. To me it must not mean so much.

And somehow, my frustration robs the day of its beauty. The

orchards now are nothing but trees in blossom. The fields are covered with flowering weeds that must be conquered before food can be grown. The mud houses that cluster around the jube are not homes, they are huts. A moment before I had been ecstatically happy; now I am miserable.

I sit down, not in the usual Persian manner, with my feet folded under me, but in Western fashion with my knees under my chin, my arms locked around my legs; and with my eyes on the deep vast reaches of the sky I wait for peace to return to me.

As I waited the sound of weeping entered my consciousness, like background music in a play. Still I sat. The crying became louder and knocked at my mind. It was incessant, almost extravagant in pitch and power. This weeping is the villagers' reaction to a death.

I jumped up and started to walk rapidly toward my home. Asghar, with a jug of water, was on his way to the chicken house.

"What is this weeping?" I asked him.

"Someone has died."

"I know that; but who?"

"I do not know, my lady. I haven't been upstream to where his body is being prepared for burial."

I did not pay attention to his words. It was later that I remembered him telling me this. "I wish that I had known before the jeep left for Damavand. Perhaps—" I turned again to Asghar. "How will they take the body to Teheran for the necessary washing?"

"They will prepare it here. They will wash it in the jube."

I started toward the mountain, walking along the spring-carpeted bank of the jube. Others were going in the same direction and soon I came upon a cluster of people crying and wringing their hands.

"Who is dead?" I asked a woman next me.

"The old father of Jamshid."

I knew this man. "The one who first knitted," I said.

"Yes. That one. He was not ill. He died without waking last night."

I could see him, the old father, with his back against the sun-warmed wall of his hut, screwing his mouth with concentration. He had survived the winter only to escape the spring. I wondered what had ever happened to him in all his life to make the struggle to keep alive worth while. But the answer was here in this little knot of women and children, in the men working near the stream. He had fathered a family who were gathered to mourn him and miss him.

"To go sleeping is a good way to be taken," I said.

I walked over to the nearly built fire though I should not have done so. A woman is supposed to take just seven steps toward the man who is dead. These seven steps say that sometime we all shall travel the path of death. I stopped behind Jamshid, who was building the fire. He looked up over his shoulder at me as his body bent toward the twigs. "He was my father," he said. And tears came from his reddened eyes.

"Can we not take your father to Teheran so that he can be bathed according to our religion?" I asked gently.

"The jube is here," Jamshid said, turning back to his task.

"He should not be bathed in the jube," I said ever so quietly. "Wherever this stream goes, people use the water for cooking and for drinking. There will be sickness everywhere."

"My father is not unclean!"

How could I say anything more? Defeated, I turned away.

When I was just a child, visiting in Abadan, I had walked out on the balcony of my aunt's house just at evening, and heard below me in the court a sort of keening—a closed, almost animal-like crying. I had gone down a step or two toward the court, and then I stopped. Kneeling beside the pool was a woman, her thin dark veil falling over her face. She was washing a child. I could see her hands going gently over the long thin limbs. The child was perhaps nine or ten, very long and slender. At first I had wondered why the child lay so quietly under the gentle hands, then I recognized that he was dead and that the mother, alone there at the pool, was preparing him for burial according to the Moslem religion.

Tears burning my eyes, I watched her every slow motion. When she washed a cheek she laid her own cheek against it and her crying rose a little higher. I saw her straighten the dark locks of his hair with her fingers, and finally wrap him in a piece of old muslin. Later, an older boy stepped from the shadows and helped the woman, bent with silent weeping, to carry the child away for his quiet burial.

I had been impressed at the time with the woman's hopeless, helpless sorrow. I had not thought of the danger of washing a dead body in a pool that was used for other purposes. Now I remembered what Dr. Birjandi had told me: "Often you will be so involved with the incident that you will be unable to see the outcome."

Today I could not interrupt the preparation of the body of the old father for burial—Jamshid and his brothers and sisters had lost the wisdom and the patience of the old one. Today this thing must be finished—but it must not happen again.

I sought out Mash'hadi Mokhtar. "Mashdi Mokhtar, do they often wash the bodies of the dead in the jube?"

"Very often. Only important persons are carried to Teheran."

"But I have not seen this before."

"I cannot tell how you have missed it. In winter, of course, when the jube is frozen, the dead must be washed in the home. This our religion allows when the winter is deep."

"But we must not use the jube for such washing."

"Now, my lady," and his voice grew gentle and soothing, "this they have done always. Oh, not in the jube, of course. In the sand bank they dig out a depression large enough for the body and fill it with water from the jube."

"And the water returns to the jube."

"Running through the sand makes it again sweet." Mash'hadi Mokhtar finished the sentence with a broad gesture of his ringed hands and a lifting of his marvelous mustache.

I did not argue with him because he knew that he was repeating a mistake many of the ignorant believe. "We must build a house for the washing of the dead."

"We cannot build so easily, my lady. Already we—"

At that moment I felt Shapoor's arm linked through mine. I felt the tingle of the thought—the dream—we had shared just that morning as we looked on the land that was really ours. Now I realized, almost startled, that never before this morning had I felt spiritually married to my husband. The words I had to say to Mash'hadi Mokhtar were the most difficult I would ever speak because I was speaking not only for myself but for one who mattered even more to me. "We will not work on my home at this time. Mashdi Mokhtar, we will build this washhouse for the dead, instead."

He looked at me curiously. "And what of your husband? Are you sure that this is what you want?"

"The council must decide, of course," I said, thinking belatedly of democratic procedures. "But for myself, I am willing."

The council, called into special session, was reluctant to build such a house. "Why, the bath is not even finished. Always, always you want a new project before the old one is completed. . . . How is this?"

There was much wrangling. "Look," I finally said, "let us leave this to the people. Shall we ask them if they wish to drink the water that has been used for washing the dead? Shall we ask them if they are willing to help in the construction of a special washhouse for this purpose? Shall we ask them if they would like to be able, winter and summer, to cleanse the bodies of their dead in the way of Islam?"

"You ask them," Mash'hadi Azzizi, one of the most loved members of the council, suggested. I wondered if he were jeering, but when I turned toward him his kind, florid face was serious and open.

"I shall," I promised.

That very afternoon I started from door to door talking of the new project. Many said they would give small amounts of money— in America you say "the widow's mite"— and some said that since they had no money they would give work. When Shapoor came home I told him that I had put off the building of our new home until this other project was completed.

"Najmeh, Najmeh!" was all he said. I sensed the disappointment in his voice—and the agreement.

Almost immediately the house for the washing of the dead was begun. It was to be a very simple structure without doors or windows. There were to be two openings, since in our religion the body may not enter in and pass out through the same door. The floor would be of hard earth and there would be a font just large enough for the washing of the body and a stone table for the other preparations. The water used would be carried from the jube but would be emptied far underground where it would be dissipated in the thirsty sand.

To Americans accustomed to transporting dead bodies by plane, burying them in satin-lined bronze caskets, these accommodations would seem primitive. But death has its own dignity.

By the middle of the month, although the washhouse for the dead was still uncompleted, the mason we had employed to build the walls of the village center came to my house.

"My lady," he said. "I have come to tell you that we will begin work on your house tomorrow."

"And what of the washhouse for the dead? What of the bath?"

He took from inside his coat a sheet of newsprint and carefully unfolded it. This paper I had seen before.

One Friday morning a young stranger had come to my house. It was clinic day and a line of people waited for their turn. When this young man shouldered his way to me I said quietly, "I am sorry. If you are for the clinic you must wait your turn," and I showed him the line that was waiting outside. I saw the look of chagrin on his face so I said, "But you are new here and so you wouldn't know this thing."

As I gave shots, cared for the sick, I caught glimpses of this man talking to the other patients under the great cherry tree. Finally when it was his turn he said, "Lady Najafi, I am a newspaperman and I would like to tell the story of this morning for my paper."

And so he had returned to Teheran and written an article. The story was called "The Angel of Sarbandan." He had sent me a copy. I wondered where the mason had got his page; from some relative in Teheran, perhaps.

"Day by day, day by day, one doesn't see and understand," the mason said, putting a finger on the often-read page. "At least you must have this home for yourself."

I was touched. How hard it is to see that which is nearest to us.

So the building began and moved forward rapidly. Each evening when Shapoor returned from Damavand and I had completed my day's work, we went together to our growing house. We wanted to build, with our own hands, our home. This way it would be ours in a very special way. Since the mason was making the walls we would build the roof.

Our house was to have a willow roof, supporting sod in the way of most buildings in the villages. Shapoor and I, in the evenings, selected, cleaned, measured and cut the willows. Every willow was straight and white and of equal size.

The plan for the building was very simple. There were to be three rooms side by side. The center room was to be a reception room and work-study-room for the women. It would be very large, comfortable, with windows on two sides. At one end of this reception room was to be a room for Shapoor and me—an intimate home that would not always be open to the public. On the other end was the kitchen, and opening from the kitchen and on the back of the house was a storeroom. A detached hayloft, hen house and latrine were also at the back of the main building.

The jube flowed behind the buildings, and irrigation ditches would transfer water from it to ditches that would pass the trees and shrubs and garden. We would have a pool, too, for beauty and for storing water for outdoor purposes. The front of the house would look out onto this pool and the garden.

Shapoor and I had decided to trim the house with fired red

brick. For this purpose we had two loads sent from Teheran. All the people in the village gathered to see the bricks unloaded. Never had they seen such fine building material! We planned to support the porch roof with two straight pillars. These we must find in the village as they could be brought from Teheran only at great expense. The search for them was an adventure. Wherever I went I studied the trees to see which two might be straight enough, tall enough, and of equal circumference. The only place I saw such trees was at the home of Mash'hadi Mokhtar, and I couldn't ask him to cut them down. For everything else I hurried to Mash'hadi Mokhtar, but not for this.

"My lady," Asghar said to me one afternoon, "I know the place." He had been looking for trees, too.

"Where?"

"At the home of Mash'hadi Mokhtar."

You too, I thought, but I did not say these words. "The trees of Mash'hadi Mokhtar are not for us."

"But they could be," he insisted. "He is going to cut them down anyway, I have heard."

And so I went to Mash'hadi Mokhtar after all.

First I admired the straightness and uniformity of the trees. Later I said that they were the only trees of such beauty in all Sarbandan. Still later I told him that I had searched all over for just such trees. I gave him the opportunity to say that for me and me alone he would cut down those trees. I did not bargain over the price he asked. I did not mind that he congratulated himself on selling to me trees he intended to cut down anyway. He had done more for Sarbandan than I would ever be able to estimate, having seen it "little by little." He deserved this triumph.

Most of the month of Ordibehesht I felt happy, alive, outreaching. This was the best month of the year for building, since the men were home from Mazandaran and the fields were still not ready for the plow. The washhouse for the dead was almost completed, our home was going up rapidly, even the village bath was progressing. In the work-study room there was always a busy buzz. Always five girls or women were working on the carpet while others sat at the smaller looms. Voices droned through the reading lessons I conducted, or chattered as women plied their needles.

I had found a small home for Zahra and her two little ones. They came to the work-study room with her in the morning but were soon at play with Little Rabbit in the yard or in his home next door.

But in the evenings I was lonely, especially when some project kept Shapoor away for several days at a time. There were no young voices in my house, no foolish laughter, no light teasing. All three of my girls were working in other villages. When the house was too quiet I thought of bringing three more girls from the work center and beginning their training; but already a plan was taking shape in my mind which would preclude this project. How I looked forward to the girls coming home for the bi-monthly meetings. They were like my own children. Farkhondeh especially I missed with an almost physical pain. I needed her warmth, her affection, to feed my own laughter and tears.

On the day the girls were expected, Asghar as usual cleaned the house, shined the samovar, raked the yard, and cooked, cooked, cooked. First Farkhondeh came in on a donkey; then Pooran, also on a donkey; and finally Effat and her little brothers on the evening bus. The girls fell on each other with tears and kisses, giggles and shouts. They ate themselves uncomfortable on Asghar's special food. They kissed me and almost kissed Shapoor until he escaped, blushing.

After our evening meal we discussed the problems each had encountered during the past two weeks. I was happy to hear them advise each other instead of always turning to me. The measure of success in training village workers was the measure of their wisdom, their independence, their competence. I was interested that each girl was advocating methods suited to her personality. Effat's nature was to advise quietly, Farkhondeh's to persuade through affection, Pooran's to show humbly. In each of the girls I saw facets of my own personality and I realized that each of us has, in some degree, all the qualities of others. It is in ourselves that we decide which quality shall dominate our lives.

These girls had come to me physically and mentally "skinny," undernourished, and now they were physically and mentally developed, well nourished. My mother, my sister, my friends had noticed the physical changes. Only I, who could see the heart uncovered, could see that the changes were not of the body alone.

After the lantern had been burning for several hours, the girls set up their beds and retired. I went to my room. Still giggle, giggle, giggle. Shapoor grew restless. "Can't those girls quiet down? Who is it that giggles now?"

I rose and went into the general room. "What is this? Tell me?" I whispered like a conspirator.

Farkhondeh made room for me beside her in bed, and I lay down, her firm, warm arm around me, and listened to the whispering.

Effat told of the son of a grocer who always found the best of everything for her when she went to shop. A farmer's son was smitten with Farkhondeh. As grandly as if it were a Cadillac, he sent a donkey to her home each morning to save her walking. But she liked a young teacher who still was too bashful to do more than say "Salaam." Pooran had not yet found an admirer, but she lived vicariously in the stories of the others. It was all foolish and beautiful and young and human! I did not care that the sky framed by the windows grew from black to dark blue, to gray, to rose. The girls were home!

For one day of their stay the girls visit with the women and take over the teaching. After two days, when they leave for their own villages, I have to turn away to hide the tears rolling down my cheeks. I do not know if the tears are from loneliness or from pride. Such emotions a mother bird must feel when she has pushed her babies over the edge of the nest and found that they can fly!

One evening, near the end of the month, Little Kadkhoda got off the bus. Asghar, buying tea in the center, hurried home to tell me the news and to report that Little Kadkhoda's face was closed and he had not stopped in at the teahouse of Mash'hadi Mokhtar.

"We will serve him tea when he passes our home," I told

Asghar. He hurried to put the water to boil.

But Little Kadkhoda passed my house with never a word.

He had gone to Teheran with the happiest face that can be worn by a young man. He had given up his position as kadkhoda in order to train for the position of co-operative specialist. Now he was returning with his face tight and full of anger and pain.

"What has come over the kadkhoda?" I asked Shapoor when he drove up in the development jeep. "Why is he back so soon?"

News travels fast in Iran. "I heard they turned him down in Teheran."

"They?"

"The Foundation had rules. Each applicant must have six grades of school."

"But that is absurd! There is no one in Sarbandan except you and me who have six grades. Any boy raised in this village is limited to four years because this is the first year we've had more than four years available."

"Don't argue with me. I didn't make the rules."

Because Shapoor's temper was short I knew that he was as concerned over this thing as I was.

"But surely they mean six years or the equivalent."

"They must mean what they say."

"He's intelligent, trustworthy; he's continued his education by himself since he finished school. Besides, if we wait for one of our boys who can finish sixth grade to grow old enough for this training—"

Again Shapoor said, "Don't argue it with me!"

"I'm going to talk with him. I'm—"

"Perhaps you have already made trouble enough," Shapoor told me.

Later, as I lay quietly in my bed looking out at the stars in the deep velvet of the night, I could not feel concerned about the delay this rejection of Little Kadkhoda would bring to a project which seemed to me so urgent. I could think only of Little Kadkhoda. He had been reluctant and I had urged him. He had asked, "What can a kadkhoda do when he is no longer a kadkhoda?" and I had brushed away his fears. I had taken for granted that the interpretation of the Near East Foundation would be the same as mine. Shapoor was right. I should have investigated and found out whether he would be acceptable before he gave up his kadkhoda position. I could have written a letter. I could have—

I did not blame him for passing the teahouse and my home with a closed, tight, angry face.

Several days later he rode to Damavand with Shapoor. I, too, went along. He did not speak to me and finally I said, "I am so sorry that I made this mistake. I did not know."

He was sitting behind me so I could not see his face but his voice was hard, accusing: "It is said that two beggars can sleep on the same rug, but two kings cannot live in the same country."

That was all.

I had been hating myself for making a mistake in ignorance when I could have found light. But he believed that I had not made a mistake. He thought that since having two kadkhodas in Sarbandan had often made my work slower, more difficult, I had purposely tricked him into resigning, knowing all the time that he would be rejected. I wanted to argue with this boy; but there was no use. Again I tried to explain, but his silence stopped my tongue.

So now he hated me and his mother stopped coming to the classes and no longer came to the women's council. I had made many mistakes, but never had I been mean, crafty. Never would I have cheated anybody in this way.

Some time later Asghar told me that Little Kadkhoda had a job taking some sheep with his own to the high mountains for summer.

Seventeen **AGAIN KHORDAD**

If it is true that this life on earth is a segment of some eternal life, without beginning and without end, we are really living in heaven when Khordad comes to Sarbandan. Everywhere is the fragrance of new-turned soil. Beans here are planted in flooded basins and the dampness brings out the rich, ever-fertile smell of the good earth. The blossoms have fallen from the cherry and apricot trees in clouds of gossamer petals, but still their fragrance seems to linger.

There is hope in the village, too. Hope and vigor and energy.

During the month of Ordibehesht the women's council met many times and began the construction of a nursery or child-care center. This was the first project the women's council mentioned after its organization. Year after year sun-baked babies had nodded on their mothers' backs or clung to their skirts as the women worked from daylight to dark in the field. "We must have a place for the babies!" This the women said over and over again. And so land for the nursery was donated and a building begun.

One room, like the storeroom at my home and at the clinic, had to be completed in order to borrow money on improved land. Like the other rooms, this one was very simple—just four walls without doors or windows. Many villagers had given money or time to its building. I myself had sent Asghar for three days to make bricks, while I did his regular chores. To the villagers a gift of

225

money is good but cold, while a gift of energy is both good and warm.

Now that Khordad was here and it was planting time, the building was still not ready for use and we had run out of money for its completion. At the request of the council I went to Teheran to discuss our needs with Mrs. Effat of the Imperial Organization of Social Services, but it was impossible to get assistance soon enough to put the nursery into use this year. Next I talked with the village council. Each gave some money, but this money was not enough. There was nothing to do but look for a building that might serve temporarily and put it in shape.

One of the council members offered her home for the season. Then what fun we had. We made baby baskets from medicine boxes and the heavy wood cartons in which dried milk is delivered. There were no car pools since there were no cars, but women took turns bringing all the tots in the neighborhood to the nursery. They were cared for by Shokooh, a kind, patient, childless woman without the strength to work in the fields herself. She was paid in produce: eggs, wheat, beans. It was my responsibility to see that the babies were fed. Sometimes the mothers came in from the fields to feed them; most often we gave them reconstituted milk, vegetable broth, other things. It was a joy to see some of the little ones turn from skeletons into round babies, almost within a month.

When the important work in the fields was done, I went from home to home urging the women to plant dooryard gardens. The year before I had planted with Asghar's help a beautiful garden and many had come to see it and to sample the vegetables which I gave to my callers. Now as I went from door to door I gave to each woman who had prepared her soil some packets of seeds. The seeds I had purchased at the bazaar and the envelopes that packaged them were the most beautiful things—outside of nature—that the villagers had ever seen. After the seeds had been put into the soil, the envelopes were saved and pasted to the inside walls of the drab houses to lend them beauty. Flower seeds I gave only to those who had first planted vegetables.

There were seeds of onions, cabbages, cucumbers, tomatoes,

carrots. These seeds were precious. While I knew that free seeds were available through one of the agencies, I found it better this first year to buy the seeds myself. They weren't to be wasted by putting them directly into the garden. Each woman who had asked for seeds prepared a hotbed to grow seedlings which could then be transplanted to the garden.

As soon as the seedlings were set out my house was filled with quarreling women. The neighbors' chickens were eating the new green plants. So I taught them to put willows lightly over the garden and build fences, if necessary, of woven willows. It was advice Shapoor and I also took in protecting the garden around our new home.

One afternoon as I walked from the new home to the one in which we lived, Mash'hadi Mokhtar stopped me with a gesture.

"Lady Najafi, it is accomplished."

"What is accomplished?"

"Come and see."

He led me to a partially constructed building which the masons and carpenters had been putting up with great speed. "A new house, Mashdi Mokhtar?"

He made a wide gesture with his hands and his gold-studded smile was wide. "Not for me, my lady. It is a home for guests. The summer is hot in Teheran but here it is beautiful. We have a bus, no? We have a road. We can have summer guests who will pay well."

"That is so."

"I will rent other houses, too, and repair them. Many go to the mountains with their herds in the summer to make cheese and oil from the milk of the sheep. These houses I will also prepare for the guests."

"We will put a great sign on the Mazandaran road. It will say *Sarbandan*," I promised him. "Many will stop, perhaps and live in the houses here, and buy food from the shops and vegetables from those who raise them. It is good."

And I thought: Motels have not yet come to Sarbandan, but when they do Mash'hadi Mokhtar will have the first one!

The village council met and discussed Mash'hadi Mokhtar's great idea. Others thought of homes of relatives or friends that might be rented for the summer. There was talk, talk, talk, but no wrangling, just the excited viewing of a new dream. At Mash'hadi Mokhtar's suggestion the council set a uniform price for summer rental and for food sold to summer guests. In this way they would protect what sometime later might be an important business in Sarbandan.

One evening Shapoor, two friends and I sat on our veranda on the chairs cut from sections of tree trunks. In a field not far from our home a group of young girls had been playing in the dusk the old, old game called, "Uncle, Who Keeps the Bread?"

"Is anybody home?" ask the girls on one side in a singsong voice.

"Yes."

"Did you braid my rope?"

"Yes."

"Did you take it to the back of the mountain?"

"Yes."

"Can we come in?"

"Yes."

"Do you want a ring?"

"Come with the voice of a—" Here the girls call for the voice of a dog, a donkey, a dove, a lamb. There is an imitation of the animal sound, young laughter. And finally at the end of the game, a "pull away."

Now the twilight had darkened into night and the girls had gone in but still their laughter, their singing, were in our ears. The sky was a great arch, bright with a million billion stars, and the moon, like the distant face of some ancient god, threw a white and fairy light over everything. In Sarbandan there are no lights on the streets; no lights in the homes except perhaps a small candle, a bit of rag thrust in a dish of grease, or a small, carefully kept lantern. Because the village is so dark the stars are clear, very clear.

The mountains, which around Sarbandan are treeless, stand black against this bright sky.

Our guests were Mr. Atree, a government official, and a doctor friend of his. Mr. Atree was a great joker and everything he said seemed funny to us. If we did not understand the point of the joke that didn't matter, since his laugh caught and carried us with him.

I worried a little for fear our neighbors, who rose with the sun to work in the fields, would think us rowdy. But still I laughed. It felt good to be carefree and relaxed. Now and then I heard Asghar, who sat on the floor inside the house, laugh in his quiet way. Because he couldn't see us, he thought we could not see him, though his legs and bare feet were directly in front of the open door.

Just when our party had reached the merriest, a young boy came running toward the house, stumbling as he ran.

My heart seemed to fall. "Again," I thought. "What is it now?" And then I was ashamed.

"Lady Najafi. Come quickly. It is my uncle, Mash'hadi Azzizi. He has a ball of fire in his chest and he screams with pain. Come quickly."

Immediately the doctor was on his feet. "I'll go, Najmeh. Sounds like a coronary occlusion, if it isn't a bad case of indigestion."

"They expect me," I told him, reaching for my sheepskin jacket.

"I'll get my bag and take care of this."

Shapoor went with him to his car, where he got out the black bag known around the world. Then my husband came back to where I sat. "There is nothing you can do, Najmeh-jun, and you are tired."

"Yes, I am tired," I admitted. We sat again, the three of us, while the doctor followed Mash'hadi Azzizi's nephew to the old man's home.

I was tired. In the excitement of guests and dinner and the unaccustomed gaiety, I had not realized it, but now I knew.

After the doctor had gone, Mr. Atree tried to pick up the mood of merriment, but the jokes fell flat even on his own ears. We were all thinking of a man who was suspended between this life and the unknown one.

Finally the doctor came back. "Not much I could do," he said. "I think the old fellow will be all right. It was a heart occlusion, all right. Thrombosis. I gave him a shot to keep his blood from clotting, and told him to stay perfectly still and not to eat."

"You are sure you told him about the eating?" I was remembering how in the village the family believes that a man should die happy. When he is near death it is ordinarily the practice to prepare him a meal which includes all of the foods he specially likes.

"I told his wife, too. Quit worrying, Najmeh!"

Soon afterwards our guests went to bed in our room and Shapoor and I made beds for ourselves in the clinic room. Our faces were in a shaft of moonlight and we could look upon the quiet sky.

Immediately Shapoor fell asleep and began to breathe evenly. I thought of Mash'hadi Azzizi and wondered how he was doing. I sat up quietly, intending to slip out and go to see for myself. If I spent the night there, no one would feed the old man. Just as I was buttoning my blouse I heard it—the unmistakable sound of the death wail raised by the family of one who has departed. I shook Shapoor. He wakened our guests; in a few minutes the four of us were on the way to Mash'hadi Azzizi's home.

There were the women of the household, standing about wringing their hands. There was Mash'hadi Azzizi looking very old with his sagging mouth and his death pallor. And there, all about him, were the remains of a banquet.

"See, Najmeh," the doctor told me. "They didn't pay attention to anything I said. How can they be so stupid?"

"Hush!" I put my hand on his arm. "They must not hear. Perhaps they are right. Perhaps it is well to die without hunger. Perhaps he did die happy."

The morning was graying as we walked back to our home. Mr. Atree tried to joke clumsily. "What a fine doctor! If you want to die tonight just call a doctor." And we laughed because we were very tired. But the words were not funny. I knew that too many of the village people would think that calling the doctor had brought the evil eye upon Mash'hadi Azzizi. Many people would tell me, "No, no doctor, Lady Najafi." And I would know the reason why.

The next morning came the procession toward the new house for the washing of the dead. The men of the village came first carrying wood and charcoal to make a fire to heat the water. Then came the sons and nephews of Mash'hadi Azzizi carrying a square of carpet upon which the dead man lay. Then, bearing a package of white cotton cloth, came his old mother—the only woman in the procession.

The washing house, for which Mash'hadi Azzizi himself had made a donation, was finished, and he would be the first to use it.

In through the door of life they carried the body, to be laid upon the stone table and cleansed according to our religion. The great toes would be bound together to keep the legs and feet straight, a bandage would be placed over the eyes, the mouth would be filled with cotton. Then the whole body would be anointed with sweet-smelling, ancient perfumes and wrapped in a large square of white cotton cloth.

In the cities special men do this service, but in the village every man helps. There are sorrow and faith and love—many emotions melted into one by bereavement. Had I been a man I would have helped with the washing, because Mash'hadi Azzizi had been my friend, always listening carefully to my words in the council, often being the first to agree with the things I thought needful. In our religion everyone must help sometime, or perhaps many times, with the ablutions of the dead. It reminds us how thin is the veil that separates mortal from immortal, and that any day can be the end of this world for us.

When the ablutions were completed, the sons and nephews again lifted the carpet on which Mash'hadi Azzizi's body was lying and carried it out of the door of the dead up the mountain trail toward the burying place. I stood off a way, as is suitable for a woman, and listened to the chant of the men.

"La Ellaha-ella Allah" (There is no God but Allah), and the

other Arabic phrase which means: We are from God and we return to Him.

Every man who hears this chant must come, his shovel on his shoulder, and join the procession to the burial place. Each woman who hears it must follow seven steps.

At the burial place a simple grave is dug by friends. There is no vault as in America, no covering the waiting earth with a blanket of green or a mound of flowers. The body is placed in this grave directly on the earth to which it will return. At each side of the head is placed a brick or stone; another flat brick or stone is placed like a bridge over these to shield the face from the earth which will fill the grave.

The burial of Mash'hadi Azzizi I did not see. I had seen many others.

For three days Mash'hadi Azzizi's family held open house in his honor. No matter how poor the family is, even if it means becoming further enslaved to the storekeeper who must be paid at harvest time, the family must do the dead this honor. I did not go to the home the first day; that day is for relatives. But after the burial, I slipped up to the house for the washing of the dead. The men had left everything in order. The thirsty soil had absorbed the water which had washed the body of my friend.

On the third day I went to the home. I took the hands of the wife. She was of the women's council and I loved her. "Oh, Lady Najafi, he was the core of my life. He was the trunk of the tree, I only the bark. What am I to do?"

Many questions I could answer, but not this one. "You have your family," I said, "and God is good."

And then I felt my own tears on my cheeks. I did not brush them away. I was crying because I had lost one whom I loved, yes, but more than this I was crying for the sweetness of the ancient customs that give security to life no matter how primitive that life can be. Above all, I was crying because this woman who had found what many women never know had lost it. Someday, we Moslems call the time *The Day,* we shall all awaken and stand. Slightly behind

Mash'hadi Azzizi will be his wife. But, oh, it is a long time until *The Day.*

That evening when Shapoor rattled up with the development jeep I ran to meet him. I put my hand in his and my head against his chest. "Najmeh-jun," he said, holding my head against him with the palm of his open hand, "what is the matter?"

"I am finding something," I told him. But I could not tell him what.

Eighteen ⊕ AGAIN TIR

Now the cherries, red-black and shining, hang like jewels in clusters from the old trees of the orchards. The apricots, smooth-cheeked and golden, await the hands of the women who move among the trees, their chadors looped like baskets at their sides. Every door-yard, which last year was of hard-baked tan earth, now is green with the swiftly growing vegetables.

It is the time for hope, for faith, for beauty and for work. This I think as I see the sleeping infants in the nursery, watch the toddlers play in the dooryard under the careful eye of Shokooh. For these little ones the world will be better than it has been for their parents. They will be different, too, freed from superstition and poverty.

As I walk toward my home I see old women with their backs against the sun-warmed walls of their houses, cutting the apricots for drying. My heart reaches toward them, too, for they have lived without complaint in a life of limitations. Abruptly I am brought back to today by the voice of Little Rabbit. "See, Lady Najafi, see! The carrot is ready for eating!" And he holds up a carrot scarcely larger than his own little finger, not much more than a thickening of the root below the fernlike leaves.

Behind him comes his aunt, Masoomeh. She is screaming at Little Rabbit, calling him a donkey and a thief. He hides behind

234

me and eats the carrot, his ears closed to her voice.

"My lady," Masoomeh says, all out of breath and patience. "You taught us how to keep the animals from our gardens with woven willows; you taught us how to keep the chickens away by placing the willows lightly over the earth. Now I am going to use the willow in another way to keep this bad boy from my vegetables!"

I remember how angered my girls were when Masoomeh took sugar from my home; how they wanted me to go and reclaim it.

"Hunger is a strange thing, Masoomeh," I say. "When one feels hunger one must eat."

"No one needs to eat my garden!"

"Perhaps if each day you give the boy a carrot from the garden he will not take it."

"Then all of the children would ask. The carrots would be eaten before they really grow."

"You are right, Masoomeh." But still I would like to save Little Rabbit's tender legs from the willow. "This time we explain. Next time we punish."

Reluctantly she agrees, and striking the air with the willow until it cracks and whistles, she walks back toward her house.

"It is not ready for the eating," I tell Little Rabbit, and I show him how big the carrot should be before it is eaten. He nods. He understands. In Sarbandan the people eat everything in season. During the season for the picking of the fruit the quantity of fresh fruit that everyone eats astonishes me. At the harvest of the wheat everyone eats bread in the same way—as if there would never be another loaf in his life.

I watched Little Rabbit trot away. He had tasted the sweetness of the baby carrot. And after all, I spoke only words.

Since everybody was busy with the fruit there were no women, no older girls, in my classes. There was no one at home to make visiting worth while. There was even, since we had renewed our campaign to put perchlorine in every family water jug, not anyone in the clinic. Shapoor and I decided to visit the village of Garmab-sar, of which we had heard but which neither of us had ever seen. The village is only about twenty-four kilometers from Sarbandan but there are no roads, almost no trails.

We set off walking and we took Pooran with us. A donkey carried our bedrolls, our food, a few medical supplies, and sometimes Pooran. How beautiful it was as we climbed higher and higher into the mountains. Sometimes we came upon little dells, fed by some mountain stream, in which the columbines stood waist high, sometimes we came upon shining emerald grass dipping down into quiet pools. And always above us and before us were the massive mountains.

At length we came into the village. It was not a small village; there were perhaps two thousand people; but it was different. The people themselves were different—beautiful, blond, taller than most people of the villages, stronger boned, really more like Europeans in appearance than Persians. These people in their remote village had scarcely been touched by the Arab invasions of more than a thousand years before. They were the original Irani, or Aryans, who moved down into Iran when their brothers continued westward into Europe. Pooran and I were dwarfed beside them; even Shapoor, who is tall but slight, seemed small.

When they spoke their language was Kurdish, which resembles Farsi enough so that it can be understood.

When I had gone into Sarbandan I had felt that life there was very primitive; the villagers had absorbed so little of modern culture. But these people not only had no sanitation, no literacy, no roads, no schools, no clinics; they had never even heard of them.

Shapoor, who is able to speak Kurdish better than I, talked with some of the men. This time there were not the usual questions: Are you an American? Are you a Communist? Did the Ministry of Education send you? Not even fear had climbed the rough trail to Gar-mab-sar. At Shapoor's suggestion two gleems were brought into the kadkhoda's dooryard, the men were called together, and we all sat down upon the gleems. Shapoor explained the village council, and at once all of the men felt that Gar-mab-sar should have a council. For seven hours there was discussion of who should belong to the council—discussion and wrangling.

Then silence fell over the crowd. An old man, his face made of wrinkled leather, came riding a cream-colored camel over the mountain and into the valley. Near the gleems the beautiful beast bent his knees and the old man dismounted. We were introduced and he bowed. He was a man who knew all about Teheran. He had been there eighty years before. Never since had he left the mountains, but his memory was keen so he did not need to go again to the city.

Eighty years! At that time Teheran was a beautiful Eastern city. No railroads, no automobiles, no Western shops and apartments, no hospitals. But even at that time there was concern over foreign influence. This, only, would the old one find unchanged.

Shortly the discussion of the council was resumed and members were selected.

After we had drunk tea and rested, the new council met, ringed by the curious who were not members. Shapoor talked to all of them of the blessings of communication with the rest of the world, and let them tell him that a road was necessary.

"You may have this road," he told them. "But you must help."

"But what can we do?" Faces which had brightened now fell.

"The government will give the money, but you yourselves must do the work."

"But we are not road builders. We do not know how to do this thing."

"You could form a class for learning. The government would send a teacher."

"A class for learning to build roads. That is good." And so the council voted to organize such a class. There was a light of excitement in all the faces except that of the old man. I turned to him. "You are not happy?"

"I am not happy with a school that teaches road building. I am not happy with such a teacher."

"What teacher do you want?"

"Someone to teach the Koran. This is of more value than the building of roads."

"This teacher we can also get for you," I promised.

But it was late. We put down our bedrolls in the home of the kadkhoda and slept.

The next morning, very early, I heard a voice. "Ooooh, ooooh, my lady!"

After I had finished my prayers I walked out into the fresh, clean morning.

"We have brought our children for you to heal!" And there, sitting silently on the ground, was a group of mothers with children—babies, toddlers, older children.

"I am not a doctor, but I will do what I can for you."

The trouble was summer complaint. Even in this high village the water from the open stream could not be drunk with safety.

I talked with them of boiling a little rice in the water all during the summer so that both the sick and the well might drink the milky fluid. I talked with them of washing the soiled clothing far away from the stream so that the water would not return to spoil the stream's sweetness. I talked with them of sanitation and I said the same old words: "It is better to keep well than to be healed."

For each child I had a shot to immunize against typhoid, that ever-present enemy of people who drink from surface streams. At first they were afraid of the needle, but I talked quietly, the mothers offered their own arms, then the arms of their children. I knew that the acceptance of the immunization was part faith in me, but even more this strange medicine was to them a new kind of amulet to ward off the "evil eye."

All morning Pooran and I worked with the women and children. Shapoor was still talking roads with the men. After most of the women had left us, a self-possessed, sallow-faced woman of perhaps forty or forty-five came to me.

"I am the wife of the kadkhoda. For fourteen months I have been pregnant."

And I asked the stupid question: "Are you sure?"

"I have other children," she said with dignity. "I know the signs." Then she hesitated. "But I have never felt life."

I wanted to tell her this life that was growing in her with the speed of its own choosing was not a child, but I did not.

"Help me, Lady Najafi. It must be born or I die."

"I cannot help you," I said. "Only in the hospital in Teheran can you receive help."

"Must I go?" Her eyes filled with fear.

I said gently, "I cannot tell you this." I could not make this decision for her. Perhaps the distention of her abdomen was due to cancer and she would die far away from her husband and her village. "Perhaps God will give you permission."

Together we opened the Koran. This would be a strange way to make a decision in America. Her fingers touched a place in the sacred book and I read the words.

"I will go," she decided. "God gives me permission." Then she turned frightened eyes to me. "If I return with you perhaps my child will be born in the mountain passes."

"Yet it would be born!" I laughed, and after a moment her laughter joined mine, but just for a second. It is a serious thing to go to Teheran when no one in one's family has ever left the village.

In the afternoon I met with the council. "Do you wish a school?" I asked.

"We wish to learn of the Koran," the men said.

"Do the women wish to sew? To learn to care better for the children?"

"All these things," the kadkhoda pushed my words away with his outturned palms, "but first the Koran."

"Then you must have a house for the school."

As I had done so many times before, I walked through the village with the council, looking for rooms that could be used for a school. There was one just being built. Since it would be clean and new and could be finished with the problems of a schoolroom in the builders' minds, it was chosen.

"For the school you must have a teacher," I said. "The teacher must have food, clothing, a donkey to ride upon."

"These things we will get for a teacher."

"Please let me stay here," Pooran begged me. "Please."

"The Ministry of Education will take over this school when it is organized," I told her, "just as it did our girls' school in Sarbandan. In that way is the teacher paid."

"Please let me stay until the school is ready for this change," she begged.

I did not need to tell Pooran to move slowly, patiently, to expect little and give much. These things she knew deeply in her own heart.

When Shapoor and I left the next morning the donkey's back was empty. I had used the medicine and left the bedding and food for Pooran. Just as we were leaving the village, accompanied by many of the beautiful, blond people crying, "Come back . . . We are glad you came . . . Come back . . . We will finish the school . . . We will watch over the 'little one' . . . We will begin the road . . ." the woman of the long pregnancy joined us. Her husband was with her and two little girls hung to her skirt. "Mama, are you coming back? When are you coming back?"

"I do not know," she said. She turned to me with questioning eyes.

And I truthfully had no answer to either question.

The villagers watched us out of sight. We waved as we topped the last hill above the village. Shapoor, the lady of the long pregnancy and I.

The way back to the village seemed longer and harder than the way up, perhaps because I was carrying a heavy heart. The woman on the donkey swayed back and forth, back and forth, but she never spoke, nor smiled, nor came alive at the beauty of the way.

"I will be glad to be home again," I told Shapoor. But before we reached our home Asghar met us. His words were for my ear.

"My lady. Ashraf is waiting to see you."

"Ashraf?"

"Yes, she came today by the bus."

"Ashraf," I said. And abruptly I felt even more weary.

Ashraf sat on the red mat in the clinic room, a cup of tea between her hands. "I made myself some tea, my lady," she said as I came in. Then, "Oh, Lady Najafi. I made a terrible mistake. I am so sorry that I went back to Teheran. I should have stayed with you and learned all that you had to teach."

"Yes?"

"So now I have come back. Now I will learn all."

My heart went out to this thin pale girl in the too-bright thin silk dress. I had made plans that would make impossible the training of other village workers. Yet—

"Why do you want to come back, Ashraf?" I asked gently.

"I have seen Effat and Farkhondeh in Teheran with new clothes, new shoes, money in their purses. I was a fool to give up these things."

She had made the wrong answer. "Ashraf," I said, "many times we can see our mistakes and turn back. Sometimes there is no second chance. In this there is no second chance."

"But, my lady—"

"I told you this when you left, Ashraf."

She fell to sobbing. "How can you be so cruel? One little mistake and—"

"Listen to me. A man is climbing the mountain. Other men have climbed this mountain before him and left a path. But this man does not follow the path. He goes a way of his own. It is not a good way. Suddenly his foot slips and he drops to a ledge only a little way below. Above him the path goes on as before. He cannot reach it now. He has left it and there is no second chance."

She broke into a wailing. Effat and Farkhondeh, she said, had turned me against her. They were never her friends. I put my hands over my ears. "Shapoor and I are taking a sick woman to the hospital in Teheran. You may ride with us. You will not need to wait for a bus." I gave her a handkerchief to dry her eyes and poured another cup of tea and put it into her shaking hands.

The next morning in Teheran we found the hospital filled. There were even beds in the garden, under awnings to keep out the sun and weather. Yet the admissions nurse looked at our patient and assigned her to a bed in one of the corridors. Because she was afraid, and because her language was difficult for the nurses to understand, they allowed me to sit beside her bed. After a time a doctor came. He had much to do but he was kind and patient. He listened to her halting sentences, then said bluntly, "This thing is not a child. It must be born with a knife."

Her eyes went to me in terror. I took the little Koran with its chain from my neck and fastened it on hers.

"What must be, must be," she agreed, the terror fading.

Before I left Teheran I went back to the hospital to ask about her. The growth had been a tumor, not a cancer, and she would soon be ready to go home. In fact she could go even now if there were roads and a suitable conveyance.

So the Koran had been a true guide. And the answer to the child's question was, "Mama will come back."

Each day seemed warmer and clearer than the last. Almost with the eye one could see the vegetables grow. Water from the jube was turned down between thirsty rows, and people who had all their lives lived on potatoes, beans, wheat and rice now ate the fresh green onion, the carrot, the cucumber, lettuce. Many things we had tried to do in Sarbandan, but this simple thing of planting seeds in the dooryard was perhaps the best.

One day as I walked toward our still-unfinished home with a basket for the gathering of some vegetables, I was stopped by an old woman who was a stranger in Sarbandan. Her bony feet were naked, her dress was worn, her eyes were weary, but there was that about the way she held her head that made me think the one word, "Queen."

"Lady Najafi?" she asked.

"Yes."

"I am of the village of Shel-shach-meh. I have come to invite you to my village since you visited Gar-mab-sar."

"You are tired," I told her. "Come to my home and we will have a tea together."

I asked Asghar to prepare abgousht as well as tea and she ate hungrily. "I come to ask only friendship," she told me.

She stayed with us for a day and I showed her the clinic, the washhouse for the dead, my chicken house, the village center, the schools where in the winter the girls and boys learned to read and write and figure, the work-study room. I had her rest on a bed which I put up in our general room and bathed her tired eyes with warm water. The next day, because Shapoor could not afford time from his work, I had Asghar bring a rented donkey and we three, the old lady, Asghar and I, started for the village. I insisted that the old lady ride.

"Why did not some man, perhaps the kadkhoda, come to me?" I asked.

"I am the head of the village."

This village was the first matriarchate I had heard of in Iran.

"All the people of the village are my children, their children, their children."

At last we came into the little village. She called everyone to visit with me, and one of her grandsons brought a rug for me to sit upon—the only rug in the village. Nearly every child in the village had trachoma, scald head, other illnesses. And there was such poverty!

To say "poverty" in a country like America means very little. It is not until you have seen children actually cry for a spoonful of rice when the mother has none to give that you realize poverty means the pangs of hunger, the warping of little bodies so that the legs and arms are like fagots and the abdomen is distended, and there is no resistance to cold nor to disease. Poverty means not enough coverings at night to sleep through from dusk to dawn in comfort, not enough clothing to keep the body warmth next to the body, not even a pair of shoes to cover cracked, bleeding, purple-blue feet.

These things I saw in this little village. I can never be really lighthearted again.

To the people I gave the few pitiful gifts I had brought on the donkey; then the old woman took me walking through the village. There was no school, of course; as for sanitation, there was not even one latrine. We stopped in to visit some of her sons and daughters. I saw not a single samovar.

"I will come again," I promised. And I did. Three times I went, taking medicine, dry milk, vitamins. I would report the needs of this village to the right agencies. I could do so little and the villagers needed so much!

To the matriarch I gave a latrine slab as a friendship gift. Asghar, with the help of some of her grandsons, dug the pit, placed the slab, built a three-cornered mud-brick wall around it. Then everyone in the village lined up to go into this wonderful new building and try out the facility!

Later the Governor visited this village. His gift was another slab.

When I told Shapoor that I was giving the old lady this slab, he laughed, and so did Asghar.

Although Tir (July) is one of the most beautiful months in Sarbandan with its green fields and gardens, its ripening fruit, its sun-warmed days and cool breeze-swept mornings and evenings, there is something about it I do not like. In the winter the flies must freeze to death. But if they do, how can they come alive again in the spring? And by summer how can they have increased until one spring fly has become a thousand summer ones? Everywhere I went with my D.D.T. Shapoor teased me about this, too. But D.D.T. was not enough. Everywhere the flies moved in swarms. Even their loud, warm buzzing sounded filthy to me. And each of these clouds seemed to rise from some open latrine.

The slab at the mosque, those at the schools and at my old home and my new one interested the villagers, especially the women. As soon as the flies began to appear I began to talk slab—slab—slab. These should have been placed before the flies came, but that is not the way my people do things. The need must be present. Right there!

One day a boy of about eleven sought me through the village. He went first to my home, next to the new home that was nearing completion, finally to the teahouse. Mash'hadi Mokhtar directed him back to my home, since he had just seen me pass. All this the boy told me between sobbing for breath, though I urged him to skip that part of the story and tell me what he had come to say. At last,

"My mother fell into the latrine. She was weak and sick. She did not have the strength. She—"

"Come," I said. "Where is she now?"

"She is in the home. But she was in the pit for many hours before anyone went into that place."

"She did not call?"

"We were all away at work. She felt pain so she left the orchard."

"I will go with you." Hurriedly I seized some of my own clothing, since many villagers do not have a full change.

When I reached the home the woman was in the yard trying to cleanse herself. I helped her, and after she was clean put my clothes on her. There was a quivering of her flesh, a paleness and coldness of her skin that worried me. Even though it was midsummer I asked her where her blanket was packed, and rolled her in it.

"Many others have done this thing. Many in Sarbandan," she told me.

"Yes, yes. You could not help it." I talked gently with her. She had been pregnant—now she was not. It was this loss that had made her faint in the latrine. How she endured this traumatic experience I do not know. But very soon her husband and sons installed a latrine slab. It would not happen again.

News, especially news like this, travels fast in the village. "Did you know that . . . ?" "Did you hear that . . . ?" All of my talk had not done so much good for the slab project. Mr. and Mrs. Koskenides of the Near East Foundation were wonderful. They sent the slabs which arrived by bus in Sarbandan. They were unloaded at my home and I delivered them to the people, two on a donkey at each trip.

The slabs that had far to go must go by the development jeep, and I was supposed to have the use of this jeep only once every two weeks. But while Shapoor was getting ready to go to his office I would whisper like a conspirator to Asghar, "Go ahead. Do. Put one in." And he'd reply by sneaking out and slipping a slab into the back of the jeep.

Shapoor, starting down the road and feeling the unusual smoothness of the ride, would stop, put his head out and call, "What, again?"

"Yes."

"Are you coming, too?"

"Yes." And I would climb in and see that the slab was delivered unbroken. One hundred and thirty slabs we placed. Not nearly one for each family, but oh, the work this represented!

On the last day of Tir the post brought me a wonderful letter. It was short—only three lines—but it informed me that the Ministry of Health would supply a resident physician for Sarbandan's new clinic!

How fruitful was the month of Tir.

Nineteen ✣ AGAIN MORDAD

Again it is Mordad (August), the yellow month of waiting. Coming from Teheran by bus I feel the air of the evening against my face. It is good to be in the mountains again! It will be good to be home in Sarbandan. In the west the sun is drowning in a sea of molten color. The mountains to the east lie half in shadow, half in the pink light of the last sun.

We round the hill and here is the village center—our home. "Stop," I tell the driver. "I will walk from here.

"Ooooh-ooooh," I cry, "anybody here?"

There is no answer. The workmen have finished for the day. I walk alone. In my dreams for this place I can see the pool, the flowers, the trees that will someday make this a garden spot. For a few moments I sit upon the steps and look out toward the hills. Peace seeps into me. The frustrations of the day in Teheran are put behind me.

Then I rise and slowly open the front door. Inside it is deep dusk; I feel, even more than I see, the simplicity and beauty. Here there are no tight wooden floors, no running water, no electricity, no furnace for the winter, no ornamentation of any kind. Yet how "right" it feels, how clean. There is still a little painting to be done, curtains to sew and to hang, furniture and supplies to put in place.

Slowly I walk through the rooms, then again I sit upon the step. God has been good to me. God, and Sarbandan.

"Najmeh-jun," Shapoor said as he met me coming from the new house to the old. "I was worried about you when the bus stopped at the teahouse and you were not on it."

"I have decided," I told him, "that in the front of our new home I will plant two rows of trees, an avenue of trees. One of these I will plant for each of my friends who has helped me in this project."

"That is good," Shapoor agreed.

For in Persia, as in other desert country, a tree is not what it is in America—something to be planted, uprooted, replaced. Tree is a symbol of life. Tree gives shade in the burning sun of a desert country; tree promises that water is near; tree is a symbol that living things can flourish in spite of an unfriendly environment. A tree named for each of my friends would be a living monument.

"What sort of tree?"

"I do not know. The poplar, I suppose. It grows quickly and points toward heaven in a way that I like."

But when I spoke of my avenue-of-memory trees to Asghar and later to Mash'hadi Mokhtar, they both shook their heads. "This is no time to plant trees," they told me. "Trees planted now would die."

"Then," I said, "we will prepare the place for them."

The next morning, paint can and brush in hand, I began the completion of the house. The painting I wanted to do myself, but it turned out that both Asghar and Shapoor assisted.

And then all the excitement of the move! For Sarbandan that day was a holiday. Nobody worked. Everybody came to see us move. The men and women stood in separate groups laughing and talking. The children, so eager to help, tumbled over each other.

The looms would be left in the house I had rented from the kadkhoda, in the room that had been built for a work-study room. Zahra and her two little ones would move into the room that Shapoor and I had used. Work on the carpet and on the other looms would go forward any time that weavers appeared and wished to work. We had recently acquired a new carpet loom—a folding affair that could be set up anywhere—which was wide enough for the making of runners. This, too, was installed in the work-study room.

The medical supplies were moved to the clinic in preparation for the coming of the resident physician. Some few things I would need by me until that time, and these we put in the storeroom at the new home. The little beds made from medicine boxes I left for Zahra and her family.

Leaving these makeshift beds, the house that had grown with me through my first year in Sarbandan, I felt as people do when they close the covers of a specially good book. It was a good thing that the children, in their awkward attempts to help, kept us laughing. If we had not laughed we might have wept. Little Rabbit decided to carry the flower pots—all of the flower pots. Twenty-six trips he made from the old house to the new and back again! Other children carried the dishes, many other things. Of course much was broken. How could that have been helped in such a holiday moving?

Asghar was worried. "We could have done these things ourselves, Lady Najafi, without all of this breaking," he told me with annoyance in his voice.

I looked at the shining faces of my helpers. "People are more important than dishes, Asghar."

How beautiful I made the big center room of the new house. The curtains at the windows were of white material with twined pink and blue flowers. Flowers like these grow on our hillsides in the spring and are called la-loos. With the same material we covered boxes to hold our supplies. Everything matched. The walls and the ceiling were painted a soft beige, like shadowed sunlight. In the center of the room we placed a long, low table. Around the walls were built low benches and behind the benches, since they were backless, were gleems on the walls. In the room, too, were the shining samovar and the turquoise candlesticks that had come from Ghom.

After everybody had admired the new home and gone to their own little houses, Shapoor and I stood together at the door and looked out over the yellow fields. Every day this view from our house would be different—every hour it would be different. This hour was for us what we had both secretly hoped it would be. The new house—the house that was not mine, but ours—gave us a sweet feeling of closeness.

When the girls came home for their regular bi-monthly meeting they were ecstatic. Never had they seen anything so beautiful, they cried. And with the girls there, filling every corner with their happy laughter, their eager questions, my dream of organizing a school for the training of village workers came to me with new power. I thought: If I could only afford to build a dormitory, provide food and clothing and allowances for the girls while they learned, pay a small staff, I could open such a school very soon. What better gift could I give Iran than more girls like these three?

Very soon the house filled with guests. "Let me buy this home just as it stands," our guests said. "This is a home where everybody must be happy."

We had known that our house would be a village center, for this we had planned it. But now it was like a hotel. We had more official guests than ever before. Always we invited our friends to be sleeping guests. The women slept in the room Shapoor and I had planned for ourselves, the men in the general room. In Iran no one minds sleeping on a floor if it is clean.

One morning several cars drew up on the road behind our house. From them came many official guests. As I hurried to greet them, I gave instructions to Asghar to commence preparations for dinner. Today we would serve at least two tables. In the villages all guests must eat in the home, since there are no restaurants, no hotels.

"While I am here, I'd like to talk with the council and such other people as are intelligent and can understand what I wish to talk about," Mr. Malak Mansoor told me. Mr. Malak Mansoor is the government head of the co-operative movement in Iran. He is an intelligent man, educated in Switzerland, who, because he owns some villages, recognizes the needs of people like those of Sarbandan.

I spoke to Asghar. He spoke to Mash'hadi Mokhtar; Mash'hadi

Mokhtar spoke to the people in and near the teahouse; each of these people took a separate route. As quickly as if we had rung a signal bell the people collected in the dooryard of the center. "How do you do it? Never in my life have I seen a village collect so quickly. They are without fright. Without uncertainty," Mr. Malak Mansoor told me.

"They have not always been like this. Our people must learn trust," I told him. And he looked closely into my face and nodded.

"I will not disappoint them," he promised.

So the people sat in the dooryard, the members of the men's council and the women's council sitting on separate gleems, and Mr. Malak Mansoor stood on the porch. For three and a half hours he talked and answered and asked questions. Four times Asghar passed among the people serving tea. The people listened carefully to his words, but they did not respond. They were cold and distant. What was this thing "co-operation" of which he spoke? Had not Little Kadkhoda been turned away at Teheran when he responded to this word by giving up his position in the village? Was it not really wiser to take care of oneself—one's relatives if one had to— and let other people take care of themselves?

This is the Persian opinion in a way that Americans cannot understand.

"Together you have made Sarbandan the most beautiful, the cleanest village in these mountains," Mr. Malak Mansoor told them.

Their faces took on no glow. They were still distant, solemn.

"Lady Najafi did all," one man said when pressed.

"Did Lady Najafi arrange for bus service for this town?"

"No," they admitted, "Mash'hadi Mokhtar arranged this."

"You have a bath almost completed. Did Lady Najafi give money for this bath?"

"No. We borrowed."

"Did Lady Najafi save for you your old bath until the new one should be completed?"

"No." (It was fortunate that he did not ask, "Has Lady Najafi kept the old bathhouse clean and usable?" or they might have told him of the whispered warning that ran through the bathhouse when I approached. "Here *she* comes. Get yourself busy with the cleaning!")

"The council did this."

"Did Lady Najafi build the girls' school? Did she insist on a woman teacher from the Ministry of Education?"

One of the women spoke, not to the group but to her neighbor, and her voice carried over the crowd. "I myself signed my name."

"Did Lady Najafi give land and money for the clinic?"

"No. We—"

And so his questions went, building into the people a feeling that they themselves had had a part in the awakening of Sarbandan.

"You have done much. You can do more," he insisted.

"But Lady Najafi showed us the way."

"Yes. You teach a child to walk. After that do you carry him?"

When the walking becomes difficult you still must carry, I thought, but I said nothing.

People in Persia love to laugh, they love to tell great jokes like the Southwestern tall tales in America, they love a celebration of any kind. But deeply they are not a happy people. It is as if this laughter, this short gaiety is a brief journey into another world for them, and quickly they must return home to the sad heart, the life of trouble. They are a pessimistic people. That they have done things once does not mean to them that they will not fail the next time. Always in my work with them I had tried to build the spirit of optimism that I found the most exciting thing in America. Optimism and hope.

Finally the discussion was ended. The council adjourned to the teahouse to talk quietly with each other about these things they had heard, to consider whether it was true or not that having made the progress they had made, progress was now unlimited. The women, walking slowly to their homes, stopped by two and threes to talk.

Later we, my official guests, Shapoor and I, sat down to dinner—a dinner that Asghar had collected from nowhere and everywhere, and Mr. Malak Mansoor went on with his talk to me.

"These people do not know their own potential," he told me.

"Yet they are learning."

"Is there one man who knows how much it costs to feed a donkey or twelve chickens for a year? Is there one who knows how much the grocer pays for the rice and how much he sells it for? Is there one who knows—?"

"Who can tell them these things?" I asked.

"Telling is not enough. These things they must find for themselves."

This I, too, had thought.

So, after the visitors had gone, again we came together. First the village council, then the women's council, then others who had been in the classes and were intelligent enough to help.

"We are going to find out many things about Sarbandan," I told them.

Their faces were dark. "Who pries into our business?" Mash'-hadi Mokhtar wanted to know. "Whose nose is it that comes into my door?"

"No one pries," I promised. Then I explained to them the plan I had spent the night in drawing up, for a study of the village.

There would be four committees. One would do research on family life, family relationships, family needs. This might have been called a "child welfare" committee had not its purposes been a little broader. Another committee would work on the cost and care of animals. What was an honest earning from the sale of cheese, oil made from sheep butter, animals for meat? Another would work on crops. How much money and how much time is spent in the raising of potatoes, beans, fruit? Just how much should be earned with the crop? And the most important committee was composed of the most intelligent people. What are the earnings of the shopkeeper-moneylender in the village? How much does borrowing cost the poor man? I knew that in many cases this borrowing cost more than 100 per cent, but the committee would learn this.

All of these committees would be given assistance by the office of Mr. Malak Mansoor. I myself would head the first committee and advise the others.

Still no one had heard of the Little Kadkhoda. He had not been back in Sarbandan. Yet perhaps this way of working toward a co-operative was better. I had wanted to give the village this good thing, wrapped in tissue and tied with ribbon, as a gift. I should have known better. Had I not learned that every project that had been successful in the village had grown out of a need the villagers themselves felt?

After the committees had reported would be time enough for the people to see that the new way, a better way, must be adopted. I was filled with hope.

And then came the note inviting me to a conference with Dr. Birjandi in his office at Teheran.

I stood before Dr. Birjandi, thinking of that evening at Fakhri's home when he had told me that I must educate my heart. Now, as then, his eyes behind their horn-rimmed spectacles were shrewd and kindly.

"Najmeh," he said, "you have done better than anyone could have hoped. I wish that this country had a hundred Najmehs."

I shifted uncomfortably. Had he called me to Teheran to tell me this?

"And I have a plan for changing you into one hundred Najmehs if you will agree."

My heart jumped. The school for training village workers in Sarbandan! Sarbandan had shown, I thought, that my way of working in a village was a good way. My girls were doing well in other villages. Dr. Birjandi was going to say that somehow, somewhere, there was money available for a dormitory and other needed facilities!

"I want you to leave Sarbandan."

I could feel the tears coming up behind my eyelids so I didn't trust myself to raise my eyes. "Leave Sarbandan?"

"I want to give you the title of Specialist. I want you to go into many villages as you did into Sarbandan, but not to stay as you have there. You could live with the people, gain their confidence, study their needs. Then you could make a report to us. On your research we could base an individual development plan for that particular village."

"Dr. Birjandi, we have just finished a new village center for which I borrowed on my own credit. It is our home. Shapoor's and mine. My husband must be considered in this decision."

"We have thought of that. There would be an assignment for him, too."

"What about my girls? I took three girls from the work center; worked with them, loved them, and trained them to carry help to the villages."

"For your girls' sake you should make this change, Najmeh. Each of them will become a village dehyar (helper). Each will receive an adequate salary."

An adequate salary? This would be the best for the girls. Yet still I could not feel that this change was for me. "But to leave Sarbandan—"

"Then the answer is 'no'?"

"The answer is—" At that moment I thought of the poor, aged woman who had come to invite our friendship, of the village where poverty lived in every hut. How limited was the help that I could give these people. A little food, a little medicine, a little hope. If I were researching villages for the government as Dr. Birjandi suggested—

"The answer is—I can't say. I don't yet know. There is too much to be considered."

"You are right, Najmeh. Of course you must have time to think, to discuss this with your husband."

"To talk, to think, and—to pray," I agreed.

Twenty ✤ AGAIN SHAHRIVAR

It is autumn, and Sarbandan and the hills that surround it are deep yellow. The leaves on the poplar trees turn faces like pale gold coins to the sun; the wheat, shoulder high, waits for the harvesters' sickle. The dooryard gardens are no longer green and the fields in which the potatoes and beans were grown now show nothing but the gold-tan of the dying, uprooted vines. Sarbandan is beautiful, always, in September; but to me this year it is wrapped in an aura of special sweetness. Always when one is preparing to say good-by, there is this special magic in the familiar that enhances the beauty and erases even the memory of ugliness.

We are leaving Sarbandan, Shapoor and I. I think I knew that I would say "yes" to Dr. Birjandi's request, even as I told him that I had not yet made up my mind.

After I returned to Sarbandan from my conference with Dr. Birjandi I lay on my bed and looked out over the dark fields. After a time the moon came up and flooded the fields and lay in a shaft of white light across the bedroom. I turned to see the sleeping face of Shapoor. Dr. Birjandi's request I must share with him, and very soon, but for now I must live with it myself.

I tried to think of reasons why I should stay in Sarbandan—reasons that were not selfish and exactly human. Sarbandan awakened was now ready to go on without me.

256

Already the resident physician had come to the new clinic. Each month he would spend fifteen days in the village. In the make-shift clinic we had given eight hundred immunizations and treated more than four thousand patients. The new clinic would serve other villages, as we had done, and with its increased facilities and cap-able doctor it could continue from where we had left off. The bath, still not fully completed, needed only the interior tile work and

that could be finished during the winter months. The house for the washing of the dead was accepted by nearly everyone. And in the village were many sanitary latrines.

There was an added class in the girls' school and already the teacher from the Ministry of Education, a strong, energetic young woman, had arrived to conduct it. A new class and teacher had been added to the boys' school and the village council hoped to add a class each year as the boys progressed, until ten years of schooling would be available. Zahra, in the original work-study room, had two hand looms and the large and small carpet looms busy from morning until night, and other carpet looms had been promised. There would be work this winter for a few more of the women who needed it so desperately. Farkhondeh could take over the social work and the women's classes and keep all of the projects of the women's council synchronized.

But more important than these physical, tangible things were the intangibles. The village council had developed harmony, initiative, optimism. Almost never did I need to say, "Come, let us do this." At council meetings the members had ideas of their own for needed projects; and some of the members, like Mash'hadi Mokhtar, had grown surprisingly astute as businessmen.

Another intangible, not perceptible, perhaps, to one who had not lived eighteen months in the village, was the change in the attitude of the men toward the women, the change in the women's attitude toward themselves. When I had first begun to teach good grooming in my classes, angry fathers came to me: "What are you trying to do to my daughter? Make her to be a prostitute?" For in Iran the women who sell their bodies to the wealthy are some of the most carefully kept women. Now good grooming, neat dressing, soft speaking, personal cleanliness were expected and enjoyed. Men were beginning to think of their women as something more than docile mates. This was a great step forward. In the village there is no word for *wife*. The village man uses the same word to mean both wife and home. Or he may call his wife by the name of his first son. This habit of speech, alone, shows the position of women. No man can say, "I love my wife," or "I respect my wife." Yet I felt a change. Someday the men could say these things.

And the women, some of them busy on the women's council, some of them earning a little at the looms, all of them taking more pride in their homes since they had learned child care, sanitation, sewing, crafts, were for the first time thinking of themselves as persons, not just women.

These intangibles I felt, rather than saw or heard.

Yet my work was not finished. We had just organized the research committees which would teach my people, more quickly than any other method, where their real needs were. I should stay at least until these studies were completed.

I got out of bed and walked over to the window. There I knelt with my arm on the casing, my chin in my hand, and drank peace from the moon-drenched world. There were specialists who could advise these committees, and I had failed in my work if the people refused to call upon these specialists and take their advice. The image of Mash'hadi Mokhtar came into my mind: his gold-studded smile under that fabulous mustache, the shrewd black eyes, the expressive hands. "Lady Najafi, it is arranged—"

But my plans for the girls' school in Sarbandan. At first this school could train village workers; later, when this need had been met, it might train teachers for the simple industries. When I had told Dr. Birjandi of my wish to set the Los Angeles Trade College down in Iran he had said, "Najmeh, Najmeh! With you first comes the donkey and then the man."

But as I knelt at my window and looked out on this loved village, any dream seemed possible of accomplishment if only I could stay in Sarbandan.

I went back to bed, but still I did not sleep. It was many hours before I realized that the dream for the school need not die. Rather the change might be a step in accomplishing the dream. Dr. Birjandi had promised that Effat, Farkhondeh and Pooran, as dehyars, village workers, with salaries from the government, would work side by side with girls who had not been specially trained in the village for village work. If the accomplishments of my girls proved outstanding—and I was sure they would—there would be a demand for other girls trained in this way. Someone else would be as eager as I for the founding of this school.

The next day I talked with Shapoor and we went together to discuss the future with Dr. Birjandi. In this talk I told him that I preferred to go into primitive areas, villages where culture had not touched, to study the needs of remote villages. Dr. Birjandi wanted me to work near Teheran where hospital and other facilities would be available and where the progress of my study could be noted by the government.

"Why not Garmsar?" he suggested.

"Garmsar?" I waited for a moment for my intuition to speak, and then I told him reluctantly, "My heart does not want to go to Garmsar. But I will take it there to find out why."

Shapoor went first to Garmsar to see what quarters might be available for us there. Oh, our beautiful Sarbandan home, lived in for less than a month!

When he returned I ran to meet him as he got stiffly from the jeep. His eyes read my question.

"Najmeh-jun, we cannot do this thing. Garmsar is awful!"

"If the village is awful we must do it," I said, trying to bring a smile to his somber eyes.

"I saw the village. There is already a team of young experts there who have set up a program. But there are flies, dirt, no place to stay—"

"I will go myself," I promised.

So, two days later, riding out from Teheran with one of these young specialists, I went to Garmsar. I was greeted by the other young men who were working there. They were intelligent, energetic, keen, but I knew at once that they saw no place in their program for women's work.

"There is nothing here for you," they told me. "But we will show you around. You won't like it, we can promise you that."

"Well, while I am here I will see all," I answered cheerfully.

First they took me to the bath. "The bath. You may go in if you wish but it offends the nose."

I went in. It was bad—but how much change had we brought to the ruined bath of Sarbandan with simple cleanliness.

Coming out I said, "But I have smelled other village baths."

"There are flies."

"There is D.D.T."

By now I sensed that the young workers felt that there was no need in Garmsar for work with the women. Either that, or they feared I would take from them something that was already theirs. All morning I trailed them, listening to stories of the difficulty of working in Garmsar. At noon they said, "We are sorry that we have no more than tea to offer you."

"Tea will be fine. I have brought food with me." Then I took a piece of plain bread from my bag.

They laughed uncomfortably. "At least we have bread and cheese," they said. But I ate my bread and drank their tea.

"May I go alone through the village this afternoon? I want to know some of the women."

They looked from one to the other. "Are you not returning to Teheran this afternoon?"

"No. This day I spend in Garmsar."

I walked about the village, calling outside the houses, "Oooooh-oooh, anybody home?" And when there was a reply I went inside the dark little houses and chatted. I praised the samovar if it was clean and shining. I praised the children if they were at home. The toddlers I coaxed out from behind their mothers' skirts and I took the infants in my arms because my arms have always been hungry for babies. One very young mother I saw who had a goiter so large that it seemed bigger than her face. I knew that she needed immediate attention and it would take some time to gain her confidence and let her develop the idea. On every side I saw evidence of a need for a program for the women and children.

At dusk I went back to the village center. "We are sorry," the young men said, "that we have no place for you to spend the night."

"Such a place is not necessary. I have my own bedroll. I could place it in the schoolroom, perhaps, or in the house of some chicken."

At this they laughed. Finally the young man who had brought me said in American slang, "You win."

It was night when I returned to Sarbandan. I tiptoed into the house in order not to awaken Farkhondeh, who had taken over in my absence. I lighted the candles in the turquoise Ghom candlesticks that stood with my open Koran on the table in the center room. Then I walked to the window. The thought seized me: *This I cannot do.* I cannot leave the cleanliness, the beauty, the love of Sarbandan to start a new fight against superstition and uncleanliness and fear! I felt empty, devoid of hope. Oh, what is the use? I asked myself. And I answered, It is foolish, crazy, without meaning.

The village lights were out and I sat down near the window that opened to the fields. I looked at the stars, like diamonds sewed to a robe of black velvet, and thought about Him who created all things. The moon had enwrapped the world and the murmur of the jube was quieter than the sound sleeping of babies.

All night I stayed awake and discussed my troubles with God and prayed to Him. I watched the sun as it rose. I performed my morning ablutions and said my prayers. I still felt utterly hopeless.

When Shapoor saw me he said, "Najmeh-jun, were they so cruel to you?" and he would have taken me in his arms but I moved away. I could not tell anyone what was in my heart. There is no word for such blackness.

"Shapoor, we will go to Garmsar. But first I must go on a pilgrimage to Karbala." Only at some holy place, I felt, could I rid myself of this overpowering sense of futility.

His eyes searched my face and he understood. "Do you go alone, Najmeh-jun?"

"You will come with me, Shapoor. Perhaps my mother and yours. The four of us."

"That is good."

In Karbala is the tomb of Ali, and near by are the tombs of my fathers.

But before we reached Karbala I was given a personal miracle.

When we arrived in Medaen (Taghi-Kasra), the capital city of the ancient Sassanide Dynasty, the darkness inside me seemed to change to tears as black clouds change into rain. My heart lightened as the tears streamed from my eyes. Dimly I saw my mother and Shapoor's with their prayerbooks in their hands. Dimly I saw Shapoor start out on a sightseeing expedition of his own. I stood still and gazed through misted eyes at the ruins of the capital of the great Anooshirvan. The shimmering of light through tears seemed to change the ruins to actuality, and this place existed whole and new and in my own time.

Once I had read in a book by Rahnam a description of this

capital and now I saw all. I repeated to myself the words of our poet, Khaghani, beautiful in the original Farsi.

> You may ridicule me for weeping over these ruins;
> Such weeping should be laughed upon.

and

> The palace was as high as the universe;
> The kings bowed at its gateway;
> I saw an owl sitting at its indented tower
> And crying, "Koo-koo-koo."

"Koo" in our language means "where" and what the owl was saying is: "Where has all the splendor gone?"

I saw in my imagination the courtroom where the king gave audience—the golden candlesticks, the suspended lanterns set with jewels, the life-sized silver camel, the horse made of gold saddled in jewel-set silver. Heavy curtains with rows of pearls set at their margins were hanging in the end of the hall. The ministers of the court—and I could see them all plainly—were standing in a line a few yards from this curtain. A high priest stood alone, and there were ranks of priests, generals, government officials.

The court chamberlain draws away the heavy curtain: "Hold your peace!" he cries. "You are in the presence of the King of Kings!"

Every body kneels and Anooshirvan ascends the emerald throne. This man is the supreme ruler of most of the known world; he is the source of law and of tradition; he is the only being whose happiness and sorrow are the happiness and sorrow of the world.

He is wearing a white robe threaded with gold and pearls, gold wrist lace and a golden belt. His trousers are of a rich, bright blue and in his ears are gold, jewel-emblazoned earrings. He wears a short, cone-shaped beard which is as soft and shining as fine silk. Above his head is suspended by a fine chain the historic crown of the Sassanide Dynasty.

The high priest offers a prayer to Ahurmazda, the God of Light, then with a voice that reveals his love and reverence he wishes the king a long life.

Now the king opens his mouth and his words echo in my heart:

"Let it be known to the people of Iran that our court is always open to them, day and night. We are always ready to listen to any petition. Whether asleep or awake, whether hunting or engaged in the games, whether in happiness or illness, every man is welcome to this court. If one man goes to bed brokenhearted I shall have to answer to the Creator of Light."

I repeated these words over and over to myself: "If one man goes to bed brokenhearted I shall have to answer to the Creator of Light." I turned to see the garden, the tall trees, the beautiful flower beds, and the marble pools with the leaping fountains.

Still my eyes were with the past and I saw, instead, the marble palace with the Kariani flag—the jeweled flag of the good omen—flying over it.

My mother touched my elbow. "Najmeh, everyone is in the bus." I turned to her my tear-washed face. "What is it? What is the matter?" she asked gently.

But how could I say, I have seen a vision? To me a miracle has been given? Instead I told her, "It is very beautiful, Mother. Very beautiful."

And so when I returned to Sarbandan the blackness had lifted from my breast. There was sorrow at leaving Sarbandan and going to a wider work, yes; but not despair. Perhaps my new work would help to bring about in some small way that day when every person in Iran can knock at some gate, just as the people did at the gate of Anooshirvan, and some man or woman of compassion will open the door of a new life for them and none shall be turned away. This I pray.

The morning that we left Sarbandan no one was inside the mud houses of the village; all had gathered in our fields to tell us good-by.

"Good-by, Lady Najafi, good-by. We love you." The men were shaking hands with Shapoor, not in the American manner but with both hands. The women, their hands busy with their chadors, looked at me and I could read their faces. And Farkhondeh, putting both her arms around my neck in a grip that could not be broken, could not speak a word.

"You are Najmeh, Farkhondeh," I told her. "I am leaving part of myself in you."

Reluctantly we got into the jeep. Mash'hadi Mokhtar came and stood beside me. There was no smile under his mustache but he said, "It is arranged. There is one who can act as secretary to the council until you return. My nephew, Malek—"

Shapoor started the car. "Come back. Come back," the children cried. A sea of faces and behind every face a story.

"Yes, yes," I promised. "We will!"

My words were more than a promise. No matter how far away from Sarbandan I might go, my home, my heart, my future would lie in this awakened Persian village.

IF YOU ARE PUZZLED

About the Spelling of Persian Words

The difficulty in using Persian names and other words in an English-language story is one of transliteration. The alphabet in Farsi (the language of the Persians) and the English alphabet are not equivalent. The Farsi language has some sounds which are most nearly expressed by a combination of English letters. We have, too, in Farsi, some sounds which cannot be accurately expressed in any way. For example, a sound somewhere between the English short *e* and short *a*. Different writers, therefore, use different letters in the transliteration of the same word. (Demavend, Damavand.)

For the transliteration in this book we have depended upon Mr. M. A. Khorouzan, a brilliant young Persian scholar who studied in England and was for a time a writer and translator for the Near East Foundation in Iran.

"In spelling I have followed the standard pronunciation of the words without paying any attention to the various dialects which are prevalent all over the country," writes Mr. Khorouzan. "I have negelected the variations introduced in the spelling of names by foreigners, except for such common known variations as Koran and Mecca.

"Some names may be spelled in several different ways, but I have tried to be consistent throughout the book. In words which re-
266

quire the usage of the sound *oo,* as found in the English word *mood,* for example, I have used *oo* instead of *ou* or *u.* (Mahmood, Mahmoud, Mahmud are all equally correct transliterations of the same name.)"

About the Religion of the People in the Persian Village

There are many good sources for learning of Islam—the religion of the Moslems. However, most Christians think of Moslems as being one body, all alike in worship. Actually there have been schisms in Islam as in Christianity.

When the Prophet Mohammad died there was a great argument about who should succeed him. Many believed that the Prophet had many times said that Ali would succeed him. Many thought that Aboubakr, the oldest of the Prophet's followers, should take his place. To prevent the group from breaking in two the leaders agreed upon a compromise. Aboubakr became the first Khaliph and he was to be followed by Omar, then Osman, and then Ali.

At this time Islam was strictly an Arabic religion. In Persia a king whose family had ruled for four hundred years reigned over a thousand-year-old empire which had extended its borders from India to Athens and had reached a high standard of culture. When Omar became Khaliph he ordered the destruction of this empire.

The Persians hated the Arabs and considered them barbarians. They had a beautiful religion of their own and resisted Islam, too, but they had to accept it or be killed. Many Persians escaped to far-off places like India. Others seemed to accept Islam but carried the teachings of Zoroaster into hiding while they waited a chance to overthrow the Arab invaders.

When the rift came between Omar and Ali the Persians were, of course, on Ali's side. Wasn't Omar their natural enemy? Wasn't Ali really one of them since his son, Hosein, had married the daughter of the last Persian king? The break that had been put off by the compromise now happened. Persia became "Sheit."

According to tradition the oldest son of each Emam, or religious leader, became an Emam at the death of his father. It was hard for the Emams to exercise the authority they thought they should have; often they clashed with the Arab leaders. When this happened they sometimes fled Arabia and settled with their families in Persia. The descendants of any Emam were called Sadats, and they could add to their names Seyed, which means Sire. A friend of mine is a descendant of Hosein, the third Emam.

Time passed and the teachings of Mohammad were combined with the older customs of the people. About the time of Queen Elizabeth I of England, a simple, virtuous, religious leader became ruler of Persia. He gave Persia a new golden age and recognized Sheit as the official religion of the Persian Moslems.

This great branch of Islam has its sects, too. One of these is the Ali-Allahis, which is described in this story.

The teachings of the Prophet Mohammad are very simple, very beautiful. Much has been added as time passed. In working with the village people I have respected their customs and traditions even though they aren't a real part of the Prophet's teachings. For myself, however, I have believed and taught the simple, true, basic principles.

About the Iranian Government's Interest in Rural Development

Although rural legislation in Iran has lagged behind urban legislation, the government is taking a very real interest in the problems of the people who live in the villages. No one knows, except people who have worked in countries like Iran—countries which are just emerging from a sort of feudalism—what difficult problems are associated with rural development.

The village men are paradoxes. Many of them still neither read nor write, although elementary education is advancing rapidly in my country, but they are really intelligent people. They often can recite for hours from the classics. They can raise more food on a given amount of soil than any other farmer in the world and yet they have little opportunity to better themselves. They love their wives and children in an almost fanatical manner, yet they must watch them die of preventable or curable diseases. They are deeply religious, yet mixed in with religion is a deep belief in witchcraft that is older, even, than race memory. And while they are not slaves, they are seldom really free.

Our present Shah, Mohammad Reza Pahlavi, in an attempt to improve the lives of such people turned over the Crown Lands Properties for distribution to the villagers. The result of such a distribution might have been to create villages of beggars, for with landlords gone where would the poor find money lenders? The farmers never, in their lives, had planned to get through from harvest to harvest without an extension of credit.

The government moved carefully. The land was turned over to an agency, Development Bongha, for distribution. A Development Bank was established and capitalized to care for the fiscal operations of the Land Distribution Program. The Lands were surveyed, broken down into small tracts, and sold to farmers at low cost and with twenty years to pay for them. The Bank also made loans to the new landholders to enable them to acquire seed and tools. Farm co-operatives were established to provide advice and to help the farmers in marketing their products.

Without the Development Bank and the Co-operatives farmers would be prey for the "bara farrish", unscrupulous money lenders and produce merchants, who would control the land through keeping the farmers impoverished.

During the premiership of Mossadegh, the Farmers' Share Increase Act was passed with the hope that it might in some way improve rural life. The bill provided that 10 per cent of the net profits from the land should be paid as special tax and returned by the government to the village for local improvements.

At first the landlords paid the 10 per cent, but later, when Mossadegh's regime fell, they stopped paying it. Even at first the collection was done in a way that would seem peculiar to Americans. There were none of the businesslike tax collections used in the United States where a form goes out by mail and is returned— as a matter of course—by mail. In Iran the whole collection depends upon the landlord's willingness to pay.

A gendarme—a law enforcement agent (rural police), the representative of the government in any situation in Iran—would call upon the landlord's agent. He would speak first of politics, maybe of mutual friends. Finally he would say, "The people here seem to be pretty bad off. No bath, no schools, no clinic. We wondered if Mr. T. wouldn't like to give his Farmer's Increase tax."

"But—" Mr. T's agent seems dubious.

"Over in the village of S. they have just built a clinic. The land has gone up in value. It has gone up more than the tax. Isn't this strange?"

"Land values up? Mmmmm."

And perhaps the agent calls this to the attention of the landlord and he makes a payment. Only he knows what the earnings are, so he alone knows the amount he should pay. He may pay. He may simply forget it.

Suppose this particular gendarme is young and inexperienced or old and courageous and pushes the collection. Next week he will find himself with a new assignment on the furthest border of the country, living with his family in a tent—perhaps.

This was the law which the council in Sarbandan studied and because most of the landlords were willing to pay the tax some money was procured for village improvements.

The government has taken more direct steps to help the villagers, too. The government's development program is based upon the theory that increased production in agriculture will raise the living standards of the farmers. The Near East Foundation was invited by our government to assist with initiating the rural improvement program and their assistance and grants from the Ford Foundation have been of immeasurable assistance.

It is a tremendous problem to bring our remote villages—much like those of Western Europe in the Middle Ages—into the world of the twentieth century.

About American Assistance to the People of Iran

Many people who hear about the problems of my country ask, "What are *we* doing to help?" A brief answer may lead those who are interested into further study.

POINT FOUR

Point Four (Asle Chahar) is not the official name of the technical co-operation program of the United States. This program has had several "alphabet" names but "Point Four" is known around the world.

When President Truman gave his inaugural address in January, 1949, he outlined four points that he thought were important for American policy. Point Four was:

> We must embark on a bold new program for making the benefits of our scientific advancements and industrial progress available for improvement and growth to underdeveloped areas. . . . I believe that we should make available to peace-loving peoples the benefits of our store of technical knowledge in order to help them realize their aspirations for a better life.

It was not until May of 1950 that Congress passed the Act for International Development. In October, 1950, an agreement was signed in Teheran by the American Ambassador, Henry F. Grady, and our prime minister—soon to be assassinated—General Ali Razmara. This agreement created an Iranian–United States Commission for Rural Improvement through improvement in agriculture, health and education. Dr. Franklin Harris, former president of Utah State University (then an agricultural college), was the first director of the Rural Improvement Project. Two years later, 1952, Mr. William Warne, who had had many years of experience in the United States Department of the Interior, was made "Country Director" in Iran.

Mr. Warne's book, *Mission for Peace*, published in 1956 by Bobbs Merrill, gives a very human report on the work of Point Four in Iran. Actually the words of President Truman in his inaugural address are an outline of Point Four's accomplishments. The enduring thing about the program is that it has been a cooperative program in which Iranians became specialists as they worked with American specialists.

THE UNITED NATIONS

The United States gives a liberal share of the money that is used by the agencies of the United Nations. Some of the agencies active in Iran are WHO, FAO, ICAO, UNESCO, ILO, UNICEF.

The assistance given me by UNICEF is mentioned in my story. Further information about the work of these agencies can be obtained from the United Nations.

THE FORD FOUNDATION

It was the Ford Foundation that helped to make my work in Sarbandan possible. Large grants to the government and to the Near East Foundation have made possible research studies on which improvement programs can be based. When the government wanted to test the theory that improved production would lead to a better life for the farmer the Ford Foundation granted $257,400 to research a few "blocks" each of about fifteen villages, 15,000 families. To free the farmers from an enslaving indebtedness to their landlords the Near East Foundation and the government began a test program comprising 1,000 families which included credit agencies for farmers, education programs, community organization of saving and credit co-operatives. For this the Ford Foundation made a grant of $177,000 to the Near East Foundation.

The Ford Foundation reports are available at college and city libraries.

THE NEAR EAST FOUNDATION

In 1946 the government of Iran invited the Near East Foundation to co-operate with Iran in initiating an intensive rural development program. The center of the Near East Foundation work is in the Varamin plains area, where I worked in the girls' school across from the village of Ghaleh Nou. Important programs which the Foundation has pushed forward are: agricultural, community development, co-operative and credit, educational (which includes teacher training, village school improvement, adult education, etc.), home and welfare, and sanitation and health.

The Annual Report of the Near East Foundation in Iran from July 1, 1954, to June 30, 1955, is especially interesting since it details progress in all of these fields.

OTHER AGENCIES

I have never come in direct contact with the Christian Missions in Iran, but I know that they have worked quietly to provide and improve hospital facilities, to conduct schools, and to initiate adult literacy programs. Dr. Elder, American Mission, Teheran, Iran, can furnish information regarding these programs.

While I have not "touched shoulders" with these missions I have known many who were educated at The American School under the late Dr. Jordan. In fact, the use of English and the knowledge of American culture gained there have helped many Iranians in their co-operation with all of the other agencies including Point Four.

The University of Southern California Institute for Administrative Affairs is interested in introducing reforms in the administrative system of the government. The Institute conducts courses in the Law Faculty of the University of Teheran and advanced students are educated on the campus of the University of Southern California to educate government administrators when they return to Iran.

There are other agencies which receive part or all of their support from the United States. The United States has been a good neighbor to my country.

OPERATION SARBANDAN

My work in the awakening of one small group of villages has been assisted by many of these agencies and by my friends. Since the royalties from *Persia Is My Heart* and from *Reveille for a Persian Village* go directly into this work, many of you have been direct contributors toward making life more livable for those who happened to have been born in a land of undiscovered, undeveloped opportunities.

Ali says: "Whoever sows good reaps his reward."

Set in Intertype Garamond
Format by Anita Walker
Manufactured by The Haddon Craftsmen, Inc.
Published by HARPER & BROTHERS, *New York*

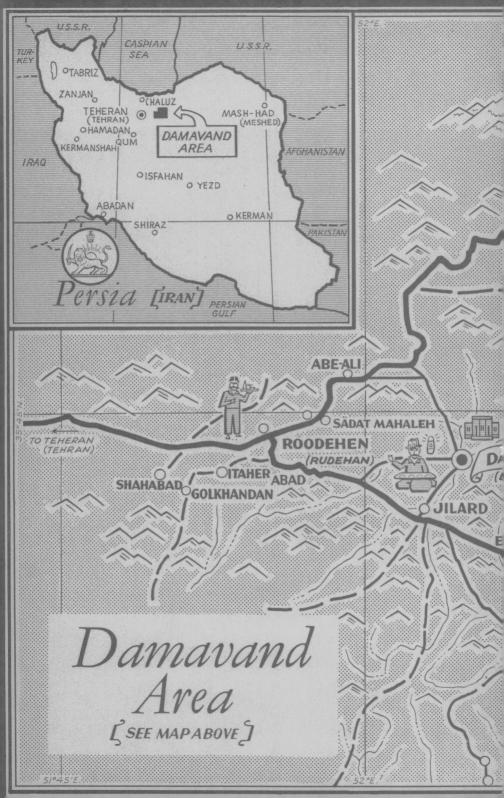

USSR.

CASPIAN SEA

U.S.S.R.

TURKEY

○ TABRIZ

ZANJAN ○

○ CHALUZ

TEHERAN
(TEHRAN)
◎ ■
DAMAVAND
AREA

MASH-HAD
(MESHED)

○ HAMADAN
QUM ○

KERMANSHAH

AFGHANISTAN

IRAQ

○ ISFAHAN

○ YEZD

ABADAN ○

○ KERMAN

SHIRAZ ○

PAKISTAN

Persia [IRAN]

PERSIAN GULF

52°E.

ABE-ALI

35°45′N.

SÂDAT MAHALEH

TO TEHERAN
(TEHRAN)

ROODEHEN
(RUDEHAN)

DA

SHAHABAD
ITAHER
ABAD
GOLKHANDAN

JILARD

*Damavand
Area*

[SEE MAP ABOVE]

51°45′E.

52°